RUGBY

A PLAYER'S GUIDE TO THE LAWS

Derek Robinson's playing career began as a junior with Avonmouth, a dockers' club in Bristol, England, and ended twenty years later with Manhattan RFC, New York. After that he refereed deep in the grassroots of the game. Being a writer, he reckoned that most players never read the rulebook because it was largely unreadable. He offered to change that and became the writer in the Rugby Football Union team that produced *The Laws in Plain English* for the International Rugby Board. (The IRB's new and simplified lawbook sprang from that version.) Apart from books on Rugby and Squash, he has written eleven novels, the best-known being *Goshawk Squadron* which was shortlisted for the Booker Prize, and *Piece of Cake*, which became a TV mini-series. He lives in Bristol, where his highly popular guide to the West Country dialect called *Krek Waiter's Peak Bristle* is even more challenging than the old Rugby lawbook was, but a damn-sight funnier.

RUGBY

A PLAYER'S GUIDE
TO THE LAWS

DEREK ROBINSON

CollinsWillow
An Imprint of HarperCollinsPublishers

Illustrations by John Gully

For their great help in the preparation of this book,
my thanks to (in alphabetical order):
R.A.B. (Jim) Crowe, Past President of the London Society of
Rugby Football Union Referees,
Peter Hughes, Past Chairman RFU Laws Sub-Committee
and Don Rutherford, former Technical Director, RFU

Any errors, inaccuracies or blemishes are
down to me and not to them

This book covers all changes to the Laws of Rugby
up to and including those made in 2001

First published in 1995 by
CollinsWillow
An imprint of HarperCollins*Publishers*
London

Second edition 1996
Third edition 1998
Fourth edition (fully revised and updated) 2002

3 5 7 9 8 6 4

ISBN 0 00 713614 5

Printed and bound in Great Britain by Clays Ltd, St Ives plc

Contents

Foreword

When someone says he's thinking of taking up refereeing and asks my advice, I always say, 'Go on playing as long as you're enjoying the game.' Make the most of it while you can!

There's another reason for that advice. The longer a referee has played, and the better he understands the game, then the more he can help the players do their stuff – provided they know the laws of rugby.

Every one of these laws exists for the good of the game. And the referee is there for the same reason – but he can't help the player if the player won't help himself. I've been lucky enough to referee 34 major international matches, including the 1995 World Cup Final. I've also refereed countless grassroot games: schoolboy, colts, students, junior club sides. Big or small, all have one thing in common. *A team that doesn't know the laws is in big trouble.*

What I like about this book is the way it not only describes each law but also explains why the law is needed; and does so with wit, imagination, and seventy excellent pictures. That's what I call user-friendly!

Ed Morrison

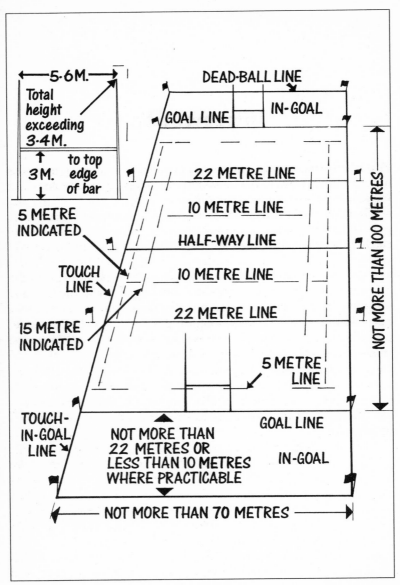

Plan of the playing area.

Introduction

There is no secret about how to play rugby, any more than there is a secret about how to play basketball, tennis, or stud poker. The laws of the game are written down for all to see. There may be many secrets about how to *win*, but there is no secret about how to play.

Moreover, it's pretty obvious that a player should learn how to play a game before he starts thinking about how to win. Any poker player who got into a game without knowing whether a full house beats a flush, or vice versa, would have a pretty unhappy time of it.

Yet it is a fact that tens of thousands of rugby players do not fully understand the laws of their game. What's more, these players have given up hope of ever knowing all the laws. They were never properly taught them when they began playing and they don't intend to start learning them now.

As a result, tens of thousands of players are playing well below their true capacity. Simply because they don't completely understand what is allowed and what is prohibited, they can never be sure that they are making the most of the first, and steering clear of the second.

This has nothing to do with a player's physical fitness, experience, or natural ability. It makes no difference whether a man is playing for a first-class club or his local pub XV – either he understands a particular law, or he doesn't. And if he doesn't, then he must be handicapped when playing against opponents who do, even if they're less fit, less experienced, or less gifted than he is. That, too, is pretty obvious.

You may think that ignorance is ignorance. Life isn't as simple as that. In rugby, there's active ignorance, passive ignorance, and cock-eyed ignorance.

Take the law of offside. A player who doesn't realise that he is in an offside position is liable to charge into the game and risk giving away a penalty kick. On the other hand, if he is not sure whether he's *on*side, he may do nothing at all. This is the result of *active* ignorance, and that's exactly what the other team likes to see.

It gets worse. Suppose he's penalised for offside play. He still doesn't know exactly what he did wrong. All he knows is the enemy is taking a pot at goal and it's his fault.

So in future he hangs back, afraid of repeating the mistake – a mistake which he can't really describe, even to himself.

Today, when kickers can slot penalties from any part of their opponents' half, indescribable mistakes are something no team can afford.

Then there's the player who doesn't take all his chances because he doesn't fully understand the laws. Often this has nothing to do with the referee. The referee applies the laws that lay down what players must or must not do. There are plenty of laws that tell the player what he *may* do, if he wants to. If he doesn't grab his chance, the game won't break down; but a good opportunity will slip away. This is the effect of *passive* ignorance – ignorance of the freedom which the laws allow.

A good example is the advantage law. A player who doesn't know how it works is not ready to seize on his opponents' mistakes and benefit from them. His failure is not that he's breaking the laws, but that he isn't getting the most out of them.

Finally, there's the player who has picked up a lot of half-baked half-truths, usually from friends who gave up playing fifteen years ago. This is *cock-eyed* ignorance.

A good example is the belief that it is always illegal for a player on the ground to pass the ball. This happens, and an opponent shouts: 'Passing off the ground, ref!' When the ref ignores him, he feels robbed. He loses heart. His cock-eyed ideas may not be illegal, but they certainly weaken his game. (If you're still not happy about passing off the ground, see Chapter 3. There *are* some occasions when it's *not* legal.)

The fact that so many players are resigned to going through their playing careers without fully understanding what they're doing is extraordinary. And yet it's true. In no other sport are the players so vague about the laws of the game. Yet the laws of rugby are not much more difficult than those of other games. Indeed, rugby is based on one very simple idea; the idea that each player should be as free as possible to get the ball and help his side score with it.

That obviously cuts out any interference with a player who hasn't got the ball. It lets everybody concentrate on the man who *has* got it. And it means that any number of players may handle, kick or pass the ball, one after another, keeping the game going continuously.

When you know the basic principles behind rugby, the laws become quite straightforward. Rugby is meant to be fast-moving and continuous, with as few stoppages as possible, so the laws are against things like deliberately lying on the ball, or refusing to let go of it when you're tackled. The aim is *positive* – to keep the game going and the ball moving, and let everyone get on with it. That's why there are clear-cut laws against foul play, such as obstruction or dangerous play.

The idea behind scrums and line-outs is simple: to restart the game, quickly and fairly, once it's stopped.

The purpose of the offside law is to keep each team more or less intact. It also gives a team space to play the ball when they've won it fairly. A man is offside when he's in front of a player on his own team who has the ball or who last played it, and for the moment he's out of the game. It's as simple as that. Without offside the game would become so scattered and confused that, like the retreat from Moscow, you couldn't see the action for the players. Offside makes the difference between an all-for-one and a free-for-all.

The law against throwing the ball forward makes sense once you understand offside. If you give a forward pass, the man who takes it must be in front of you. And if you mustn't throw it forward, you obviously shouldn't *knock* it forward either; hence the law against the knock-on.

These laws are both simple and useful. If you abolished offside, allowed forward passes and ignored knock-ons, the result wouldn't be better rugby; it would be a kind of sloppy handball.

The need for laws about scoring, kicking and the in-goal (where scoring takes place) is pretty obvious. Finally, there is the advantage law, which can trump nearly all the rest. This simply allows the referee to let play continue when one team breaks a law and their opponents take advantage of this. The advantage law covers ninety-nine per cent of all rugby.

True rugby can be played only if the players know the laws and honestly try to follow them. Accidentally breaking the law is bad luck; deliberately doing so is trying to distort the whole shape of the game. It's cheating in its most childish form because in the long run the player is only cheating himself. It's the players who benefit from the laws so it's up to the players to apply them.

That's why there's only one referee for thirty players. If everyone uses the laws and doesn't abuse them, one referee is all you need.

The better you know the laws, the more you'll enjoy the game. If the French, Italians, Poles, Japanese, Rumanians, Portuguese, Fijians and God-knows-who-else can master them, so can you. There is no secret about rugby, but before you start thinking about how to win games, you should make sure you know what the game itself is all about. Winning rugby starts here.

1
Offside in open play

Not at scrums, rucks, mauls or line-outs

'More players have nervous breakdowns trying to understand the offside law,' a research expert recently reported, 'than get kicked to death by green canaries.'

Which is a pity, because offside is basically simple. In open play, you are offside when you are in front of a player of your own team who has the ball, or who last played it. ('In front of' means 'nearer your opponents' dead-ball line'.) And you must not take part in the game in any way until you become onside again.

This means much more than not touching the ball or the opponent who has the ball. It means that when you are offside because a team-mate behind you has kicked the ball ahead of you, then you must not even move towards the ball. Move *back or sideways*, if you wish, but not towards the ball or the enemy waiting to play the ball. He may be fifty yards away. Tough luck. You can't take a step in his direction until you've been put onside. You can't do anything at all to influence the course of the game except breathe in and out. Temporarily, you are on ice.

What's more, if you are offside and you are near where the ball is about to land, you must beat it fast, until you're at least ten metres away. More on that later.

Take comfort. There is nothing to be ashamed, disgusted or suicidal about in being offside. Everybody is offside at some time or other. You get into trouble only when you try to take part in the game before you have been put properly onside.

Two kinds of offside

The ball is behind you

Firstly, there's offside because a team-mate behind you has the ball or has just passed it or dropped it. The point is he touched it last and it's still behind you. You're in an offside position but you can go where you like, provided you don't obstruct an opponent. Also, you must not play the ball if it comes your way. For instance, if a team-mate behind you knocks-on in your direction, you'd better leave the ball alone, or you'll be in trouble. Even if an opponent grabs it, you can't immediately grab him. You're still offside and out of the game until you've been put onside.

There's no penalty, though, for being in an offside position as

Offside when in front of the ball. A player is offside when he's in front of a team-mate who has the ball. In this situation, the offside player is free to go anywhere, provided he doesn't interfere with play by obstructing an opponent. Starbursts indicate offside players.

Offside when behind the ball. A player is offside when a team-mate behind him has kicked the ball ahead of him. In this situation, the offside player must not move towards the ball. He must stand still or move back, until he's put onside. Starbursts indicate offside players.

long as you don't get involved in play. If the ball's behind you, you're certainly not obliged to stand still.

The ball is in front of you

Second, there's offside because a team-mate behind you has kicked the ball and put it in front of you. This is the situation already described, where you must not move towards the ball or your opponents who are waiting to play the ball. Even if they don't catch the kick, even if they let it bounce, the offside player must not go forwards.

The kick may be huge. The nearest opponent may be half the field away. It makes no difference. Anyone who is offside when a team-mate boots the ball over his head must stand still (or move backwards) until he's been put onside. If he takes a step forward, he may be penalised.

What good does offside do?

It is not hard to see the reason for the offside law, once you see the mess we'd be in without it. If players could station themselves anywhere in the field, no matter where play was, you would have some of them camping permanently on their opponents' goal-line, just waiting for the ball to be booted their way. Players would be scattered everywhere, and both sides would constantly kick ahead in the hope of reaching someone and getting an easy score. Rugby would be basketball or, worse still, soccer.

As it is, offside does not paralyse a player; it just keeps him quiet (off-the-side) until he has been put onside and has thus rejoined the team (on-the-side). Offside in French is *hors-jeu* – out of the game. That says everything.

That justifies most offside. But what about the situation where an offside player can't even take a step forward, just because a team-mate behind him has kicked ahead? The kicker may be in one 22, and the catcher in the other. That's a big gap. What's the harm in letting an offside player close the gap by a few paces?

Go back a few years. Teams (especially in Australia) worked out a way to stifle an enemy attack. The full-back put in a long, high kick. While the ball was in the air, the rest of his team raced after it.

As the laws stood then, they were all offside but not liable to penalty because they took care to stop when they were at least ten metres from the catcher. He caught the ball, looked up and saw a line of opponents spread across the field, so close he could see the whites of their eyes. Attacking prospects: poor. So he booted the ball back from where it came, hotly pursued by *his* team. And so on. It was aerial ping-pong. It was not rugby. The lawmakers changed the law. 'You want to kick possession away?' they said. 'Fine. But only your onside players can chase it. The others are out of the game, until they're put onside.'

Being in front of the ball does not make you offside

You're only offside if you're *in front of a team-mate who has the ball,* or who last played it. (This is in open play, remember.) So if your opponents have the ball you can be well in front of it – nearer their goal line – and you're not offside. Sometimes this *looks* wrong. Suppose Reds are playing Blues. A Red attack breaks down. Blues come away with the ball, passing and running and gaining ground. A Red attacker (ex-attacker) chases after them. He is, of course, in front of the ball; that is, nearer Blues' goal line. Blues drop a pass. The Red player arrives and grabs it. The crowd howls: *Offside!* They're mistaken. Who last played the ball? His opponents did. And that's what matters.

Readers write

T.D. of Leatherhead writes: You can't tell me that refs apply the offside law as strictly as you make out. I'm talking about the situation where a player kicks ahead, over the top of his team, and you say they have to stand still.

D.R. Or move back.

T.D. And if one of them so much as takes half a pace forward, he gets penalised? I don't believe it. Besides, there's up to fourteen offside players. The ref can't watch them all, can he?

D.R. You'd be surprised how much a good referee can see. Still, you have a point. But remember, advantage may apply. What matters is whether or not an offside player moving forward is liable to influence play. For instance, if he's near the right-hand touch line while his opponents are successfully attacking down the left, the ref may ignore him and let them carry on enjoying themselves.

* * *

R.S.J. of Northampton writes: Changing the law of offside in open play hasn't worked. You still get the full-backs kicking the ball from 22 to 22, each hoping the other will knock-on. It's boring.

D.R. Don't tell me. Tell them. There's nothing in the law-book that forces teams to play good rugby.

2
Onside in open play
The ten-metre law • Also penalties

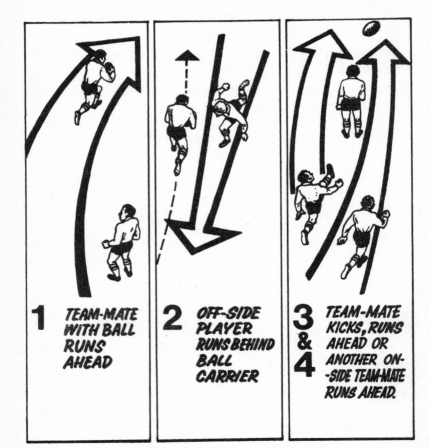

1 TEAM-MATE WITH BALL RUNS AHEAD

2 OFF-SIDE PLAYER RUNS BEHIND BALL CARRIER

3 & 4 TEAM-MATE KICKS, RUNS AHEAD OR ANOTHER ON-SIDE TEAM-MATE RUNS AHEAD.

If you are not in front of a team-mate who has the ball, or who last played the ball, you are onside. ('In front' means 'nearer your opponents' dead-ball line'.) Onside means you are not offside, so you can take part in the game.

I'm still talking about open play. Scrums, rucks, mauls and line-outs are different.

When you're offside, there are *seven* ways of getting yourself put onside.

Four depend on what your team does. *Three* depend on what your opponents do.

Put onside by your own team

1. When a team-mate, carrying the ball, runs in front of you, he puts you onside.
2. When a team-mate who kicked the ball when he was behind you, now runs in front of you, he puts you onside.
3. When any other team-mate who was onside when the ball was kicked, now runs in front of you, he puts you onside.
4. When you run behind any one of these team-mates, he puts you onside.

Put onside by your opponents (but not under the Ten-Metre Law)

In this situation, you're in front of a team-mate who has kicked ahead. An opponent gets possession of the ball (he catches it or picks it up), or he intentionally touches it.

1. When an opponent runs 5 metres with the ball, he puts you onside.
2. When an opponent plays the ball – kicks it or passes it or just plain drops it – he puts you onside.
3. When an opponent intentionally touches the ball but doesn't catch it, he puts you onside.

(Opposite) Put onside by your team: 4 ways. In general play, an offside player is put onside when (1) the ball-carrier runs in front of him, or (2) he runs behind the ball-carrier, or (3) a team-mate kicks ahead and runs in front of him, or (4) any other team-mate who was onside when the ball was kicked runs in front of him.

Put onside by an opponent: 3 ways. In general play, an offside player is put onside when an opponent (1) runs 5 metres with the ball, or (2) kicks or passes it, or (3) intentionally touches it but doesn't catch it. (None of this applies to an offside player within 10 metres of where the ball lands.)

Onside balances offside

The laws try to discourage you from getting offside by making you do a little penance before they let you back into the game. You have to return to your team, or wait until your team (in the shape of an onside player) comes up and joins you. Note that, in a kick-ahead situation, you can be put onside by any other player on your team who was onside when the ball was kicked. So even if the kicker is brought down as he makes his kick, and is unable to follow it up, any player level with him or behind him can run forward and put his team-mates onside.

In short, you can be put onside by any player who is himself onside when the ball is kicked.

But *until* you're put onside, you must keep out of the game and give your opponents room for one free go – a chance to start something without fear of interruption from you. Only when one of them has run five metres with the ball, or passed it, or kicked it, or done *something*, can you come out of your trance and join in the action again.

And sometimes you cannot even do that, as we shall now reveal.

The Ten-Metre Offside Law

If you're offside because a team-mate behind you has kicked ahead, and you're within ten metres of an opponent waiting to catch the ball, there's only one thing to do: get the hell out of it. Nothing your opponents may do can help you here. You must *immediately* retreat from where the ball is about to land, until you're ten metres (or more) from that spot.

This ten-metre line used to form an imaginary circle surrounding the opponent waiting to catch the ball (or the ball itself, if no opponent had arrived yet). That's all been changed. Now the ten-metre line is an imaginary straight line running right across the field from touch line to touch line. The line is ten metres behind the point where the ball lands. 'Behind' means towards your goal line.

If events are moving so rapidly that you cannot *avoid* being less than ten metres from the opponent when he catches the ball (or from the spot where the ball lands), then just beat it as smartly as you can, and the referee won't say anything. However, as you depart, steer clear of your opponents, especially the man about to catch the ball. Take the shortest route out. Look where your opponents are and avoid them.

It's worth repeating. When you are offside under the Ten-Metre

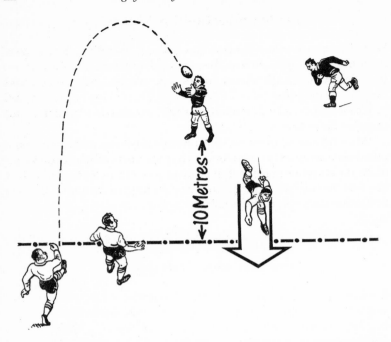

The Ten-Metre Law: Act 1: Beat it! When an offside player is in front of an imaginary line ten metres from an opponent waiting to catch the ball, he must immediately retreat behind that line. Until he does, nothing his opponents do can help him.

Law there is only one thing to do: immediately and quickly retire ten metres from the waiting opponent. It's worth repeating because what you *must* do is not what you *want* to do. Here is an opponent waiting to catch the ball, and here you are near enough to close in and clobber him or at least to hang around and look threatening; naturally you don't want to run away. It's a strange and unnatural reaction. But it's what the law says you must do, and do at once. This is the only occasion in the game of rugby when the ball is in open play and you are required to run *away* from the action. The habit does not come easily. You just have to work at it.

Onside under the Ten-Metre Law

Retiring ten metres does not, of course, automatically put you
onside and therefore back in the game. All it does is keep you out of
trouble. If you don't retire ten metres you are *criminally* offside, and
liable to be penalised. After you've retired ten metres you may still
be offside, depending on what else has happened in the game, but
at least you're safe.

While you *are* retiring ten metres, the only way you can become
onside is through your own efforts or the efforts of an onside team-
mate: either you can run behind him or he can run in front of you; it
adds up to the same thing. So if he follows up fast enough, you
might not need to cover the full ten metres.

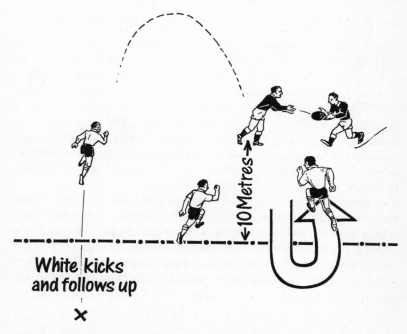

**White kicks
and follows up**

×

*The Ten-Metre Law: Act 2: Onside is possible again. Once an offside player has
obeyed the Ten-Metre Law, he can be put onside by a team-mate or an opponent, in
any of the usual ways.*

Suppose, for instance, that you are in front of your full-back when he puts up a high kick ahead. You discover that you are only a few feet from an opponent who is getting ready to catch the ball, so you immediately turn and run. Meanwhile, your full-back has been hotly pursuing his kick, and before you've had time to cover more than about five metres, he passes you. This puts you onside; you can stop beating it and join in the game again.

Once you *have* retired the full ten metres, you're in the same position as any other offside player, so you can be put onside by your opponents as well as by your team-mate. If one of them runs five metres with the ball, or kicks or passes or drops it, or intentionally touches it, you can go straight back into the game. But *until* you've retired your ten metres, nothing your opponents do can put you onside. Nothing.

The reason why

The Ten-Metre Law makes sense. As an offside player you must not take any part in the game; and your opponent cannot be expected to concentrate on catching a greasy ball coming out of the sun if you're standing right next to him, breathing hard. Of course, *you* know you're offside, so *you* know that you are not going to lay a finger on him. But *he* doesn't know that, and your magnetic presence might make him nervous. Or you might accidentally get in his way. Or simply not get *out* of his way. So the laws say you *must* get out of his way *before* he gets the ball and keep on getting out of it until you're ten metres off.

There's one small exception to this. Suppose an attacking player kicks the ball, an opponent charges it down, and another attacking player who is within ten metres of the opponent plays the ball. No crime has been committed. The opponent wasn't *waiting to play the ball,* so the Ten-Metre Law doesn't apply; and the second attacker was put onside when the opponent intentionally touched the ball.

Two rules to remember

1 If you are offside and less than ten metres from an opponent waiting to catch the ball, you can never be put onside by any action of your opponents, so don't wait for it. Don't wait for anything. Clear off.

2 Any *other* time you are offside in open play, you are *always* put onside the moment an opponent kicks, passes or intentionally touches the ball. (But see Chapter 9.)

The penalty for offside

There are, in fact, *two* penalties for offside play, and the unpenalised side can choose which one it wants.

You will remember (how could you ever forget?) that you are penalised for offside when you are in front of a player on your own team who has the ball or last played it, and you try to take part in the game.

Now the penalty – and pay attention, because this isn't as easy as the rest – the penalty can be *either* a penalty kick where you (the offside player) took part in the game *or* a scrum where he (your team-mate) last played the ball.

Remember that it takes two to make offside – you, and your mate who had the ball behind you – and the penalty is either a kick where you are now, or a scrum where he was then.

If this all sounds a bit overdone, believe me that it makes good sense in practice, and it's worth understanding, because one day you might be captain of a team when an opponent gets done for being offside and the referee will look you straight in the eyes and say: 'Kick or scrum?' And if you shrug your shoulders and say you haven't the faintest idea, the ref is going to give you a very old-fashioned look and the selectors are going to give you a very modern rocket.

Here are two examples which show you how the kick-here-or-scrum-there penalty works out. Blues are playing Whites.

1 From a scrum on the Whites' 22-metre line, Blues win the ball, which goes to the Blue fly-half. He kicks ahead, not very well, and a White player catches the ball. A Blue forward who is in front of the kicker (and therefore offside) makes a tackle. Now Whites can *either* take a penalty kick where the Blue forward went wrong *or* a scrum at the place where the Blue fly-half kicked ahead. Since the scrum would give them only a few extra metres, and since they are defending, they probably choose the penalty kick.

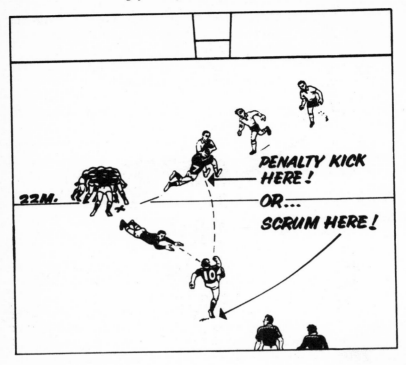

Penalty for offside play: kick or scrum? The Black flanker, obviously offside, tackles an opponent. The referee offers the White team a choice: either a scrum where the kick was made, or a penalty kick where the tackle happened. They probably take the kick.

2   Near his own goal-line, the Blues' full-back kicks for touch, misses, and the ball goes to a White player. A Blue player is less than ten metres from him. He makes no effort to retire and he's penalised for offside under the Ten-Metre Law. Whites can take *either* a penalty kick where the offside Blue player was standing *or* a scrum where the Blue full-back kicked. The penalty kick would be in mid-field, perhaps too far out for Whites to kick a goal, but the scrum would be near their opponents' goal-line; so Whites might well choose the scrum.

Penalty for offside play: scrum or kick? A big kick by the Black full-back finds a team-mate, miles offside, about to clobber an opponent. Whites' choice is either a penalty kick where the player was offside (midfield) or a scrum where the ball was kicked, near the posts. They might prefer the scrum.

Accidental offside

What happens to a player who is offside, who is really sincerely making every effort not to interfere with the game, but who, despite himself, gets involved in it? (For instance, when a team-mate who has the ball bumps into him.)

You will be relieved to hear that the laws treat him with dignity and restraint. Provided the referee is satisfied that the team in possession gained no advantage from the accidental offside, he lets play go on. If, on the other hand, he considers that it has improved their chances, he orders a scrum, with their opponents putting the ball in.

Readers write

P.J. of Swansea writes: What if a player kicks ahead and then runs forward to put his team onside, but he does his running in touch? Is that OK?

D.R. There's nothing to stop him running in touch (or even in touch-in-goal), but in order to put a player onside the runner must be in the playing area.

P.J. Why?

D.R. Because that's where the game is played, dummy.

*   *   *

M.N.T. of Wimbledon writes: This is about the Ten-Metre Law. Suppose the player waiting to catch the ball is standing a yard from touch, and there's an opponent right next to him. If that opponent steps into touch, he can't be penalised for being within ten metres, can he?

D.R. Who says?

M.N.T. A bloke I met in the pub.

D.R. The whole point of the Ten-Metre Law is to make sure an opponent can't influence the catcher by being, or staying, near him. If this opponent steps into touch, I'd advise him to keep moving.

M.N.T. The ref might penalise him for leaving the field without permission.

D.R. Nobody said life was easy.

3
The tackle

One of the big things about rugby, as we never tire of repeating, is that it should be fast-moving and continuous, with as few stoppages as possible.

On the other hand, the big thing about the tackle is that it latches on to something that is moving fast and stops it dead.

Clearly, tackles must be made; but then the game must go on. That is what the law of the tackle tries to bring about. This, too, is quite simple, as long as you know *what is a tackle and what is not*.

For a start, a tackle must be in the field-of-play (the stretch between the goal-lines). You can't be tackled in an in-goal. Brought down, yes. Tackled, no.

Tackled: ball touches ground. If the ball-carrier is held by an opponent in the field-of-play, and the ball touches the ground, then he's been tackled.

Tackled: player on one knee. If the ball-carrier is held by an opponent in the field-of-play, and he's on one knee (or both knees), then he's been tackled.

If a player with the ball, in the field-of-play, is held by an opponent and brought down, he's tackled. It's very straightforward. Grab the ball-carrier and bring him to earth, and the law says you've tackled him.

What the law actually says in so many words is that he's tackled if he is held and 'brought to ground and/or the ball touches the ground.' You might think the ball couldn't touch the ground unless the player holding it had also been brought down, but believe me, anything's possible.

If you want to know what 'brought to ground' means, it means 'no longer on his feet', which is probably what you thought it meant. But what if he's on one foot and one knee? Or on both knees? Or sitting on his duff? Or on top of another player who is on the ground? Has he been brought to ground and therefore tackled? Yes, he has. If he's not up, he's down. Simple as that.

If an opponent lifts the ball-carrier off his feet, this is not a tackle, and play goes on.

Immediately you're tackled, both you and the tackler must try to make the ball available so that play can go on.

The key words in the tackle law are *held* and *brought to ground*. One is no good without the other. If a player dives at an opponent and knocks him over without holding him, it's not a tackle, and so the opponent need not let go of the ball. He must do *something* – he can't just lie there, thinking beautiful thoughts – but he's free to throw the ball to a team-mate, or to get up and run with it. In this situation, there is nothing to stop him passing off the ground: nothing.

The working of the tackle law is really very simple and obvious. When play can reasonably go on, the law lets it go on. When the tackled player hits the deck, it makes him let go of the ball so that someone else can play it. Immediately.

There are two reasons why the laws says *immediately*. One is so that other players can grab the ball and keep the game going. The other is so that you aren't turned into a basket case by opponents who are looking for the ball. As usual, what's good for the game is good for the player, too.

Hang on. Not so fast. Let's go back a bit. The tackled player must make the ball available. What exactly does *available* mean?

It certainly means a lot more than just letting go of the ball.

If you're tackled, the laws allow you to *pass* the ball provided you do it immediately. (Hard to imagine a player passing the ball the instant he hit the deck because his legs had been scythed from under him; but there are other forms of tackle. A tackled player on

Tackled: lying on another player. If the ball-carrier is held by an opponent in the field-of-play and he's lying on another player (including that opponent), then he's been tackled.

one knee might be able to get an immediate pass away.)

Or the laws allow you to *release* the ball provided you do it immediately and then get up or get out of the way if you can. The word 'release' has an interesting pair of meanings. You can release the ball by *putting it on the ground in any direction.* Or you can release it by *pushing it along the ground in any direction,* except (of course) forward. You may have noticed that the direction preferred by most tackled players is towards their own team.

A tackled player must not place or push the ball into touch.

Right then, onwards. You are tackled, you let go of the ball. Fine. What next?

The next player to play the ball – whether he picks it up, passes it or kicks it – *must be on his feet.* Rugby is a game where you run with the ball, and you can't run on your knees. That goes for you, for the man who tackled you, and for anyone else who turns up. Find your feet before you look for the ball.

Normally, of course, the tackler and the tackled man have their faces in the mud, so it's the third man up who gets the ball. This player has achieved mythic status in refereeing circles. 'Third man

Tackled: sitting. If the ball-carrier is held by an opponent in the field-of-play, and he's sitting on the ground, then he's been tackled.

Third man up must be on his feet. After a tackle, the next man to play the ball must be on his feet and stay on his feet.

up must be on his feet,' referees tell anyone who will listen. When the ball gets released from a tackle, the referee takes a keen interest in the next man to play the ball. Never mind how far the ball may be from the tackle – if the next man is not on his feet, or if he was on his feet until he dived on the ball, the referee hammers him. This makes sense. When the tackled player makes the ball available but the next man up promptly makes it unavailable, play grinds to a halt.

The tackle law is very simple. If you're not on your feet after a tackle, you can't do anything. You can't play the ball. You can't even touch it. You can't tackle an opponent who gets the ball. You can't even *try* to tackle him. There's only one thing you *can* do: get up. So do it.

Tacklers: now hear this!

What's sauce for the ball-carrier is sauce for the tackler. If they both go to ground with the ball, the tackler must act fast. He must let his opponent release the ball. In fact the tackler must completely let go of the tackled player, and do so at once. Then he must get away from him, and from the ball. If he can get up, he should get up, for the very good reason that he can't play the ball until he's on his feet. Both players – the tackler and the tackled man – have a duty to make the ball available, by releasing it and getting clear of it. (But note that if the tackled player is lying within reach of a goal line, an opponent can legally pull the ball from his hands to prevent a try or touch-down.)

Join the tackle from your side - not theirs!

A tackle has happened. You are not the tackler or the tackled player, but you want to get there, join the action and play the ball. You must do this from your side of the tackle. You must arrive behind the ball, and behind the tackler or tackled player who is nearest your goal line. If you join the tackle situation in front of the ball, or in front of the tackler or the tackled player, you're liable to be penalised.

This is an important change. It means that players heading for the tackle situation may have to circle around in order to get stuck in from their team's side. At first sight, this seems similar to the offside law at ruck or maul, which tells players either to join it from behind the hindmost team-mate in it, or to get behind the offside line through that team-mate's hindmost foot. But there's a big difference. There is no offside line at the tackle situation. Any player who's not involved in it is free to go anywhere (always assuming he's not offside under the laws applying to open play). It's only at or near to a tackle that players have to join the action from their own side. Which raises the obvious question: how near is 'near'? The Laws say 'within one metre'. Most referees work on the idea of a 'tackle zone' that extends from the back feet of the tackler(s) to the back feet of the tackled player, and covers a space one metre wide on either side of them. Any player who wants to join this 'tackle zone' had better do so from the direction of his own goal line. Sometimes, of course, the ball gets knocked or thrown from the tackle. It might get knocked or thrown ten feet from it, in which case the 'tackle zone' is history, we're back to open play, and any player can make a bee-line for the ball (provided he's onside under the usual open-play laws).

Use it. Don't abuse it.

The whole idea of this new tackle law is to get the ball back into play more quickly. So, if you win possession at the tackle, you must play the ball - run, pass or kick - immediately. You can be tackled by an opponent coming from behind his side of the `tackle zone'. What you must not do is get the ball and go to ground without being tackled. Rugby is meant to be played by players who are on their feet. The laws say so.

Scoring while tackled

You can score a try even though you are tackled. If sheer momentum takes you from the field-of-play to the goal-line, dragging the tackler behind you, certainly you can score. Alternatively you can reach out and score even if the tackle has stopped you dead, just short of the line – provided you do it immediately. Full details are in the chapter on Scoring.

Brief reminder

None of the above applies to the in-goal. A tackle, legally speaking, is only a tackle in the field-of-play, which is the area between the goal-lines. Once you cross the goal-line there is not much point in expecting a bloke to drop the ball just because you've got hold of him, so the law is completely different there. (See the chapter on in-goal play.)

Tackling has not always been the humane and enlightened affair it is today. Back in the 1850s, when the game was still a kind of student demonstration at Rugby School, a player who was 'collared' could cry, 'Have it down!' and put the ball on the ground for a scrum. If he didn't, his opponents could shout 'Hack him over!' and start kicking. They hacked only from the knee down, and they weren't allowed to hold *and* hack at the same time; still, they sometimes hacked for up to a quarter of an hour before they got the ball down. Today's law achieves the same result about three hundred times more rapidly and five thousand times less painfully.

The penalty for breaking any part of the tackle law is a penalty kick where it happened.

4

The player and the ball on the ground

Forget tackles. This has nothing to do with being tackled or making a tackle. This is about what happens when a player with the ball goes to ground, or when a player goes to ground in order to gather the ball, and what he must do next.

He must act immediately.

Falling on the ball – for instance, to stop a forward rush – is all right. Lying on the ball stops the entire game, and is all wrong.

Once you've gone to ground and got the ball, it doesn't much

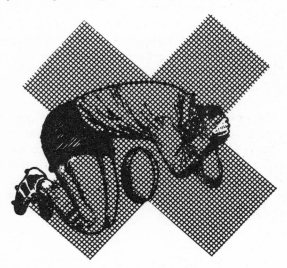

Don't lie on or around the ball. It's not enough to avoid lying on the ball – you must also do all you can to get up or roll away from it. This player isn't touching the ball, but he's obviously obstructing others who want to get at it.

matter what you do as long as you do it at once. You have a small choice. You can either get to your feet with the ball, or pass it or release it while you're on the ground. And if you pass or release it, you must also get up or move away from it, immediately.

The All Blacks, who are a poetic lot, have a charming couplet:

Do not lie upon the grass,
You cannot ruck when on your arse.

Don't tell me that it doesn't rhyme, or that they are daft about rucking in New Zealand. The verse tells an eternal truth, which is that rugby is meant to be played by players who are on their feet. Anyone who makes the ball unplayable by falling down, or by staying down, is bad news.

Don't lie near the ball

If you're not going to play the ball, you must, if you can, get up or roll away from it. What you must *not* do is drape yourself around the ball and lie there until help comes. Even if you are the last defender and the enemy is two feet from your line, you must not lie on the ball. It ruins the game and – unless the referee blows up smartly – it may do considerable damage to you, too.

Don't fall over a player with the ball

If you can't lie near the ball, then it's no surprise that intentionally falling over a player on the ground with the ball (or near the ball) is just as bad. The key words are 'intentionally falling'. That's what the referee is liable to penalise. The moral is: make an effort to stay on your feet. After all, that's where the game is played.

5
Somebody blundered: Part I

Four principles sum up the things you must and must not do in rugby:

1 The only way to gain ground is to run or kick. You must not throw or knock the ball forward.
2 You can grab an opponent, or get in his way, only if he has the ball.
3 Even so, you must not play dangerously.
4 You must do all you can to keep the game as fast-moving and continuous as possible.

If you follow these simple principles, you'll be all right – in theory. Still, it won't do any harm to go through the charge sheet with a powerful lens and a fine-tooth comb.

Throw-forward and knock-on

Penalty: scrum.

Throw-forward

You must not throw the ball forward. 'Forward' does not mean 'in front of you'; it means 'towards the enemy line'. (If you have crossed the enemy line and are unselfishly donating the ball to a team-mate, just don't throw it towards the enemy dead-ball line.) Picture an imaginary line running through the ball, parallel to the goal lines, and make your pass go along or behind that line, and you should be all right. If the ball hits the ground and *bounces* forward, your pass is still okay. The laws try to regulate what you do, but nobody on earth can say what a rugby ball is going to do next. If you make a pass which starts travelling through the air quite legally but then gets blown forward by the wind, it too is okay.

It has been argued by people who have nothing better to do, that when two players are running upfield absolutely level with each other and one gives a pass, the ball must go forward if it is to arrive where and when the other player is due to arrive, even though the first player is still running level with him. Other people disagree, and draw little diagrams with their beer on the top of the bar to prove it by trigonometry.

It doesn't matter terribly much, because when you start cutting it as fine as that, the decision really hinges on how much dust there is in the referee's left eye. That's where all the really important trigonometry takes place. It doesn't much matter whether or not you make a forward pass – what matters is whether the referee *thinks* you did. Moral: make it easy for him to approve.

One tiny detail: if you hand the ball to another player, this is a pass. If the player is in front of you, he's offside and the upshot is a scrum for accidental offside, unless he did it on purpose, in which case it's a penalty kick.

Knock-on

If you can't *throw* the ball forward, then you must not *knock* it forward, either. Stands to reason. To qualify for a knock-on, you don't actually have to *knock* the ball, or punch it, prod it or even give it a good hard slap. A knock-on need be nothing more than a clumsy fumble in the general direction of the enemy camp.

A knock-on needs three things. First, the ball hits your hand or arm (or vice versa). Second, it goes forward: towards the enemy's dead-ball line. (You can knock-on in his In-goal, remember.) Third, you fail to catch it again before it touches the ground or another player.

The knock-on law isn't interested in distance. A knock-on is a knock-on, whether the scrum-half nudged the ball half an inch or the winger elbowed it six feet. Furthermore, the law doesn't care how many times you lose the ball. Whether you're fielding a kick or taking a pass or scooping the ball up from the ground, you can fumble and juggle it till your captain's hair turns white, but provided you don't drop it altogether or let it touch another player, this is not a knock-on.

Exception: charged-down kick

If you succeed in charging down an opponent's kick, this is not a knock-on – even if the ball hits your hand or arm and goes forward and hits the ground – provided you didn't try to catch the ball. If you succeeded in catching the ball you must have bionic eyes and hands like flypaper.

No deliberate knock-ons

The laws say that a knock-on (or a throw-forward, come to that) must be unintentional. If you interrupt an enemy pass by sticking your great fist out and deliberately knocking the ball forward, you're asking for trouble. Similarly, if you see the opposition coming at you from all sides and you get rid of the ball by throwing it forward, that's bad news. In either case the penalty is a penalty kick and the referee may even award a penalty try.

Knock-on: second bite at the cherry. If you accidentally knock the ball forward, but you catch it before it touches the ground or another player, then this is not an infringement, and play goes on.

Charge-down: not a knock-on. If you charge down a kick and knock the ball forward, this is not an infringement, and play goes on (provided you didn't try to catch the ball).

Out there in the sweat and mud of battle, nobody talks about a throw-forward. Everyone calls it a forward pass – everyone but the lawbook, and the lawbook has a good reason. A pass involves two players. A throw-forward does not. The law doesn't care what you are trying to do, or whether you have a team-mate at the other end of it. If the ball leaves your hands and it's thrown forward, that's enough.

Mind you, I have seen players claim that a throw-forward was really a knock-on, and not even that, because they caught the ball, sir. (Players always say 'sir' to the ref when they're on dodgy ground.) What happened was the player reached far behind him to take a terrible pass, biffed the ball ten feet forward, and ran on and caught it. Nice try. But if the ref says that it was a throw-forward, you'd better believe him.

If you must fumble, fumble backwards

A knock-on does not have to be knocked, but it does have to be *on*. Suppose you take a pass or field a kick when you are facing backwards, towards your own line. You can juggle with the ball, fumble it, drop it and it's all perfectly legal. The game goes on. Unless the ball bounces *forward* – towards the enemy line – from a hand or arm, then it's not a knock-on.

A couple of laughably obvious points which nobody but a raving perfectionist like yourself would bother to read:

A rebound – off the chest, for example, or the shoulder – is not a knock-on; it's a rebound. If, however, a rebound ricochets off a chest and hits a hand or arm *and then* bounces forward, it *is* a knock-on. What often happens is that a player fails to catch a ball, which hits his chest and bounces forward, leaving him wheezing pitifully, the spectators demanding a knock-on, and the referee, quite rightly, doing nothing. Incidentally, it's perfectly legal to *head* the ball in rugby. You can even head the ball forward, into touch. I saw it done once, in an international match. By Gareth Edwards of Wales. Very enterprising fellow, Gareth.

In case you have just joined us at this point, here is a news summary. A player throws-forward or knocks-on when he throws or knocks (or even fumbles) the ball in the direction of his opponents' dead-ball line – unless (in the case of a knock-on) he catches it again before it touches the ground or another player. The penalty for this lapse is a scrum where it happened, with his opponents getting the put-in.

And now, back to our regular programme.

Readers write

L.C. of Leicester writes: Last week I saw the referee explaining the tackle law to the captains. I was brought up to believe he wasn't allowed to do any coaching before the match. Has that been changed?

D.R. No. 'Coaching' means giving tactical advice before the match, and referees are not allowed to do that; but they are allowed to give *instructions* to the teams in advance, especially if this will increase the players' safety. The tackle law is a good example.

6
Somebody blundered: Part II

Foul play

The Foul Play Law has three separate parts: (1) Obstruction, (2) Unfair Play and Repeated Infringements, and (3) Dangerous Play and Misconduct.

Now that's a mouthful. Some bits stick in the throat more than others. The difference between them tells us a lot about the laws and what they're out to do.

Take **Obstruction** (example: running in front of a team-mate carrying the ball). This is trying to play the right game in the wrong way. If caught, you get penalised with a penalty kick.

Next is **Unfair Play** (example: throwing the ball into touch) and **Repeated Infringements** (example: persistently feeding the scrum crookedly). This is all about distorting or evading the laws, not necessarily with physical violence. If caught, you get penalised with a penalty kick. Keep it up and you'll get a yellow card.

Last and worst is **Dangerous Play** (example: late tackle) and **Misconduct** (example: taunting an opponent after you've scored.) This is not playing the game at all. If you're lucky you only get warned and penalised with a penalty kick. Do it again and, if you're lucky, you get penalised with a penalty kick (perhaps even a penalty try), maybe yellow-carded, or sent off for good and carpeted before the Disciplinary Committee. (If you're unlucky you get a large knuckle sandwich from the opposition. The laws forbid retaliation, but don't push your luck.)

This three-way split reflects the aims of the Foul Play Law.

The laws as a whole are against wrongdoing, and wherever it rears its ugly head the lawbook delivers a crisp penalty kick or free kick. But if the player was taking an active part in the game when he committed Obstruction, the laws consider a penalty kick enough. 'The lad did wrong,' they reason patiently, 'but at least he wanted to get on with the game. Now perhaps he'll know better.'

By contrast, anyone guilty of Unfair Play or Repeated Infringements is trying to rewrite the lawbook in his own favour – for instance, by persistently getting offside at scrums or line-outs. The laws take a dim view, and they discourage him with a penalty kick. 'Change your ways,' they add, 'or we might be obliged to dispense with your services altogether.'

The really big guns come out against Dangerous Play (such as kicking an opponent) or Misconduct (such as kicking him while the ball is out of play). This isn't mild cheating by someone who doesn't understand the game. This is a bloke being so stupid, negative and pernicious that he's really sabotaging the game. He's not so much playing bad rugby as playing anti-rugby, so he's a menace to all concerned. The laws not only penalise him with a penalty kick but also require the referee to warn him. If he commits a similar offence (note that word *similar*: it doesn't have to be precisely the same offence), then the laws say he *must* be sent off. If his first offence was bad enough, he can be sent off there and then, without warning.

Rugby is a tough, physical game. It demands self-discipline. The laws come down hard on a player who can't control himself. 'That joker is going to spoil it for everyone,' they brood, worriedly. 'If he wants to indulge his sordid whims he'd better take up alligator-wrestling. Next time he tries to throttle the scrum-half, have him quietly removed.'

Obstruction

1 Running for the ball

When you are running for the ball, and an opponent is also running for the ball, you must not charge him or push him *except shoulder to shoulder*. Now, you very rarely see this shoulder-to-shoulder stuff done, and when you do somebody in the crowd usually takes exception to it; nevertheless it's perfectly legal as long as you keep running for the ball. It can be very effective, too, especially if the other bloke trips over his own feet.

Shoulder-to-shoulder charging is legal. If you and an opponent are both running for the ball, it's perfectly legal to charge him – but it must be shoulder-to-shoulder and you must keep running while you do it.

2 Offside player obstructing opponent; 'scissoring'

If you are in front of a player on your own side who has the ball (which makes you offside, right?), you must not stand or move in such a way that you obstruct an opponent who's trying to get at him. This is pretty obvious: if you're offside, you have no business interfering with the course of the game, and here you are, blocking the tackle.

Notice that it's up to you to *avoid* interfering with play. It is possible to obstruct an opponent simply by *being* in his way as well as by *getting* in his way. If you're offside and in his way at all, it's your job to get out of it – not his job to go around you.

3 Obstruction during a kick-ahead

The high kick-ahead is a tactic you often see in rugby. Usually a defender is waiting to catch the ball, while opponents are racing towards him. So far, so good. Trouble arises when team-mates

Blocking the tackle, a.k.a. 'scissoring'. If a player moves or stands in front of a team-mate who has the ball, so as to prevent an opponent from getting to him, that's obstruction – called 'scissoring' because the obstructing player often crosses the path of the ball-carrier.

appear in front of the catcher. They zigzag busily, running back and forth as if pursued by bees. What they are doing is making it difficult for opponents to reach the ball or the catcher. This is obstruction, and illegal. So is standing in front of (and near to) the catcher. This amounts to forming a shield to protect him.

4   Running into your own scrum or line-out

If you have the ball after a scrum or line-out, you must not try and crash through your own forwards in front of you. Same applies to ruck or maul. It's obvious: they must be offside, and you are bringing them into the game. Slightly less obviously, you are using them as a shield to keep the horny hands of the enemy off you; and since in rugby every man should be free to grab the man with the ball, provided he can catch him, what you are doing is wrong. Nevertheless, it's amazing how many players cannot resist taking the shortest route to the enemy line by ploughing straight through their own forwards.

Incidentally, the laws have laid down that a player carrying the ball can never be penalised for obstruction. If anyone gets penalised it's the team-mate he runs into.

5 Flanker swinging out from a scrum

When your side has hooked the ball in a scrum and it is coming out of the back row, the flanker – the man on the outside of the scrum – must not swing further outwards to stop the opposing scrum-half

Flanker obstructs scrum-half. A flanker (No. 6 here) must not swing out from the scrum in order to prevent the opposing scrum-half from getting past him. The flanker can pack at any angle, but he must not then widen the angle.

from coming round and zeroing in on your scrum-half (if he's got the ball) or the ball itself (if he hasn't).

There's nothing, except the length of his arms, to stop a flanker from packing on to the scrum at a wide angle if he wants to. The law simply says that, once the ball has been heeled, he must not move out to an even wider angle.

And there's another side to that coin. The flanker must not swing out to obstruct the scrum-half, but equally that scrum-half must not lay hands on the flanker – or any opposing forward – to give himself leverage as he follows the ball when it's being heeled through the scrum. Handling a flanker like this is misconduct, for which the punishment is a penalty kick.

Unfair play

Unfair play is what happens when a player plays unfairly. And if you think that's a pretty broad definition, well, so it is. The Unfair Play Law is one of those handy catch-all regulations that the referee can call upon in an emergency. Such as…

1 Offending on purpose

A player who intentionally breaks any law is guilty of Unfair Play. Referees, you see, have the power to look into men's souls and divine their intentions.

Sometimes that intention is pretty obvious. Suppose you get the ball inside your 22 at a moment when five hulking opponents are bearing down on you. You've just sprained your ankle, so it seems unlikely that you will jink past them all. Inevitably, you will get flattened, they will get the ball, and after that, nothing stands between them and your goal line but twenty feet of autumn mist.

Suddenly you see a team-mate to your right. He's ten feet in front of you, but unmarked. If you give him a forward pass the referee is bound to notice, and a scrum will at least give your team a chance to re-group. So you cleverly throw the ball forward.

The referee whistles and gives your opponents a penalty kick, maybe even a penalty try. Rugby works on the assumption that players try to uphold the laws, even when they're feeling desperate.

Intentionally breaking a small law is a big deal. The Foul Play Law says a player must not intentionally infringe any Law of the Game. Here you see a player, about to be overwhelmed by opponents, intentionally throwing the ball forward in the hope of getting a scrum. A penalty kick is more likely; perhaps even a penalty try.

If you intentionally break a law for which the usual penalty is only a scrum, you are distorting the game, and you'll be made to pay for it.

2 Time-wasting

Wasting time is a fairly pointless way to behave; if you don't want to play, what are you doing out there in the first place? Especially as the referee is going to penalise you for unfair play. Let's face it, intentional time-wasting is hard to hide. Throwing the ball in the wrong direction when your opponents have been given a penalty kick is an obvious delay. So is not forming a scrum or a line-out. So is delaying a drop-out. The penalty is at least a free kick. It might be a second penalty kick, and a penalty try is not impossible.

That's *intentional* time-wasting. There is also the other kind, of which quite a lot goes on. Some players waste time simply by not doing all they could to get on with the game. There is a slow way to put the ball into a scrum, and a fast way. The slow way is for the forwards to pack down and the scrum-half to start looking for the ball. When he locates it – cleverly camouflaged on that patch of mud, ten yards away – he *walks* over to it, picks it up, drops it, retrieves it, reads the name on it in case it's the wrong ball, and *walks* slowly back to the scrum.

Correct me if my arithmetic is wrong; but that leaves sixteen forwards impatient for action, and thirteen backs standing around scratching themselves, while one scrum-half carries on the game at a steady limp. I don't care if he is getting his breath back, it's still a pathetic waste of twenty-nine players' time. What's more, it is, strictly speaking, illegal.

The laws are liberally spattered with the key phrase, 'without delay'. The ball must be put into the scrum without delay. In fact, the laws say that it shall be put in without delay *as soon as the two front rows have closed together.* So any scrum-half who waits until a flanker has finished blowing his nose and leaned on the nearest rump before he puts the ball in, is wasting time. Any hooker who has a lengthy discussion (or even two) about the line-out signal, before throwing in the ball, is wasting time. Any team which is awarded a penalty kick and then democratically debates what to do with it, is wasting time. Nobody ever scored a try while the ball was out of play.

I am not suggesting that everything should be done at a gallop. All I'm saying is that, if players were as alert when the ball is dead as they are when it's alive, then we would see shorter stoppages and more game. (Amazingly, even at international level, the ball is actually in play for only about one-third of the game.) As it is, they often regard the sound of the whistle as a signal to stop thinking.

The referee has a duty, under the laws, to see that the game goes forward 'without delay', and if he thinks you're acting unnecessarily sluggishly, he is right to award a free kick just to goose you along a bit. And the fact that you didn't *know* you were acting all constipated is neither here nor there: one disadvantage of sluggishness is that very often you're too sluggish to realize just how sluggish you are.

3 Throwing into touch

Intentionally throwing (or knocking) the ball into touch is also Unfair Play. If you want to put the ball into touch you must either kick it there or take it there in person. Throwing into touch is the easy way out. This also applies to intentionally throwing the ball into touch-in-goal or over the dead-ball line. The penalty is a penalty kick.

If, however, you try to give a pass to a team-mate who turns out to be not there, and you throw the ball straight into touch, this is not intentional, so you won't be penalised.

Persistent offending

Or, as the laws call it, Repeated Infringement. This is pretty basic stuff. The laws of rugby are a description of the game. Change the description and you change the game.

Players who persistently break a law are, in effect, trying to change the game. They may be doing it for their own advantage, for example, by barging in the line-out. Or they may be doing it simply because they don't know any better. (There are hookers like that.) The effect is the same: it distorts the game, and by distorting it, ruins it for everyone. The prop forward who won't let the ball into the scrum is damaging the chances of *both* teams to get on with the game. Ignorance is no excuse: the damage is the same whether he knows what he's doing, or not.

That is why the referee is given large powers to deal with this sort of thing. Not surprisingly, he is required to apply a stricter standard in senior matches: when a player breaks the same law for the third time, the referee must warn him about it, and if that doesn't work he can even send him off. In more junior rugby, where the percentage of dipsticks is higher, the referee usually warns the player first and then, if he doesn't improve, warns his captain that the player will have to go off unless he can be rendered harmless. The captain, if he has any brains, gives the offender an immediate posting to the wing, followed by an early lesson on the game.

Certain problem areas seem to breed repeated infringements – the scrum, line-out, ruck/maul, and the offside laws. A set of backs who persistently wander over on to the wrong side of their offside line can stifle attack after attack. I know they get penalised, and that might mean three points against them, but then again it might not; and in any case their opponents would sooner have seven points from a converted try, thank you very much.

One difficulty is that sometimes it isn't always the same player getting offside. When the same offence is shared out by a team, what can the referee do? A great deal. He can take a long, cool look at the way a number of different players have committed the same offence, and if he decides that it adds up to repeated infringement, then he can give the team a general warning. After that he has no choice. The next player to repeat that offence – even if he personally is doing it for the first time – must be sent off. Referees are not out there to make friends. They're out there to apply the laws of the game, and the laws give them considerable muscle to do it.

Dangerous play

1 Don't strike an opponent

And it's no good saying you hit him because he wouldn't let go of the ball. You're not allowed to thump *any* opponent, with or without the ball, at *any* time.

Players on your own side are different, but not much. (I once reffed a match in which a captain whacked one of his forwards before I could penalise the chap for a minor piece of foul play; so I didn't.) There's no specific ban on clouting a team-mate, but the Foul Play law says you must not do anything against the spirit of good sportsmanship. Is it unsportsmanlike to give a colleague a poke in the chops? I suppose it might be. If he's smaller than you, for instance. On the whole, it's safer not to belt anyone.

2 Don't hack, kick, stamp on or trip anyone

That's pretty simple. It was not always so.

As late as 1866, all that the laws of the game as played at Rugby School said about hacking was that you could not do it on or above the knee or with the heel, and you couldn't hold *and* hack, unless, of course the victim stupidly refused to release the ball, in which case you could settle down and batter him to a pulp.

In 1874 the Rugby Football Union declared that hacking and tripping were absolutely prohibited under all circumstances, a sure sign that a lot of it was still going on.

Today, of course, hacking is definitely out … Well, let's not get carried away; you don't see many manufacturers of shin-pads selling matches in the street; so let's say that any hacking is accidental rather than intentional.

Then there's stamping.

While you contemplate the grisly spectacle of one player stamping on another, you might like also to ponder what the law of the land says about negligence.

It says that everybody has a duty of care to his neighbour. This means that you must not behave in such a way that another person gets hurt. Do something which you know might be harmful, and you're guilty of negligence. What's more, you're just as guilty if you don't know and you don't care whether or not it's harmful. So where does stamping fit in?

Take a player who treads on an opponent to make him release the ball. That player knows he's doing harm; he must know; he can

Reckless = dangerous = foul play. Dangerous use of the boot is banned. This includes – for example – taking a wild and reckless kick at the ball when it's close to an opponent. Dangerous play is not necessarily malicious. It can also be careless. Players have an obligation to avoid both.

see what he's doing. Now take another player who charges into a ruck and then tramples on an opponent who happens to be underfoot. This player can't see where his boots are going and he doesn't care, as long as he gives the ruck a good shove. Which player is guilty of stamping?

Both are.

The first player may claim he was simply trying to winkle out the ball, which his opponent should have moved away from, according to law. The second player may defend his action by saying he was half-buried in a ruck, so he couldn't be expected to know what his feet were doing, and anyway his opponent was offside.

Neither excuse holds water. An opponent's offence cannot justify dangerous play; and it's a player's responsibility to *know* where his boots are, and to control what they do. Any player who stamps on someone is acting recklessly. Boots, and especially studs, can do great damage.

This is one area where the laws of the game overlap with the laws of the land. You might have a rush of blood to the head and end up in court; maybe in jail. Others have. Remember that, when you put your boots on. It's a game. It's not a war.

Lastly, there's tripping. Tripping is done with the foot. If you trip over somebody's hand or arm, that's your fault, not his.

3 Do not tackle dangerously

What is or is not a dangerous tackle is a matter for the referee to decide, but I can tell you that there are five kinds which bring the whistle to his lips like a flash. They are: early tackling; late tackling; high tackling; tackling an opponent as he jumps for the ball; and stiff-arm tackling.

Early and late tackles are doubly illegal – you're playing the man without the ball – and they are dangerous because your opponent has no chance to brace his body for the impact. In this respect, a late tackle can be worse than an early one, because the player has *relaxed* after giving his pass.

A high tackle is a tackle above the ball-carrier's shoulders, known in the trade as 'clotheslining', because it has the same throttling effect as running into a clothesline. You must not tackle an opponent around his neck or head. That includes yanking him

Dangerous play. An early tackle – like this, before the opponent has caught the ball – is dangerous and illegal. So is a late tackle, after he's passed or kicked.

by the collar. It also includes *trying* to tackle high. Even if he dodges and you grab sweet fresh air, you can still get penalised for making the attempt.

If an opponent is jumping for the ball – at a line-out, say, or when fielding a kick – it is dangerous play to tackle him while his feet are off the ground. That includes tapping or pulling his feet or legs. Why? Because he might land on his head. Satisfied?

'Stiff-arm tackle' is a slightly misleading term. The tackler can do it to the ball-carrier – but the ball-carrier can do it to the tackler too, so sometimes it's not even a tackle. What happens is one player hits the other with a stiff arm. When the tackler does it, he usually sticks his arm out where the ball-carrier's head runs into it. When the ball-carrier does it, he usually whacks the tackler with a rigid forearm. Either way it's dangerous play.

Avoiding causing injury is one of the responsibilities of playing rugby. Nobody expects a tackle to be pleasant or even painless, and one of the hazards of jinking your way through for a brilliant solo try is getting rudely dumped on your ass in the middle of it. But let us remember why we are playing this game; what the object is. The

Dangerous play. A high tackle – around the neck or head – is dangerous and illegal. You must not grab an opponent above the line of his shoulders, or by his collar.

aim in rugby is to win the ball and score with it. You get no thanks and no points for putting a player out of action. It's getting the ball that counts.

Once you find yourself making a tackle *in order to injure the player*, instead of *in order to get the ball from him*, then you are heading for a disaster the memory of which may haunt you for the rest of your life.

4 Don't bulldoze

Tackling was invented to stop the man with the ball. If you don't try to grab him but you simply charge into him or knock him down, this is dangerous play. After all, you can damage a player just by bulldozing into him. Similarly, it's dangerous play if you charge into a ruck or maul without binding onto a team-mate.

Dangerous play. Tackling a player while his feet are off the ground (because he's jumping to catch the ball) is dangerous and illegal. You must wait until he lands before you tackle him.

It's also possible for the ball-carrier to be guilty of dangerous play. Take the hand-off, which is normally used to fend off a would-be tackler from the side, not the front. If the ball-carrier finds an opponent dead ahead, and he runs at him with an arm stuck out like a battering ram, the referee might well judge that battering has no part in the game, and penalise him.

5. Don't obstruct him after he's kicked the ball

If you think you've been here before, well, you have. This is more of the same old stuff about not charging, tackling, holding, prodding, barging or in any way molesting a player who hasn't got the ball – in this case, an opponent who hasn't got it because he has just kicked it.

What is so special about this offence is the penalty: *either* a penalty kick at the place where you did it *or* a penalty kick at the spot where the ball comes down. Why should this be?

The thinking behind this law is as follows. Suppose you are a three-quarter belting down the wing, ball neatly tucked under the outside arm. Out of the corner of your eye you see an opponent, hurtling in for a tackle. Meanwhile, hobbling at top speed down the middle, as you know from past experience, is your entire pack of forwards, baying for blood. It is but the work of a moment to extract the ball from the armpit and cross-kick it smartly into their immediate future – say, about fifteen metres in front of them.

Eager to the point of rashness, of course, they are all slightly offside at the moment you kick the ball. Being decent, law-abiding types, they skid to a halt. So it's up to you to carry on flashing down the wing until you've caught up with them and put them onside.

Right now is when your opponent, foiled of his tackle, runs directly in your path. Obstruction, of course; but look at the effect! Not only has he stopped you from taking part in the game; he has

Obstructing the kicker: a choice of penalties. When a player kicks the ball, and is then obstructed by an opponent, that player's team can choose to take the penalty kick either where the obstruction happened or where the ball landed. Not much doubt which one they choose here.

also effectively stopped you from putting your forwards onside. So he has quietly killed your brilliant cross-kick, and with it perhaps a chance of a try. By God, skinning with a blunt putty-knife is too good for the swine.

What the law lays down, to discourage this kind of obstruction, is that the innocent party can choose to take its penalty kick in one of two places, as already described. If the player who obstructed the kicker did so to nullify a cross-kick, then the law makes sure he fails by giving his opponents the chance of a penalty kick in the middle, where the ball landed. On the other hand, it may be that the cross-kick was a wild one and came down in a poor place from which to take a penalty, so they have the option of taking it from the spot where the player was obstructed.

You can see this would work out just as well if the kicker put in a kick-ahead instead of a cross-kick, before he was obstructed. Also there's always the penalty-try law, which applies when foul play robs the attacking team of a probable try.

In case anybody is wondering what happens if the cross-kick or kick-ahead comes down close to touch, or in touch, the answer is the optional penalty kick is given 15 metres in from touch, opposite where the ball landed or crossed the touch line. And if the kick-ahead landed in the in-goal or touch-in-goal or on or over the dead-ball line, the optional penalty kick is given 5 metres from the goal line, opposite where the ball crossed that line, and at least 15 metres in from touch. Don't try to memorise this formula; you'll only strain your brains. Leave it to the referee. He knows his stuff.

One last thought about alleged obstruction after a player has kicked the ball, and also about alleged late tackles.

Sometimes the kicker invites trouble. He knows the tackler is closing in, and he delays his kick to the last micro-second. By then the tackler is flying. He's in mid-air. Don't ask him to go into reverse. Or perhaps he's square in the ball-carrier's path, poised and ready to try and charge down the kick if he can't make a head-on tackle. Next thing you know, the kicker's kicked and the tackler's tackled him. Or the kicker's kicked and he has instantly collided with his waiting opponent.

I don't think that was a late tackle; I think it was a late kick. I don't think the collision was obstruction; I think the kicker got his timing wrong. Tacklers have rights in this world, too, and kickers should not expect tacklers to do them the favour of backing off and giving them extra space and time to kick.

6. Don't touch him unless he's got the ball

This gets right to the heart of the matter. If rugby is to be a wide-open, man-to-man contest for a bit of streamlined leather, people have got to be free to try to intercept the ball (or the ball-carrier) just as fast as their puny limbs and wheezing lungs can carry them. What you cannot have is other players reaching and pawing at them, lurching into them and seizing handfuls of hair, clothing or fatty tissue, or simply sneaking up behind and unloading a large shove in the small of the back. I mean, it's hard enough to run right across a rugby field after a heavy meal and wearing someone else's

Off-the-ball obstruction. Except at scrums, rucks or mauls, it is illegal to hold, shove or interfere with any player who hasn't got the ball. That includes grabbing his jersey, his shorts, or even his hair. By law, it's dangerous play. Referees take it seriously.

boots, without being got at by some grasping saboteur who isn't even looking for the ball.

Similarly it is wrong to obstruct an opponent who hasn't got the ball and wants it, simply by being or getting in his way. Sometimes, of course, it's difficult to get *out* of his way until you know which way he's going; but not always. If you are standing right between him and your team-mate who has just caught the ball and fallen flat on his face with it, don't put your hands on your hips and wait to be asked to move. Just move.

Keen students of the printed word will be asking themselves, at this point, if they haven't been here before. Doesn't it all seem terribly familiar? A sense of what the French call *déjà vu?* (They play rugby too.) Well, yes and no. Our recent skirmish with the law of Obstruction included a warning against offside players obstructing opponents by getting or being between them and the ball. That's what you're thinking of. Why then, you ask, go over it all again? Two reasons.

First, there is a difference. The Obstruction offence talks about *offside* players who *obstruct* an opponent. The Dangerous Play offence covers *any* player, offside or on, who obstructs or *lays hands on* an opponent. Now this is much worse. It is at least under-standable that an offside player – by definition usually in front of a team-mate with the ball – might get in an opponent's way. It's wrong and it can't be allowed to pass, but it's understandable. But a player who hasn't even the excuse of being offside, and who not only obstructs an opponent but actually tries to distract him from the game by using force – now there is a bloke who is asking for trouble. He's in line for a penalty kick plus a warning or even a sending-off. There is no room in the game for private revenge. If you can't get the man with the ball, then don't get anybody.

That's the second reason for re-hashing this subject. It is important because it is absolutely basic, and therefore worth repeating a few times. The simple charm of rugby is that anyone can lay claim to the ball, and everyone else enjoys the same freedom to go after him and get it back. Don't try and stop them.

And don't imagine you can get around the law by grabbing a player's jersey instead of the player. Clothing counts, too.

In fact it hurts to have to tell you that there is one occasion when you can, lawfully, hold an opponent who hasn't got the ball, and that is in a scrum, ruck or maul.

Don't get too excited about it, though. As privileges go, this is worth about as much as sitting next to the driver on the bus. Besides, your opponents can do it to you, too.

7 Don't collapse the scrum (or ruck, or maul)

Telling a forward not to collapse the scrum is like telling a human pyramid not to scratch itself: horribly obvious. And yet it needs to be said, because you do see forwards doing it, for instance when their opponents have won the ball and are trudging relentlessly towards a pushover try.

Well, it's no good; you must not intentionally collapse a scrum. (If you merely come to pieces under the strain, that's different.) It's dangerous, and it negates the whole purpose of having a scrum, which is to have a scrum until the scrum is over. In this respect it's rather like travelling on the Tube, going to pop concerts, or making love: they're all scrums, and you simply have to see them through to the end.

8 Don't do anything dangerous

A few more insanities to avoid. Don't jump on a ruck or maul. Don't, if you are a front row of a scrum, rush against your opponents. Don't, if you are a front-row player, lift an opponent off his feet or force him up and out of the scrum, commonly called 'popping'. Once he's off his feet, he's helpless, and 'popping' him could seriously injure him. All these madnesses are classified as dangerous play and will get you penalised.

9 Don't retaliate

You must not do anything that is dangerous to an opponent. Sometimes it is difficult, I know; but the fact that some bloody idiot is behaving like a bloody idiot does not entitle you to behave like a bloody idiot. What's more, if the referee has penalised your opponent's idiocy, and you then retaliate, he may reverse his decision and penalise you instead. So keep your cool and collect the points. Winning is the best revenge.

10 'Flying Wedge' and 'Cavalry Charge' banned

Usually these tactics are used when the attacking team is awarded a kick near the goal line. For a 'Flying Wedge', they take a tap-kick, players bind onto the ball-carrier in a wedge formation, and they try to drive him over the line. For a 'Cavalry Charge', attacking players form a line across the field, some distance behind the kicker. At a signal, they charge forward, the ball is tap-kicked and one player takes a pass at speed. Both the 'Flying Wedge' and the 'Cavalry Charge' are dangerous and illegal at all age levels.

Misconduct

1. Do nothing contrary to good sportsmanship

As if you would.

2. Don't start anything while the ball is out of play

This is another of those splendidly vague laws which every civilized nation keeps tucked away in its hip pocket to deal with lunatics and hotheads. It simply says that, while the ball is out of play, you must not obstruct, or molest, or interfere with, or spit at, or denounce, or make up obscene limericks about, any opponent. Nor must you commit any sort of misconduct. (Try and get round *that*.)

The penalty kick is given not where the offence took place but where the ball would next have been brought into play. If, for instance, your opponents kicked the ball over your goal line and you touched it down, and an opponent came up and molested you right in the solar plexus, you would take the penalty kick from your 22-metre line, since you would otherwise have had a drop-out. If the ball goes into touch and there's some hanky-panky before it's thrown in, the penalty kick is given fifteen metres in from touch.

Finally – and just to lumber your echoing skull with some data which you will probably never use – if the referee gives a penalty kick, or awards a free kick, and an opponent blows a fuse before the kick is taken, the referee awards a second penalty kick, ten metres in front of the first kick, and this second kick replaces the first one.

In this and all other cases of Dangerous Play and Misconduct, the penalty kick is only half the penalty. The referee can send the player off, there and then. If not, he *must* warn him; and if the player does it again, he *must* send him off. That means he stays off for the rest of the game and, depending on the Disciplinary Committee's feelings, probably for several other games, too.

Red and yellow cards. The Sin Bin

When the referee sends a player off, never to return, he shows him a red card. When the offence is not serious enough for a red card but too serious for just a penalty kick, the referee shows the player a yellow card and that player is, so the lawbook says, 'temporarily suspended' – or, as you and I say, sent to the Sin Bin. Typical yellow-card offences are professional fouls (such as failing to release the ball in a tackle because opponents are likely to score a try), and persistent infringement (such as repeatedly getting offside). A second yellow card in a match means an automatic red card.

A yellow-carded player leaves the field for ten minutes of play. That means play. The half-time interval and recognised delays don't count. If a player goes to the Sin Bin two minutes before half-time, he must serve the remaining eight minutes of his sentence when the second half starts. If play stops for an injury or for a permitted delay (such as replacement of players), then Sin Bin time stops accordingly. All of which makes sense. Incidentally, there is no Bin, as such. The yellow-carded player just leaves the field and stands in the rain, looking martyred.

Footnote

There is only one judge of fact and of law during a match – the referee. The lawbook says so. Therefore you're wasting your time if you try to argue with him, because (a) he won't argue back and (b) he won't alter his decision. The laws say he *cannot* alter his decision, except in two cases, both involving a touch judge.

If the referee blows his whistle for something and then sees that a touch judge has his flag up, he can accept that the ball went into touch first and change his decision to a line-out. (Mind you, he can also overrule the touch judge.) In certain top fixtures, where the appointed touch judges are also qualified referees, they can help the referee by signalling if they see dangerous play or misconduct take place. When he next stops the game, he will go over and ask what happened, and then make his decision accordingly. In top fixtures where a Video Official (also a referee) has been appointed, the referee can delay his decision while the official studies video evidence. This usually concerns play in or near an in-goal when the referee was unsighted. Was the player in touch when he grounded the ball? Was it a try or a touch-down? Was the ball dead? Was the kick at goal successful? That sort of thing. Finally: match organisers may appoint a timekeeper to announce the end of each half.

Readers write

A.W. of Llanelli writes: I know you're not supposed to charge an opponent who's got the ball. You're always supposed to tackle him. But it never gets penalised, does it?

D.R. That depends on the circumstances.

A.W. Well, years ago, in an international, J.P.R. Williams shoulder-charged the winger into touch. He had to. It was a try, otherwise.

D.R. You're saying he had no choice. Maybe – but bulldozing the ball-carrier when you could tackle him is still Foul Play.

*   *   *

J.W. of Hawick writes: Is it a high tackle when the ball-carrier ducks at the last second?

D.R. Let the ref decide.

J.W. I mean to say, the tackler might be six-foot-four while his opponent's only four-foot-six.

D.R. Then the tackler should bend his knees more, shouldn't he?

7

Scrums

Including offside

I could write a whole book on scrums, and most of it would be junk.

It's one part of the game that has been turned into a special subject all on its own. Some people become experts in the scrum the way others spend their lives learning all there is to know about wallpaper, or the sex-life of the bloater. And it's about as big a waste of time as eating gravy with your fork.

Scrums are very simple. There is no secret about them. You can understand all, provided you use a little common sense and remember the ancient Chinese saying:

Only reason for scrum is re-starting game quickly and fairly.

Now, then. If that is its purpose, what is its shape? We all know what a scrum looks like – eight compressed men growing shorter and wider in an effort to telescope eight other compressed men – but what must you have, and what can you do without? It is (as you're probably starting to discover) all quite simple.

What is a scrum?

A scrum must have eight players from each team: no more and no less. Each front row must have three players. Each second row must have two locks. Each lock shoves on and binds on the prop in front of him. Flankers and No. 8 bind on one or both of the locks. Players must stay bound until the scrum ends.

The scrum begins as soon as the two front rows come together. The law says that from this moment the scrum-half *shall* put the ball in *without delay*. If he hangs around, picking bits of mud off the ball and waiting for his hooker to get comfortable, he is wasting time. He should be penalised, with a free kick.

Players often get upset about this, and usually for one of two reasons. They argue either that the scrum-half has to trundle off and get the ball, which takes time, or that the back-row forwards have to get themselves sorted out, which also takes time.

Both observations are true as far as they go. What they overlook is the fact that scrum-halves and back-row forwards can hustle pretty damn fast when they really want to. If they would only put a bit of ginger into their trundling, then half a second after the Front

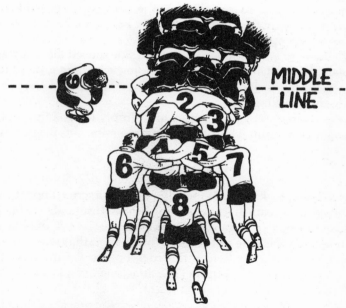

Bird's-eye view of a scrum. The scrum-half stands at least one metre from the mark on the middle line. (This imaginary line is beneath where the front rows' shoulders meet. The mark is in the centre of the line.) His head must not touch the scrum or enter the tunnel. Props (1 and 3) bind on the hooker (2), who binds on them. Locks (4 and 5) bind on each other and shove on the front row. Flankers (6 and 7) bind on the locks and shove on the props. No.8 must bind on the locks with at least one arm. All players in the scrum must bind onto it, using the full length of the arm.

Five went down the other forwards would be bound onto them. And half a second later the scrum-half would have the ball in.

It all depends on your attitude. If you regard a scrum as a kind of tea-break – a chance to lean on someone and get your breath back – then obviously there is no hurry. If you regard it as a piece of well-greased machinery for getting the ball into play, then you want to see it working quickly. Without cursing in my uncontrollable fashion, the laws leave no doubt that they are against tea-breaks.

Who puts the ball in?

Let's leave abortive rucks and mauls aside for a minute. Apart from them, the team not responsible for the stoppage that led to the scrum is the team that puts the ball in. For instance, if a player knocks-on, his opponents get the put-in.

Where there's any doubt about which side caused the stoppage, the team that was moving forward before everything ground to a halt gets the put-in. If neither team was moving forward, the put-in goes to the attacking side.

If the referee stops play purely and simply for an injury, play restarts with a scrum. The team last in possession gets the put-in.

Scrum after ruck

If the ball gets stuck in a ruck, the referee orders a scrum and the put-in is given to the team that was moving forward immediately before the ruck stopped. If neither team was moving forward (or if the ref can't decide), then the put-in goes to the team that was moving forward immediately before the ruck began. Failing this, the attacking team gets the put-in. (The attacking team is always the team in its opponents' half of the field.)

Scrum after maul

This is more complicated. For one thing, a maul comes to an end *either* when the ball becomes unplayable *or* when the maul stops moving or collapses. That's when the referee must blow up and order a scrum. (To be absolutely sure that it's come to a halt, he's

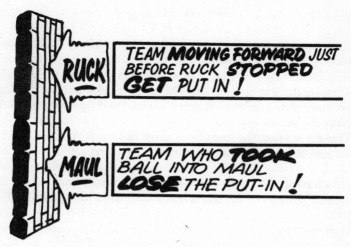

Bent arrows. When the ball fails to come out of a ruck or a maul, the referee orders a scrum. After a sterile ruck (ball on ground), the put-in goes to the team moving forward just before the ruck stopped. After a sterile maul (ball held), the team that took the ball into the maul loses the put-in to its opponents. A scrum from a maul resulting from a ball caught direct from an opponent's kick may be different: see text.

advised by the laws to allow a five-second pause before he blows his whistle.) The team that puts in the ball is the team that did *not* have the ball when the maul began. Use it or lose it. Sometimes the referee can't tell which team had it; in that case, the team moving forward before the maul came to a halt puts in the ball. If neither team was moving forward, the put-in goes to the attacking team.

There's more. A maul that forms after a player catches an opponent's kick-ahead may be a special case.

Suppose a player fields a kick-ahead, direct from his opponent's boot, and before he can move, players arrive and a maul forms. The maul goes nowhere or the ball fails to come out. The referee orders a scrum. In this case, the team of the player who originally caught the ball gets the put-in.

This exception does not apply to a ball caught from a kick-off or drop-out.

The front row

The front rows are the heart of a scrum. This is where it all happens. The rest is just horsepower.

Each front row must have three players in it – no more and no less. These three must link together firmly, so that they don't fall apart, and must combine properly with their opponents, so that nobody dislocates anything.

This means that the front rows must not form up some distance apart and charge each other. (An Irish forward actually broke his neck doing this in 1924.) And it means that the players must interlock naturally, with opposing heads next to each other. Two front-row players of the same team with their idiot heads locked together just break everything apart.

Within living memory, scrums collapsed, repeatedly. They no

Opposing heads must alternate. The heads of the two front rows must interlock so that adjacent heads belong to opposing teams.

sooner assembled than they disintegrated. Throughout the land, front-row forwards stuffed their faces into the mud, got up, heard the ref tell them not to do it again, and promptly did it again. And again. And again. Meanwhile, halfbacks and threequarters were being stretchered off with hypothermia.

That is why the scrum law now takes so much trouble over instructing front rows about staying on their feet.

For a start, the scrum-half should have the ball in his hands, ready to feed the scrum, before anyone thinks about making a tunnel. Then the two front rows should be standing not more than an arm's length apart, already crouched and in a position – when the referee calls 'Engage' – to meet. (If they're ready to meet. It's not an order. It's permission.) And when the front rows meet, each player must keep his head and shoulders no lower than his hips, thus ensuring that all six backbones are more or less horizontal.

The law about binding does two jobs. It keeps the front row intact, and it stops the hooker from swinging like a trapeze artist.

Every player in the front row must bind, and keep on binding, around his mate's body. The props latch on to their hooker, the hooker clamps both arms around his props. They must all bind around the body – *not* across the shoulders – so that they grip at or below armpit-level. If they do this properly, the scrum won't disintegrate and the hooker cannot swing into the middle of his opponents' second row.

The tunnel

The only reason for having the two front rows is to form a tunnel for putting the ball into, quickly and fairly. Therefore, like all good tunnels, this one must be open and dependable.

All front-row players must have their feet on the ground. Their feet must not be crossed, and they must be in a position to shove. That is what the law says. It doesn't say they have to shove, but it does say they have to be *in a position* to shove, and to shove forward.

A quick experiment against the nearest wall will prove that the only way to shove forward is to place the feet towards the rear. How far to the rear is a matter of taste, but an angle of forty-five degrees is one that appeals to many referees with long experience in the

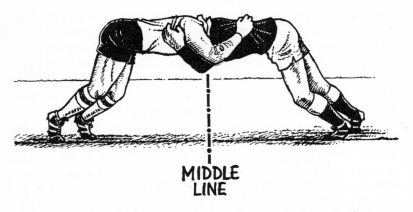

**MIDDLE
LINE**

Scrum-half's view of the tunnel. This shows (more or less) how the front-row players must have their feet back and in a position to shove, so that the ball can be put into the middle of the tunnel. Note that the left arm of the loosehead prop (black shirt) must be inside the tighthead prop's right arm. A prop must not pull his opponent down. Note also the horizontal backs: spines in line.

shoving business. Other referees feel that forty-three degrees is quite adequate, or that on a wet day forty-nine degrees is the absolute minimum. It's all a bit academic, because the laws also say that front-row players must keep their feet back far enough to allow a clear tunnel, come rain or shine. So that clinches it. Keep your size elevens pulled back so that the referee can see plenty of daylight on the other side, and you'll be all right.

If all this makes the front row of a scrum sound as balanced and sober as a Baptist missionary reunion, that is unfortunate, because it doesn't work out that way. Veins bulge, joints crack, discs slip, strange animal noises are heard, and – to paraphrase Dylan Thomas – steam comes gushing out of their nostrils. Considerable heaving and grinding take place.

Nevertheless, despite all the sado-masochism, the front rows have a duty to keep the tunnel standing and open. The hooker, for instance, must not hang entirely from his props: some of his weight must always be on his own feet. The tighthead prop must bind on his opposing loose-head prop by putting his right arm *outside* the loose-head's arm and gripping the back or side of his jersey. The loose-head prop must bind on his opposing tighthead by putting his left arm *inside* his opponent's right arm and gripping the back or side of his jersey. Neither prop is allowed to grip his opponent's arm or his opponent's sleeve, chest or collar. Props must not use their arms to pull down. And if all these detailed rulings strike you as being a bit longwinded, take it from me they're worth it. Their purpose is to avoid a lot of ill-tempered wrestling and some serious injuries too.

With each pack weighing well over half a ton, the pressure on the front rows is hefty enough already, without prop forwards trying to force their opponents' heads into the mud by dragging them down. A deliberately collapsed scrum is a temporary pain in the neck to other players, but it could be a permanent pain in the spine to a doubled-up prop.

A front-row player must not at any time – either before or after the ball is in – take both feet off the ground at once, or deliberately do anything else that might make the scrum collapse, such as twisting his body or forcing it downwards. Also once the ball is in the tunnel, he must not kick it back out again.

This is all pretty obvious. A scrum is to heel the ball. You can't have people deliberately preventing either the scrum or the heel from taking place.

Use it or lose it

When the ball is put into a scrum, and the scrum doesn't move and the ball doesn't immediately come out, then the referee will whistle, order another scrum and give the put-in to the team that was *not* in possession at the stoppage. Similarly, if the scrum moves, then stops, and the ball doesn't immediately come out, the team *not* in possession will get the put-in at the re-set scrum. Ditto if a scrum is wheeled through more than 90 degrees; the new scrum is where the old one ended and the team not in possession get the put-in. If neither team has won possession in any of these scenarios, the same team keeps the put-in. No longer can a team run down the clock by hiding the ball in the scrum or endlessly wheeling. Now, if you don't use it, you lose it.

The second and back rows

A scrum has a maximum and minimum of eight players. All eight must bind. You are not in a scrum unless you have at least one hand and arm *around the body* of a team-mate. Resting your hand lightly on the small of his back is not binding, either legally or physically.

If you are a flanker, packing in a 3–4–1 formation, you must bind around the second row, not the prop. This goes back to the principle of a three-man front row. A flanker who attaches himself to a prop-forward is creating a *four*-man front row. Another thing: as long as the ball is in the tunnel, only the front-row players may play it. No poaching by flankers or locks. Not surprisingly, second- and back-row forwards must not do anything which is banned in the front row. They must not collapse the scrum, or put the ball back in once it's out of the scrum, or handle the ball in a scrum, which (amazingly) includes picking it up with the legs.

Scrums: where?

You can have a scrum anywhere in the field-of-play – and nowhere else. So touch lines and goal lines are death to scrums.

The scrum should go down as near as possible to where the stoppage happened. If this is less than five metres from a touch line then the scrum is formed five metres from touch. This means there is a clear space five metres wide between the touch line and the scrum when it forms. Similarly, if the stoppage is near the goal line, then the scrum is formed five metres from the goal line - but that distance is measured, not from the nearest part (which would be the defending No.8's feet), but from the middle line of the scrum - the line where the front rows meet. It makes a difference.

The scrum must stay where it went down until the ball goes in, and it must be fairly square, too – not in shape but in position. The referee will make sure the tunnel is roughly parallel with the goal-lines when the scrum-half feeds it. He won't allow either pack to try to shove their opponents into the car park before that happens. The game restarts where it stopped. A team that heaves the scrum away from the mark before the ball can be put in will get penalised.

And now – for I see that the scrum-half has, at last, retrieved the ball from the sewage farm behind the pavilion – we might let him have a little go at throwing it into the tunnel.

Putting the ball in

This, it goes without saying, he should do honestly and fairly, so that both hookers get a good chance to hook the ball, and before we go any further I just want to say that if there is any more of that coarse, cynical laughter I shall go back to writing TV commercials. It's not my fault that all scrum-halves are cheats, rogues and con men. It must be something to do with their genes.

Mind you, the law as it is written doesn't leave the scrum-half much room for manoeuvre, although this hasn't noticeably stopped him trying. What it says is this:

The scrum-half must stand at least one metre from the mark on the middle line - the line where the front rows' shoulders meet. This is a change. The old law said 'one metre from the scrum'. Since the mark for a scrum is in the centre of the middle line, the scrum-half

Photofit of a scrum-half at the put-in. Note that he holds the ball with both hands, midway between knee and ankle, so that it is parallel to the ground, and puts it in straight (no backward movement, no dummying) along the middle line, so that it passes the nearer prop before it touches the ground.

can now stand closer. He must hold the ball with both hands so that, lengthwise, it is parallel to the ground and over the middle line. He must hold it midway between knee and ankle. Then, *without dummying or moving the ball back,* he must put the ball in quickly and straight down the middle line, so that it touches the ground just past the first prop forward. Thus, it must travel at least the width of the prop's shoulders into the scrum. He must release the ball while his hands are outside the tunnel.

And until it leaves the scrum-half's hands, no front-row forward may raise a foot.

You would think that that spelt it all out clearly enough, wouldn't you? And yet getting the ball into the scrum has caused more problems than any other single aspect of the game. Players complain that no two referees apply the same interpretation. Referees complain that players don't follow the law. Spectators just complain, not that anyone cares about them.

If it's any consolation, life was always thus. Down through the years men have aged and withered under the strain of finding a better way to put the ball into the scrum. In 1920 New Zealand suggested that the referee should do the job. In 1929 the International Board thought scrum-halves were standing too far away and throwing too hard. In 1931 the law was changed to make the scrum-half 'gently propel' the ball in. That didn't work very well, and next year the IB warned against 'throwing the ball into the scrummage with unnecessary force'. In 1934 the Rugby Football Union was explaining that 'gently propel' now meant that 'the ball is not put in at excessive speed'. In 1937 the scrum-half was told to put the ball in 'fairly, at moderate speed'. That didn't work, either, and in 1939 an RFU committee suggested scrapping everything and just telling the scrum-half to stand a metre away and pitch the thing in, since that was what he was doing anyway.

Ulster wanted the speed to be 'slow' instead of 'moderate'. Wales, however, liked 'moderate'. Scotland ignored the speed question and asked for several other changes. Leinster, Munster and Connaught each had their own ideas, and so did Hitler.

Hitler's proposals held attention until 1946, when the entire scrum law was considerably tidied up. This worked quite well, and in 1947 a South African suggestion that the ball be *rolled* into the scrum got nowhere, thank God.

The law today says that the ball should be put in quickly, and if you want to know what that means, it means 'at a quick speed as distinct from a slow speed'; so you can see that things haven't changed all that much.

The best advice for any scrum-half is simply to try and look at things from the referee's point of view occasionally. What does the referee want? He wants the scrum-half to get on with it and put the ball in as soon as the scrum is ready. He wants him to put it in hard enough to get past the loose-head prop, but not so hard that it rockets out the other side.

He would *like* him to put it in fairly – straight down the middle line of the tunnel – but he will usually settle for having it put in not too unfairly. He might let you steal an inch or so, but if you try and shoot the ball under your hooker's feet *and* the referee's eye, he is likely to feel insulted. It all boils down to this: don't be greedy.

Hooking the ball; foot-up

The ball must go into the scrum fairly (or not too unfairly), and it must come out in a similar way.

By common consent the hooker is responsible for this, since the ball must pass the loose-head prop, and the hooker is the next man in line. But the law which governs the hooker's actions also applies to the rest of the front-row players.

The hooker must not strike until the ball has touched the ground. After that he can go for the ball with either foot, provided he doesn't take both feet off the ground at once.

You will recall that the scrum-half is under orders to put the ball in quickly. People have calculated that if he does, and if it goes where it should, and if the hooker does not strike too soon, then the whole thing is impossible because the ball will have flashed across his bows before he can get a foot to it, such being the laws of nature. Other people have proved the same thing with motion pictures of the ball beating the hooker comfortably and barely getting trapped by the far-side props as it makes its bid for freedom.

What they are getting at is that any hooker who actually hooks the ball first time must have struck too soon, and thus be guilty of

A bad case of foot-up. This is what the scrum-half sees when his hooker, instead of letting the ball get right inside the tunnel, strikes too soon. Not a wise move.

foot-up. It may be so. Nevertheless, every week-end tens of thousands of hookers do manage to satisfy the referee *and* hook the ball, so there must be a way. What that way is, exactly, is something to be forged in the heat of battle; but a handy slice of advice for hookers is the same as the maxim for scrum-halves: don't be greedy.

Purists may consider that cynical, but then no purist was ever a hooker. Or *vice versa*.

Hookers tend to be the forgotten men of rugby, rather like miners, doing cramped and exhausting work where no one can see; so they might appreciate this small historical note, just to show that things could be worse. At least as late as 1889 the object of a scrum was not to hook the ball backwards but to hack it forwards, until you had kicked it right through your opponents. This might take some time – five minutes, ten? – because what with all the hacking going on, somebody was bound to miss the ball, and that might lead to deplorable retaliation, which in turn provoked more of the same, so that even when the ball did come out, views continued to be exchanged quite frankly and fearlessly in the depths of the meeting. Today's scrums have their share of crunch, but at least it's usually a short, sharp crunch.

Heeling the ball

One reason why the crunch is short and sharp is that it is now very easy to heel the ball from the scrum. It can come out anywhere except by the tunnel. You can heel the ball out between the prop's legs, or between the prop and the flanker, or through the flanker, or the second row – anywhere at all, as long as it's behind the tunnel. The scrum-half can put the ball in and have it heeled out to him half a second later, only a couple of feet away.

If the ball comes back out of the tunnel, the same scrum-half puts it in again, and on the same side. This applies if it goes right through the tunnel. If no front-row player touches the ball, and the prop on the far side sticks out a foot so that the ball goes behind it, this is *not* heeling, and the ball gets put in again.

However, there's an interesting variation on this. It's the kind of thing that has specialists in the finer points of front-row play chuckling with delight, like tax accountants who've just discovered another loophole. It has to do with advantage.

The advantage law says that advantage does not apply when the ball comes out of the tunnel at either end, *not having been played*. Note carefully those last four words. They make all the difference. You cannot have an advantage (in law) unless somebody's done something wrong. Now, suppose the scrum-half feeds the ball into the scrum crookedly; that's an offence. But suppose the ball is then played by any of the front-row players (which side they're on doesn't matter) and suppose it then pops out of the tunnel, where a flanker (say) who is an opponent of the feeding scrum-half unbinds and snaps it up. The referee can play advantage and let him go.

Another example: the scrum-half feeds, and the opposing hooker strikes too soon. His foot kicks the ball back out of the tunnel and into the same scrum-half's hands, and the scrum-half runs with it. The referee's entitled to play advantage, because (1) somebody infringed and (2) the ball was played before (3) it came out of the tunnel.

If the ball is heeled back by the second row, the number eight forward can detach himself from the scrum and pick it up, even though it is in front of him. By breaking from the scrum, he has in fact placed the ball outside it.

Ball in, ball out. In (A) the ball is still in the scrum, so the scrum-half must not handle it. In (B) the No. 8 has moved his right foot up, so that the ball is now out and the scrum-half can legally pick it up.

Picking the ball out

Normally, of course, it's the scrum-half who does the snapping-up, and he does it only when the ball has come right out of the scrum. Handling the ball in the scrum, you will remember, is illegal, and that goes for the scrum-half as much as the forwards. If his forwards heel the ball with all the free-flowing ease of cold treacle, that's just too bad: he'll have to wait for it. Even if it's lying right between his number eight's feet, within easy reach, the scrum-half must let it come to him, and not go in after it.

There is an easy test to decide whether or not a scrum-half is picking the ball out of a scrum. You say to yourself: if the ball were left where it is, and if an opponent were to come thundering round the scrum, would he be offside? If the answer is yes, then the ball is still in the scrum.

Not every scrum-half thinks this way. A good few feel that the ball is in the scrum until such time as they pick it out. It's an attractive theory, if you're a scrum-half, but not if you're an opponent – or a referee.

Scrum offside

There are two separate offside laws for scrums. One applies only to the scrum-halves. The other applies to everyone else.

Scrum-half offside

For scrum-halves, the offside line runs through the ball itself. As long as the ball is in the scrum, each scrum-half must stay on his own side of it.

This can make life a bit difficult for the scrum-half whose side *has not* heeled the ball. There he is, edging his way around the perimeter of the pack, trying to stay onside and yet also trying to get close enough to pounce when his opposite number grabs the ball. If he is too eager he will overstep the ball while it is still in the scrum; if he is too cautious it will pop out while he's out of range. He has to walk the fine line between giving away a penalty kick and giving away possession.

This assumes that the ball is heeled quickly, something which last happened in November 1937. When the ball comes back slowly, the scrum-half on the non-heeling side has more time in which to follow it through. However, even if he can see it, he must not try to kick it out of the scrum.

Both scrum-halves are forbidden to kick the ball while it's still in the scrum. What's more, the scrum-half who *didn't* put the ball in is not allowed to circle around to the *opposite* side of the scrum and patrol that area. On that side, he can go no further than the rest of his backs – which means staying behind the tail-end of the scrum, until the ball is out.

Not so the scrum-half who put the ball into the scrum, though. He is free to stroll around to the opposite side whenever he likes (provided, of course, he stays behind the ball in the scrum). And if

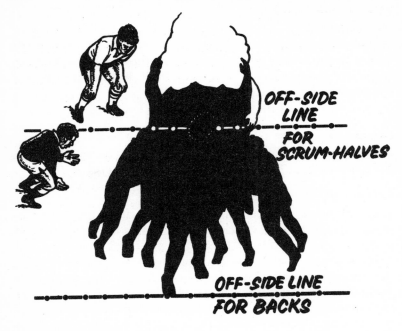

Scrum offside lines. While the ball is in the scrum, each scrum-half must stay on his own side of the ball. All other players (normally the backs) must stay behind the tail-end of the scrum until the ball comes out.

his forwards are skilled enough to channel the ball out through the south-east corner of the scrum, there's precious little the opposing scrum-half can do to prevent him from snapping it up and putting it to work, what with that back row shielding him like a set of flying buttresses. It all means that any pack of forwards which is good enough to hook the ball and heel it intelligently can pretty well guarantee their scrum-half perfect possession.

What's more the scrum-half whose team wins the ball is granted one small advantage by the law. When the ball is still in the scrum, he can plant one foot in front of it without being offside. (This is to help him get his pass away.) The opposing scrum-half must keep *both* his feet behind the ball, or he's offside.

'Offside trap' banned

One thing a scrum-half must not do is try to lure his opponents offside. In the past this has been the cause of much bad acting. While the ball was held in his back row, the scrum-half would exercise his arms, as if passing to his outside-half. It's now illegal for a scrum-half to do anything to make his opponents think the ball is out of the scrum when it's not. The offside trap is dead.

Offside for the rest

For everyone except the scrum-halves, the scrum offside line runs through the tail-end of their side of the scrum. (Thus there are *two* offside lines, one for each team.) Normally, when the scrum forms properly, the line runs through the feet of the number eight forward, since these stick out furthest. Until the scrum ends every player who is not part of the scrum must keep both feet behind this line (or behind his goal line, if the scrum is straddling it). The scrum ends when the ball is heeled out, so the side which gets the ball starts off with anything up to ten or twelve feet of clear ground between it and the nearest tackler (except for the opposing scrum-half)– enough space to start an attack.

This is what the law wants to happen. Its aim is to nail the back row to the scrum until the ball comes out – the only exception being the hindmost player (usually the No. 8), who can unbind from the scrum if he has the ball at his feet. But neither the No. 8 nor the flankers, at either end of the scrum, are allowed to break away early. The back rows must bind and remain bound until the ball is out. If a team wins possession in a scrum, its flankers or No. 8 can no longer detach themselves in readiness for a back-row attack. Similarly, the opposing team cannot detach its back row to form a defensive barrier. The glory days of the marauding back row are gone.

This is nothing new. The lawmakers have been balancing attack with defence ever since the game began. Fifty years ago, the off-side line at scrums ran though the ball; and so it moved with the ball in the scrum. Wing forwards (as flankers were known then) could break and follow the ball as it got heeled through their opponents' scrum, until they were poised, itching

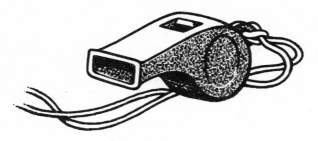

You get only one referee at a match. You can make the best of him, or you can make the worst of him – but you won't change him. If you cause him problems, he's likely to pay more attention to you than to your opponents who are not causing him problems. Is that going to help you win the game? Moral: Think what you like, but keep your big mouth shut.

to pounce on the scrum-half. If he avoided their clutches, the outside-half got the ball with little space to work in.

Life wasn't much easier at line-outs. The offside line ran down the line-of-touch, which meant that it was possible for the opposing three quarters to stand toe-to-toe. With no maximum length for the line-out, wing forwards were free to roam and cause havoc in midfield. The wonder is that halfbacks and centres ever had a chance.

Eventually, the lawmakers restored some balance. Offside lines got pushed back to the hindmost foot at the scrum (and ruck, and maul) and to a line ten metres behind the line-out. The second rows were obliged to remain bound to the scrum. (Within living memory, only the front row was necessary to form a scrum, and it was not unknown for a captain with a weak scrum to pull out his back five and tell them to go off and tackle somebody.) The changed laws created space for the team that won the ball: twenty metres of it at a line-out; three metres or more at a scrum.

For a while, the balance was good. Then, gradually, three things happened. First, back-row players got fitter and faster. They made space shrink. Secondly, they stopped even pretending to shove when it was the opposition's put-in at the scrum; instead they broke off and plugged a few gaps in defence. And thirdly, coaches got better at coaching defence rather than attack. As a result of all this, the midfield became crowded with players once more. Attacks were stifled. The balance was lost again.

Hence the lawmakers' introduction of an eight-man scrum bound solid until it ends. This makes a difference three ways. The team winning possession should be able to get the ball back and out fast, before the opposition can use an eight-man shove to disrupt the heel. With the opposing flankers pinned to the scrum, the half-backs should have more time to make their moves. And with the No. 8 a fixture at each end, the scrum becomes a yard or two longer – which widens the gap between the offside lines and thereby creates more space for attack.

And in case you're wondering what happens when a team is down to fewer than fifteen players because of injury or sending-off, they're allowed to reduce their number in the scrum accordingly.

When the scrum turns: the 90-degree law

Once upon a time, back in the days when all decent rugby shorts reached the knee and well-bred scrum-halves wore mitts, there was a referee's nightmare called The Rotating Scrum.

What happened was the scrum wheeled until it had made a half-circle. The scrum offside lines were supposed to run through the tail-ends of the scrum, but now the tails had become the heads. What if a flanker were to break? Which way should he run to get onside? Forward or back? Who could go where? And why?

At this point the referee usually awoke, bathed in a cold sweat.

All that, thank God, is a thing of the past. If a scrum is wheeled through more than 90 degrees (a quarter circle), so that the middle line – the line of the scrum-half's feed – has moved beyond a position parallel with the touch lines, then the referee calls a halt, blows up, and re-sets the scrum. He does this at the place where the old scrum ended (which may be some distance from where it began). Whichever team had won possession in the old scrum, their opponents get the put-in at the new one. If neither team had possession, the put-in stays with the team that previously had it.

90-degree wheels seem to arrive in clusters, like meteorites or buses. Meanwhile no rugby gets played. That's when the referee is liable to point out that any team which intentionally wheels the scrum 90 degrees or more is guilty of Unfair Play, and there are penalties for this. Sanity soon prevails.

As for players not in the scrum: wheeling changes nothing. Scrum-halves must stay behind the ball, and other backs must stay behind their tail-end of the scrum. As the scrum rotates, that tail-end might no longer belong to their No 8. It might conceivably attach to a lock, or even a prop. Makes no difference. The offside line runs through the hindmost foot. That's the law.

Penalties for scrum offences

Wrongdoing in or around a scrum is penalised *either* by a penalty kick *or* by a free kick.

The free-kick offences are for what you might call 'technical mistakes'– crooked feed; hooker striking too soon; front-row feet blocking the tunnel; kicking the ball out of the tunnel; putting the ball back in the scrum; any delay; working the offside trap; and so on. It's also a free-kick offence if a team shoves the scrum off the mark before the ball is in.

Scrum-linked crimes that lead to penalty kicks are the more serious things – one front row charging another; any player binding illegally; 'popping' an opponent; twisting or dipping so as to collapse a scrum; handling the ball in a scrum; flanker widening his angle to obstruct opposing scrum-half; and all sorts of offside.

These are all a threat to the player or the game, or both. Interesting to note that the law book devotes three pages to describing how the front rows should bind, but only three lines to how the rest of the scrum should bind. If a flanker can't bind, the scrum won't fall down. If a prop slips his binding, it might. That's why props have to be far more intelligent than flankers. I know. I was one.

Readers write

M.F. of Cork writes: I never heard such fairytales as that stuff you wrote about scrums.

D.R. Give me an example.

M.F. For a start, the scrum-half never stands one metre from the mark, he always stands closer. And he always feeds his own hooker, and the hooker is never in a position to shove. If his props were to let go of him, he'd fall down sideways! Don't you ever watch TV?

D.R. Anything else?

M.F. Front-row players never bind around the armpits. Most of them haven't got arms long enough. And their shoulders are usually lower than their hips. Every prop tries to pull his opponent down. It's a private battle up front, isn't it? Who needs laws?

D.R. The players need them because sometimes everything goes to hell, the ball never gets into the tunnel, the scrum keeps collapsing, and so on. Players get hurt. That's when the referee uses the laws to rebuild the scrum from scratch. And he needs laws to stop players cheating. For instance, a hooker who slips his binding is getting an unfair advantage, because he can strike further and faster.

* * *

T.W. of Queensland writes: When is the ball out of the scrum? I've seen it lying in the same spot for a long time before the scrum-half picked it up. If it was out, why didn't the other scrum-half go for it?

D.R. I've often asked myself that question.

* * *

D.S.K. of Harrow writes: This is about the scrum-half who didn't put in the ball. What's to stop him running wide, ready to tackle the centres? If he stays behind the ball, he's onside.

D.R. The lawmakers thought of that one. They ruled that the scrum-half must either stay near the scrum or get behind his scrum's offside line.

8
Rucks and mauls

A ruck
Puts the ball in the muck,
Whereas a maul
*Requires hands on the ball.**

Rucks

If you have thoroughly read and completely understood all the preceding guff about scrums – all right, don't lie to me – you won't have any trouble understanding rucks.

A ruck is simply a scrum with all the starch taken out of it. Its purpose is the same – to get the ball back in play – and most of the laws that cover a scrum apply to a ruck.

The big difference, of course, is that you can't have any specialists in a ruck, which is simply a first-up, first-down affair. This cuts out all the scrum-half / hooker / flanker / number eight rubbish, because none of those gents is recognisable in a ruck. And we are spared the pomp and ceremony of putting the ball in, since the ball is already in. This effectively eliminates any special scrum-half offside law, because after all *any* player could be scrum-half at a ruck, so no favoured treatment is going to be handed out there. There is only one offside law for rucks, and it applies to everybody.

* Anonymous Japanese haiku.

What is a ruck?

First things first, however. What exactly is a ruck? It's important to know this, because you are not, for instance, allowed to handle the ball in a ruck. On the other hand, if you hesitate to grab the thing because you aren't sure whether or not a ruck is taking place, you could be missing a slice of glory. So pay close attention.

To have a ruck, all you need is one player from each team in the field-of-play, on their feet and shoving each other, with the ball on the ground between them.

If any other player joins the ruck, he must bind on to a team-mate; but the heart of a ruck is simply a pair of opponents, shoving over the ball on the ground. If they are not opponents, or if they're not shoving each other, or if the ball is not on the ground, or if it's on the ground but not between them, then it's not a ruck, and you can go where you like and do what you will (subject to the other laws, of course).

What makes a ruck. This get-together meets all the requirements of a ruck: ball on the ground, in the field-of-play, with opponents over it and shoving each other. The offside lines run through the tail-ends of a ruck. You must either join it, from behind your own offside line, or get behind it. If you join it, you must do so alongside the hindmost player – not in front of him. You're not in a ruck unless you're bound onto it. Shoulders must be no lower than hips.

Offside at a ruck

The ruck offside lines run through the tail-ends of the ruck, just as they do in scrums. If you are not in a ruck you have a choice. You can *either* get behind its tail-end (if you're not already there) and stay behind it, *or* you can join the ruck. If you want to join it, you've got to start from your team's side of it. Then find your hindmost team-mate in the ruck and get stuck in alongside him or behind him. Do not join the ruck in front of him, or you'll be offside.

This is important. Often there is an attractive opening halfway up the side of the ruck, just tailormade for you to slot into. Don't be seduced. The laws says that anyone joining a ruck must add himself to the tail. Same applies if you leave a ruck. First, you get behind your offside line, and do it fast. Then, if you want to rejoin, attach yourself to the nearest team-mate at the stern. The ball may be elsewhere. It may be very elsewhere. Forget it.

If you're not in the ruck, stay behind the offside line until the ruck ends, which is when the ball comes out.

Rucks tend to take place unexpectedly, of course. It is not uncommon for a whole slew of players to be caught offside when a ruck suddenly breaks out. Nor will they suffer for it, necessarily. Provided they don't hang around, and provided they do their little best to scurry back where they belong, the referee will look upon them charitably. It is when he sees them shambling back, and notes that they are not displaying that bustle and vigour of ten minutes ago when they thought they were going to score a try for the first time in twelve years – *that* is when he gets impatient and starts handing out penalty kicks.

When you come to think of it, there is precious little point in ruck-mooching and risking getting caught for being offside. If you're going to get stuck into a ruck, you might as well pull your finger out and *do* it. If you're not, then you might as well prepare to make yourself useful when the ball comes out. If it comes out on your side, you'd better be behind it, for obvious reasons. To join a ruck, you must bind onto a team-mate as you arrive. If you simply charge into a ruck or maul without binding, this is dangerous play.

There are various other things to say about rucks – things like: don't handle the ball in a ruck; don't make the ruck collapse; don't jump on a ruck; don't fake a pass from a ruck – the Offside Trap is banned at rucks as well as scrums; if you're on the ground get away from the ball ... but you know all that stuff by now anyway.

In any case, it's all common sense. As we said before, a scrum is to heel the ball away. You can't have people deliberately preventing either the scrum or the heel from taking place – and that applies to rucks too. Much scoring comes after rucks, so every player should understand them. That means backs as well as forwards. There is no class discrimination at the bottom of the heap.

Mauls

The big difference between a ruck and a maul – listen, because I'm not going to say this again – is that for a ruck the ball must be on the ground, whereas for a maul a ball must be carried. *A ruck needs only two players, whereas a maul must have at least three: one from each side around the man who is carrying the ball, in the field-of-play, and all of them*

What makes a maul. A maul is like a ruck except that the ball is held, not on the ground. It needs at least one player from each team plus the man with the ball, all caught up in the maul or bound onto it. The offside lines run through the tail-ends. You either join the maul (from behind your offside line) or you get behind it. You must join alongside the hindmost player, not in front of him.

OFF-SIDE LINE

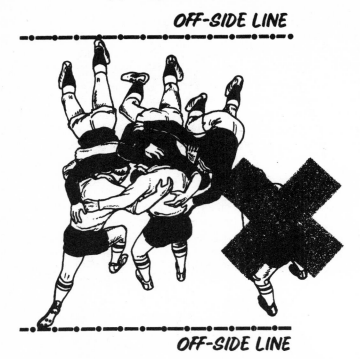

OFF-SIDE LINE

Ruck and maul offside. This handy all-purpose illustration could be a ruck (ball on ground) or a maul (ball held). Offside is the same for both. The offside lines run through the tail-ends of the ruck or maul (through the hindmost foot). Any player in front of his team's offside line must get behind it, fast, or he may be penalised for loitering with intent to spoil his opponents' possession. The player marked with a cross is loitering. He's in trouble.

wrestling for possession. You are not in a maul unless you're caught up in the struggle or bound on to it.

Maul offside

The offside law for mauls follows the same lines as scrum and ruck offside. The offside lines at a maul run through the tail-ends of the maul. And – just as with a ruck – you have a choice. You can *either* get behind the maul and stay there until it ends, *or* you can join it. If

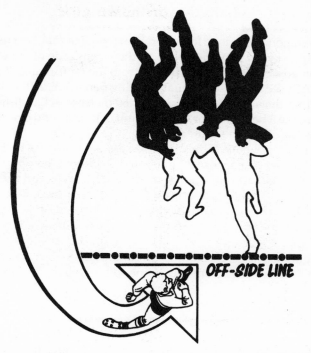

OFF-SIDE LINE

Leaving and rejoining a ruck or maul. This overhead view shows a ruck or maul. The offside law is the same for both. A player in a ruck or maul who wants to leave it must first get back behind his team's offside line. This runs through the tail-end. Then he can rejoin it, provided he does so alongside the hindmost player – not in front of him.

you join it, do so alongside or behind your hindmost team-mate in the maul. If you want to pull out and rejoin it, unplug yourself and retire behind your offside line first; then plug in alongside or behind your hindmost team-mate, but not in front of him. All very familiar, isn't it?

I said a lot about players who get caught in an offside position when a ruck breaks out and then get into hot water for loitering. Exactly the same applies to mauls. So does the banned Offside Trap. Faking a pass from a maul is illegal.

Loitering on the wing

When someone gets done for loitering at a ruck or maul it's usually a forward, caught hanging about on the wrong side of the offside line. Sometimes it's a centre who has crept too far forward. But you don't often see a wing-threequarter being penalised. After all, he's so far from the action – perhaps 50 or 60 metres – what difference does it make if he's a step or three in front of the tail-end of a ruck or maul on the other side of the field?

Ask his opponents. If they win possession, move the ball wide, and suddenly see the enemy winger closing down their options, it's because he had an unfair start on them. (Referees call this 'The Banana Effect' – when the wing is offside he's in front of his centres, and the backline curves like a banana.) Thus an offside player loitering on the wing can be as damaging to an attack as if he were loitering on the fringe of the ruck or maul. By cutting down his opponents' options, he's damaging their chances of attack. The offside line stretches from touch line to touch line, and there's a good reason for that.

Scrum after ruck or maul

I know we did all this in the chapter on scrums, but a quick round-up would do no harm.

When the ball in a ruck is unplayable, the put-in at the scrum goes to the team that was moving forward just before the ruck stopped. Failing that, it goes to the team moving forward just before the ruck began; and failing *that*, to the attacking team (the team in its opponents' half).

When the ball in a maul becomes unplayable, or when the maul stops moving, the put-in at the scrum goes to the team that was *not* in possession of the ball when the maul began. If the ref can't decide, then the team last moving forward gets the put-in; failing that, it goes to the attacking team. The put-in following a maul after a kick-ahead has been caught may be different.

So, here's a summary of the round-up. After a ruck, the team finally moving forward gets the put-in. After a maul, the team originally in possession does *not* get the put-in. They didn't use it, so they lose it. Makes you think.

The pile-up

After scrums, rucks and mauls, there is a fourth type of steaming heap to be seen on the rugby field. It's known as a pile-up. You won't find the word anywhere in the lawbook, but every referee knows what it looks like; so we might as well cover it here.

Rucks and mauls have this in common: the players are on their feet. Sometimes the irresistible force hits the immovable object, and the object moves. The feet lose their footing. Civilisation crumbles. Next thing you know, bodies are stacked horizontally like logs of wood. What is the referee to make of this? It's not a ruck, nor a maul. It's a pile-up.

If he reckons the ball will pop out fairly immediately, he might give it a brief chance. If it doesn't, he must blow up and order a scrum. However, he has a couple of other shots in his locker. If he reckons a player is lying on or near the ball when he could get away if he tried, the referee can penalise him. If he reckons a player intentionally fell on or over the pile-up, thus making the ball even more unplayable, he can penalise him.

The referee should not delay. Because the pile-up is a helpless mess, there's a big risk someone might make it even worse with his boot. The pile-up is a clot in the bloodstream of the game, and the referee has a powerful de-clotting agent: his whistle.

Readers write

P.N. of Manchester writes: I saw a bloke convert a try by standing with his back to the posts and drop-kicking the ball over the bar with his heel. Brilliant!

D.R. What's that got to do with rucks and mauls?

P.N. Nothing. My point is, the ref disallowed it. Why?

D.R. Because it wasn't a legal kick. The laws of the game say a kick means hitting the ball with your foot or leg, anywhere between the knee and the toe but not the heel. Back-heeling the ball over the bar is a fancy trick that scores *nul points*.

* * *

C.G. of Natal writes: Let's get this straight. Handling the ball in a ruck is wrong, but the scrum-half can use his foot to winkle it out of the edge of a ruck. Yes?

D.R. Yes. But if he sticks his foot in front of the ball in a ruck, and he's not binding on the ruck, he's offside.

C.G. What if he uses his hands to drag the ball out?

D.R. Unwise. You can't handle the ball in a ruck.

C.G. But the scrum-half can reach into a maul to get the ball.

D.R. Of course. The ball's being handled in a maul, anyway.

C.G. Can he put his foot into a maul?

D.R. Are you crazy? He'll pull a hamstring.

* * *

P. de B. of Paris writes: Quelle est la raison de la décision du 'put-in' dans la mêlée aprés un "maul" abortif, par contraste avec un 'ruck' abortif?

D.R. C'est simple. Parce que le ballon est par terre pendant un 'ruck', aucune équipe ne peut l'avoir en sa possession. Alors, l'equipe qui avance au début, merite le 'put-in'. Mais, pour faire un 'maul', un joueur doit avoir le ballon dans les mains. Donc, l'arbitre pense: 'Faisen quelquechose, ou perds-le!' Si cette equipe ne peut pas recycler le ballon, le 'put-in' est donné à leurs adversaires - comme il se doit.

T.F. of Bradford writes: What was all that about?

D.R. The reasoning behind different put-ins at scrums after rucks and after mauls. A player actually carries the ball into a maul, so it's reckoned to be his team's fault if they can't get it out again. That's why they lose the put-in. But neither team possesses the ball when a ruck forms (ball on ground), so if it doesn't emerge, the team going forward before it stopped deserves to get the put-in.

* * *

H.A. of Cambridge writes: At a kick-off or a drop-out, the team receiving the kick often catch the ball and immediately bind onto the catcher and form a wedge. That's not a maul, is it?

D.R. No. A maul must have an opponent in it.

H.A. So there's no maul offside line, then.

D.R. Correct.

D.R. And any player on the kicker's team can legally go around the wedge and grab the ball.

D.R. He'd be a brave man. But you're right. If the kicker's team don't want to create a maul, then no maul exists, and their players are free to go anywhere.

* * *

A. McL. of Kelso writes: If the pile-up is so frequent, why isn't it in the laws?

D.R. I sometimes wonder that myself.

* * *

N.J.M. of Dorset writes: What if the ball-carrier in a maul goes to ground? Falls to his knees, for instance. It's not a ruck, but it's not a maul either – the ball-carrier should be on his feet in a maul. What next?

D.R. Unless the referee sees that the ball is likely to come out at once, he blows up and orders a scrum.

9

The law that nobody knows

Offside and onside following a quick ruck, maul, scrum or line-out

Nobody knows? I exaggerate. At the last count, four people did actually know this law: two referees, a sportswriter who has since left the country, and myself.

You may remember that earlier we said that in open play – not during scrums, rucks, mauls or line-outs – you could be offside only if you were in front of someone on your team who had the ball, or who played it last. That is what we said and we make no apology for it, because it's true – 99.9 per cent of the time.

There is just one situation, however, in which it isn't true. You can be offside, *even though your opponents have the ball and no scrum, ruck, maul or line-out is taking place,* if they have just forced a snap scrum, ruck, maul or line-out between you and your line, won the ball and started an attacking movement. In that situation you are offside and there's nothing you can legally do until they have put you onside, which they can do only by kicking the ball or running five metres with it. Passing the ball does *not* put you onside, not after they've forced a snap action and won quick possession from it. Understand?

No. As I thought. From the rows of sagging jaws, glassy eyeballs, and calloused thumbs scratching numbed skulls, I can see that we have achieved something less than total, blinding comprehension. Perhaps we should try it again, this time more slowly.

For a start, let's narrow it down to rucks and mauls. I suppose it's conceivable that this law might apply to a scrum or a line-out, but it's highly unlikely because everything would depend on a player taking so long to catch up with play that the scrum or the line-out could begin and end while he was still trying to get back to it. Possible, but very improbable. Rucks and mauls, on the other hand, are much more spontaneous affairs. It's not unusual for a player to find himself a long way on the wrong side of (say) a ruck. While he's running towards it, his opponents win the ruck and start passing the ball. He's offside, and nothing he does can change that. Only his opponents can put him onside, by kicking or by running five metres with the ball – not by passing it.

Picture this. Blues are playing Whites, and all the action is inside the Blues' half. Suddenly, a Blue player breaks clear and puts in a tremendous kick ahead. The Blue team races upfield and catches the White full-back in possession. A maul forms. Blues win the ball, get it out and start an attacking movement.

At this point some White defenders arrive on the scene, pounding back to help save the day. Obviously they *were* offside during the quick maul, but the maul is now over. On the other hand, would it be fair to let them rush into the game and destroy the Blue

Act One: The big Blue breakaway. A White attack fizzles out in the Blue half. Blues win the ball and a Blue player puts in a huge kick, deep into the White half.

Act Two: Blues beat Whites to the maul. The White full-back fields the kick. Blue players arrive, tackle him and force a maul. White defence is slow getting back.

attack? An attack which the Blue players sweated for and earned by being faster and more quick-thinking than Whites?

Wouldn't it be like rewarding Whites for being slower, and might it not be an incentive against hurrying back to join the maul or at least to get behind it where they're onside? After all, if the leisurely defender can turn up and immediately tackle an attacker, he might deliberately take his time, reckoning that Blues are going to win the ball anyway, and he can do more damage if he catches them starting an attack and tackles from behind than if he hurries and gets in front, where they can see him.

Clearly, slow play cannot be allowed to succeed at the expense of fast play. So the sluggish defender is made to pay for being late. An offside defender retiring towards a ruck or maul is covered by the appropriate offside law while the ruck or maul is going on. But, if his opponents have won the ball, and he's still slogging back, he's covered by the Forgotten Law of offside, which says he must not interfere with play until he's been put onside.

Only his opponents can do this. There is no offside line for him to retire behind. The only way he can become onside is for an opponent to kick the ball, or run five metres with it. Until then, the defender can only wait and curse, and he'd better do *that* under his breath.

In general play, a player is always put onside the moment an opponent plays the ball; for instance, by passing it. But this is not general play; it's a sort of untidy aftermath; and the leaden defenders don't get let off so easily. They must concede their opponents at least a run of five metres or a kick before they can interfere. A pass alone is not enough to put them onside; neither is two passes, nor three nor four. Only a kick or a five-metre run will do the trick.

The situation outlined above (Blues versus Whites) doesn't often happen. There isn't usually such a great difference in speed and stamina between the attacking and the defending sides. But there is

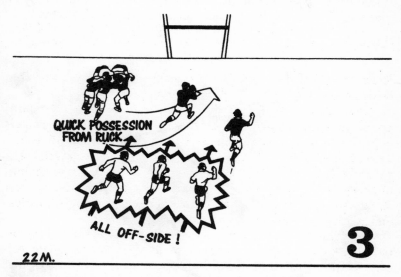

Act Three: Blues attack, Whites arrive, offside! Blues win quick possession and pass the ball. As they attack, White defenders arrive. They are offside. They must not take part in the game – even though the maul is over – until a Blue player kicks or runs 5 metres with the ball. This puts them onside. Nothing else does.

one aspect of the modern game where this particular offside law does increasingly apply, and that's the quick heel from a ruck following a scrum or line-out.

Say that Blues heel from a scrum and the ball reaches their fly-half, who gains fifteen metres and is tackled. Immediately, the Blue back-row zeroes in and rucks for the ball. They heel it out and are ready to start another passing movement when the White forwards arrive on the scene, too late to ruck but eager to tackle – and all offside.

Now, the ruck (or maul) is an important part of the game. Fast second-phase possession is the best way to revive an attack, when the defence has been sucked in by the ruck (or some of it, anyway).

Knowing this, a couple of the defending forwards may decide to take their time about covering across the field after a set piece, on the principle that the best time to reach a ruck is just after your opponents have heeled from it. Which is true as far as it goes. It just doesn't take into account the basic nature of the game. Rugby is meant to be a fast-moving, attacking game, and the Forgotten Law

First Phase: scrum ball – stand-off break – tackle. From a scrum, the Blue stand-off gains 20 metres and is tackled. The Blue back row, backing up fast, reach him and ruck. White forwards are just leaving the scrum.

PHASE 1

Second Phase: ruck ball – attack – defenders arrive – offside! Blues win the ruck ball quickly. White defenders reach the scene just as the Blues are beginning a passing movement. Whites are offside and must not interfere – even though the ruck is over – until a Blue player kicks or runs 5 metres with the ball. This puts them onside. Nothing else does.

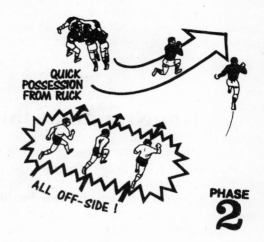

of offside exists to protect that aim. It is very seldom applied, but it's always there, if needed.

It was needed in the England-New Zealand match of 1993. England suddenly broke out of their half and took play deep into the visitors' half. Just as England heeled the ball from a ruck, Sean Fitzpatrick (the All Black captain) arrived. The ruck was over. He knew he was still offside – his hands were raised in that familiar (but futile) gesture. He touched nobody, but he got in the way of the England scrum-half. And he got penalised for it.

Maybe more people know the law that nobody knows than I give credit for.

Readers write

L.G. of Chipping Sodbury writes: I've read that chapter three times and I still don't understand it.

D.R. Are you complaining or boasting?

10
Touch, and the throw-in

Touch

Where is it? Touch is the area beyond the sides of the field-of-play, and there's not much more to be said.

Two things save touch from being a complete waste of time. One, it provides somewhere for spectators to stand. Two, it marks a definite boundary to the field-of-play, without which everybody would be on the point of collapse after about four minutes.

Once the ball goes into touch it becomes dead, and play is restarted by throwing the ball in. The touch line is in touch, but the corner-posts are not – they are in touch-in-goal, which is a different story.

The ball alone. When the ball is in free flight (not held by a player) and it touches a touch line, or the ground (or anything on the ground) beyond the touch line, then the ball is in touch.

Note that being in touch is *not* a matter of crossing the touch line; it's a matter of landing on or beyond the touch line. If the ball flies through the air and crosses the touch line but swings back or gets blown back and comes down in the playing area, play goes on.

The ball carried. When a player is holding the ball and he touches a touch line or the ground beyond it, then the ball is in touch. Similarly, when the ball held by him touches a touch line or the ground beyond it, it's in touch.

But note the word 'ground'. If a tackler sweeps his opponent off his feet so that the tackler ends up in touch but he is *underneath* his opponent's legs, while the upper half is still in the playing area and still holding the ball – that ball is not in touch. The ball-carrier's feet and legs are over the touch line *but they haven't touched the ground*. If he can reach the goal line, he can score a try. Rory Underwood did exactly that when playing for England. All credit to the touch judge for knowing his law.

So it's contact with the ground on or beyond the touch line that matters. Let's assume the player himself is not in touch. If the player carrying the ball holds it over the touch line, it's not in touch. If it falls out of the sky beyond the touch line and he catches it without putting his feet on or over the touch line, it's not in touch. The same applies to touch-in-goal. He doesn't even have to catch the ball: he can reach across the touch line (or the touch-in-goal line) and knock it into the playing area, as long as he doesn't knock it forward. Or he can leap into the air and knock the ball inwards while his feet are off the ground, provided both his feet land in the playing area.

Indeed, even stranger things are possible. If the player is in

Beyond touch isn't necessarily in touch. For the ball-carrier to be in touch, his body or the ball must touch the touch line or the ground beyond the touch line. If the ball-carrier is tackled and the tackler ends up in touch underneath the ball-carrier, then the ball-carrier has not touched the ground. He's not in touch. He can score a try. It's happened.

Out may still be in. The ball is not in touch just because it's falling beyond the touch line. If a player who has both feet in the field-of-play catches the ball, the ball is not in touch. Alternatively, he can knock the ball in-field. If he jumps and catches the ball, it is not in touch provided, when he lands, his feet are in the playing area.

touch, but the ball is not, he can legally reach across the touch line and hit the ball with his hand, or he can kick it, and provided it hasn't crossed the plane of touch, it won't be in touch.

If he grabs it, of course, it will.

Remember always: the touch line itself is in touch. If the ball (or your boot if you're holding the ball) so much as brushes the chalk, then it's in touch.

That makes it dead. The throw-in brings it back to life again.

The throw-in

Where is the ball thrown in?

The question, you may have spotted, is not 'Where is the line-out held?' That too is a good question, and we'll get round to it soon. But when the ball goes into touch, a line-out is not always essential to get it back in play. You can have a throw-in without a line-out; so let's first sort out what the law has to say about throw-ins. The key phrase is 'gain in ground'.

Rugby is basically a game of handling and running. Agreed, there are moments when you have no choice but to bang the ball into touch, but the laws discourage unlimited touch-kicking.

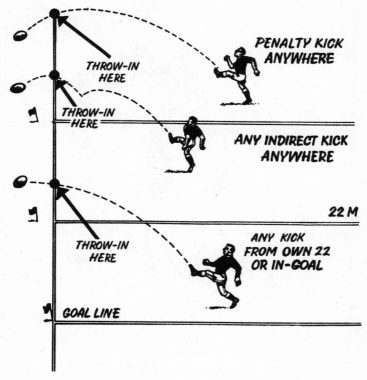

When touch-kicking gains ground. From the bottom upwards: When a player inside his 22 or in-goal kicks directly to touch, he gains ground. This also covers a free kick awarded inside the 22. If he kicks indirectly to touch (ball bounces in the field-of-play) there may be a gain in ground. When a player takes a penalty kick anywhere and kicks directly or indirectly to touch, there can be a gain in ground, and his team takes the throw-in.

It boils down to this. Outside your own 22, if you kick directly into touch – that is, if the ball doesn't touch the ground or another player before it goes out – then your kick gains no ground for your side: the ball is thrown in opposite the place where you kicked, not at the place where it went out. Inside your own 22 or your in-goal, you may kick directly into touch and still gain ground, provided you personally didn't take the ball into the 22. If you carry or knock

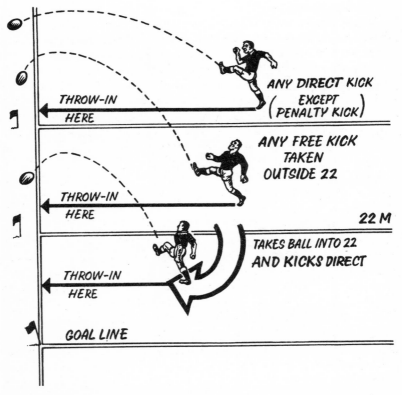

When touch-kicking gains no ground. From the bottom upwards: When a player takes or puts the ball into his 22 and then kicks directly to touch, he gains no ground. Outside the 22, any free kick taken directly to touch gains no ground. Any kick (except a penalty kick) taken outside the 22 that goes directly to touch, gains no ground.

or kick the ball into your 22 and then you kick directly to touch, there's no gain in ground.

The only exception to this is penalty kicks. From anywhere on the field, a penalty kick into touch can result in a gain in ground, because the ball is thrown in at the place where it went out. This applies whether the penalty kick went directly into touch (on the full) or it went indirectly into touch (bounced first in the field-of-play). What's more, the kicker's team always gets the throw-in after a penalty kick to touch.

Free kicks are not an exception. Outside your 22, if you bang a free kick directly into touch, you gain no ground. Inside your 22, it's different; a free kick can gain ground just like any other kick – with one proviso. The free kick must have been *awarded inside* the 22. If your free kick is awarded *outside* your 22, you're entitled to take the kick as far behind the mark as you like; but if you cross your 22-metre line and then hoof that free kick directly to touch, you gain no ground. The throw-in will be opposite the place where you kicked.

What's going on? I'll tell you what's going on. The lawmakers want to discourage a team that's been given a free kick in midfield from retreating into their 22 in order to kick for touch. This was slowing down the game. The entire kicking team had to run back so that one man could boot the ball. Then they all ran forward again, for the throw-in. Tedious.

Naturally, any touch-kick which bounces in the field-of-play, or any grub-kick which goes into touch, gains ground for the kicker's side. The ball is thrown in where it crossed the touch-line. And that applies if the ball touches an opponent, too. It's a direct kick to touch only if the ball touches nothing at all on its way.

If you kick directly to touch and actually find touch behind you, then that's where the ball is thrown in, not opposite where you kicked. You get the worst of the deal, whatever it is. And if, from a kick-off, you kick the ball directly into touch, your opponents can (if they wish) take a line-out opposite the place where you kicked, i.e. on the halfway line. Similarly, at a 22 drop-out, if the kick goes directly into touch, the other team can (if they wish) take a line-out where the ball went out. It rarely happens. Still, a team monopolising the line-outs might prefer it to a scrum on the 22.

The throw-in: a round-up

Gain in ground. The throw-in happens at the place where the ball went directly into touch from any kick made inside the 22 (except a free kick awarded outside the 22) and from any penalty kick made anywhere. There can also be a gain in ground if the ball goes indirectly into touch – after first touching the ground or an opponent.

No gain in ground. Except for a penalty kick, if you're outside your 22 and you kick directly to touch, there is no gain in ground. This includes a free kick. If you take the ball into your 22 and kick directly to touch, there is no gain in ground. If you're awarded a free kick outside the 22 and you take that kick directly to touch from inside the 22, there is no gain in ground.

Quick throw-in

All it takes to throw the ball in from touch is the ball and someone to throw it. A line-out is an optional extra. If play moves so fast that most players are left far behind when the ball goes into touch, then the laws do more than allow a quick throw-in. They encourage it. Provided the line-out hasn't formed, the team with the right to throw in has the freedom to make a quick throw-in anywhere on the touch line between the place where the ball went out and their own goal line.

Think of that. Blues are playing Whites. The Blue full-back kicks from just inside his 22. He has dynamite in his boot. His kick finds touch deep in the White half. That's where the ball crosses the touch line, but where it lands is much further on. A White player catches it, runs to the touch line and takes a quick throw-in at a place only a couple of metres from his goal line. His full-back catches it and – with the aid of a following gale – hoofs it deep into the enemy half. Or he runs with it, jinks and swerves and side-steps through the entire opposition and scores the winning try. Listen, anything's possible. The point is, the White team used the freedom the laws gave them, and didn't wait for a line-out. Indeed, the player taking the quick throw-in need not wait for a team-mate. He can throw the ball in 5 metres, nip in-field and snap it up himself.

What's interesting here is the way the laws define the stretch of

Quick throw-in: how it's done. Play can re-start without a line-out. You can take a quick throw-in provided you use the same ball that went out and nobody else has touched it. You must throw it in straight, and at least five metres. A team-mate to catch it is an optional extra. You can run in-field and play the ball yourself.

5 METRES

touch line that's available for a quick throw-in: it's anywhere between the player's own goal line and the place where the ball went into touch. Now, that place may be a long way from where the ball would have been thrown in at a line-out. Take the example I just invented, Blues against Whites. Suppose the Blue full-back kicked from *outside* his 22. And suppose his kick went directly into touch. No gain in ground: the line-out would be opposite where he kicked. But if Whites attempt a quick throw-in, the furthest point upfield they can do it is where the ball went into touch. Worth remembering.

The freedom to take a quick throw-in is lightly hedged around with restrictions. You must use the same ball that went into touch. Nobody else must have touched the ball; that includes spectators. Notice that word 'touched'. If a team-mate even side-foots the ball to the thrower-in, that kills any chance of a quick throw-in. (If either of these things happens, any attempt at a quick throw-in is

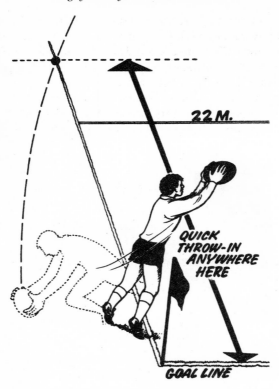

Quick throw-in: where it's done. You can take a quick throw-in without waiting for a line-out to form. This quick throw-in can be taken anywhere on the touch line between the point where the ball went into touch and your own goal line. You must use the same ball that went out, and only you must have touched it.

disallowed – yet oddly enough the same team gets the throw-in at the subsequent line-out.)

A quick throw-in has to be straight, and it has to go five metres before the ball is played. If not, the opposing team gets the choice of *either* a line-out *or* a scrum on the 15-metre line – and note this: that line-out or scrum will not be where the regular line-out would have happened; it will be where the quick throw-in went wrong. You don't need much imagination to realise that this point could be a very long way from where the line-out would normally have been held. So it pays not to be sloppy when you take a quick throw-in.

One last thing. The line-out job description which you will read in the next chapter – all about the position of the furthest player, and the maximum distance of fifteen metres from touch, and so on – none of that applies to a quick throw-in. If you want to take a quick throw-in and you see a friendly face waiting twenty or thirty metres infield, chuck him a straight ball and the law will smile upon you both.

Readers write

C.M. of Hammersmith writes: Can you take a quick throw-in after an opponent's been tackled into touch? He held the ball in touch, so if you take it, it's been handled twice, hasn't it?

D.R. Technically, yes. But this is an exception. When an opponent's tackled into touch he must release the ball at once. If you take a quick throw-in, that's legal.

* * *

B.M. of Llanelli writes: A free kick's not much use if you can't score from it, is it? You can't even kick it direct to touch outside your 22 and gain ground. When I was a boy, a free kick was worth having.

D.R. It still gives you a bit of breathing space. It also creates a 10-metre gap between the teams. That's something. And if you're awarded a free kick just outside your 22, and you tap-kick and pass the ball into the 22, a team-mate can kick direct to touch and gain ground.

* * *

E.H. of Manhattan writes: I used to know a chap who could run down the touch line, with one foot in play and one foot out, dribbling the ball and always keeping it in the field-of-play.

D.R. Not easy, but legal.

* * *

A.K.K. of Chicago writes: If a team takes a quick throw-in, but they use the wrong ball or if it's been handled twice, the referee orders a line-out and he gives the throw-in to the same team. That's generous, isn't it?

D.R. Some might think so. Don't blame the referee; he's only doing what the law says. The thinking behind that law is this: play has not re-started, because the wrong ball was used. Therefore no offence took place, and so the same team keeps the throw-in. It's like an attempted drop-out taken from the wrong place. The game has not re-started, so the drop-out is taken again.

*   *   *

T.F.W. of Wellington writes: If there's a tree overhanging the field-of-play, and the ball hits a branch, is it in touch?

D.R. That's for the captains and the referee to decide, preferably before the kick-off.

*   *   *

A.C. of Liverpool writes: If two players (opponents) are holding the ball as they go into touch, who gets the throw-in?

D.R. The attacking team. That's the team in their opponents' half. Same applies when the referee can't decide who took or put the ball into touch.

*   *   *

R.H. of Exeter writes: If the ball goes into touch and bounces off a tree, can a player take a quick throw-in?

D.R. Yes. Same applies if the ball bounces off the clubhouse, or off an advertising board.

11
The line-out

The line-out is simply a way of getting the ball back into play, quickly and fairly, by throwing it along the line-of-touch. This line must be at least five metres from the goal line, so as to make room for the line-out. Play can restart without a line-out: *See Quick throw-in*. You can't take a quick throw-in once the line-out has formed, and there are certain guidelines about a formed line-out.

Usually, and especially towards the end of the second half, when the knees are buckling and hot flashes streak across the eyeballs, your average line-out begins to look like a bus queue in a typhoon.

All the faults which the players have been trying to avoid suddenly take over.

The line-out *should* be formed opposite the place where the touch-judge is signalling – but the players shamble up to a nearby spot and hope that the touch-judge will move over to them. The front of the line-out *should* be at least five metres from the touch-line – it's not; it's four, or three. The two lines *should* be straight and parallel to the goal-lines – but one line is pure switchback, and the other points right at the corner flag. There *should* be a clear space one metre wide down the middle – but it's clogged with bodies.

This is not the ideal way to restart the game.

The ideal line-out is a very simple thing. It is two straight lines, with a clear space of one metre (a yard and a bit) between them, one line per team and at least two players per line. The front of the line-out is at least five metres from touch, opposite the mark signalled by the touch-judge, and the back is no more than fifteen metres from touch.

Except after a penalty kick to touch, the man who throws the ball in is an opponent of the side which last touched the ball when it went out. It makes no difference if they didn't mean to touch it, or if

The line-out: before and after taking the medicine. Two views of a line-out – one all wrong, the other rather better. A line-out should have two single, straight, parallel lines, with a clear gap of one metre between the lines. The line-out should be at right angles to the place signalled by the touch judge. No player in the line-out should be less than five metres or more than fifteen metres from the touch line.

they were reluctantly forced into touch while holding the ball – they still lose it. Deciding which side throws the ball in is simply a matter of deciding who last touched it, and giving it to the other side. (The benefit of the doubt goes to the attacking team.)

The player throwing in – usually the hooker – must stand in touch and throw the ball so that it goes at least five metres at right angles to the touch-line before it touches a player or the ground.

Now, the laws say that he has to throw the ball *along the line-of-touch,* which is an imaginary line running through the touch-judge and across the field, parallel to the goal lines. (So it follows that the line-out forms up on either side of the line-of-touch.) The purpose of a line-out is to re-start play quickly *and fairly.* Both sides must be given a reasonable chance of getting the ball, and if there's a small gale blowing from left to right, it's obvious that a short, hard throw stands a better chance of landing in the right place than a long lob.

If the player throwing in makes a hash of it – stands in the wrong place, or doesn't throw it five metres, or doesn't throw it in straight – the other side can choose either to take the throw-in themselves or to have a scrum fifteen metres in. If they decide to have a second throw-in and they too get it wrong, then the referee orders a scrum.

As the hooker stands poised to lob the ball, picture the scene: two single, straight and parallel lines, starting five metres in and separated by a healthy respect for the invisible line-of-touch. Bear all that in mind while we have a bash at the next bit, which affects so much of the line-out that we might as well do it now: the dreaded (but really simple) *line-out offside.*

Line-out offside

'People,' Marx* once observed, 'come in two sorts. There's the workers, who do the grafting; and there's the rest, who get the benefit.'

He was talking, of course, about the line-out, which is divided for the purposes of offside into:

1 those taking part
2 those not taking part.

* Dr Henry Marx, perhaps the heaviest-ever forward to play for Rutland.

Those taking part are all the players involved in throwing the ball in, catching it, and disposing of it. In chronological order they are the man with the ball (and his opposite number), all the forwards standing in the line-out, and the one player of each team in position to receive the ball from the line-out – usually (but not necessarily) the scrum-halves.

Those not taking part are all the others – the backs (stand-offs, centres, wings, full-backs) and any forwards who have chosen not to join the line-out.

Where the backs can stand. The offside line for players not taking part in the line-out (usually, but not exclusively, the backs) lies ten metres behind the line-out – or it is the goal line, if that's nearer. Until the line-out ends, all players not in it must stay behind that line. The only exceptions are the scrum-half, who can stand between the two, and one opponent (usually the hooker) of the player throwing in the ball. This opponent can be in the 5-metre area.

A serious case of impetuosity. Until the ball is thrown in, the line-out offside line runs down the middle. Once it's thrown in, it runs through the ball. Either way, the nearest White player has gone too far. In his desire to cream the stand-off he has got himself thoroughly offside.

Offside for those taking part in the line-out

Until the ball is thrown in, the offside line for those taking part is the line-of-touch. No player must put a foot across this imaginary line, unless he's jumping for the ball; and if he jumps and misses he must hustle back without delay.

As soon as the ball is thrown in and it has touched a player or the ground, the offside line runs through the ball itself. Every player in the line-out must stay on his own side of the ball until the line-out is over. (And if you don't know when that is, don't worry, we'll get to it later.)

So offside for players taking part in a line-out is quite straight-forward. Until the ball is thrown in, keep behind the line-of-touch; after that, keep behind the ball.

Offside for those not taking part in the line-out

The offside line for players *not* taking part is even simpler. It's a line ten metres behind the line-of-touch (which is like saying ten metres behind the line-out) and parallel to the goal lines, or the goal-line itself, if that happens to be nearer. And as before, all players *not* taking part in the line-out must keep both feet behind their offside line until the line-out is over. (In the case of the goal line they can keep both feet *on* the line, since the line is in the in-goal.)

If you have this situation clearly imprinted on what for want of a better word we may call the mind, you will see that it creates an area up to twenty metres wide between the opposing back-lines. Whichever side wins the ball from the line-out is rewarded with a healthy acreage of sod in which to start hatching its devilish plots before the foe can pour across no-man's-land and start making nuisances of themselves.

This is what the law is for. There is no point in winning the ball if you get a tackle like a Turkish earthquake immediately after it. Once the line-out is over the forwards can set off and do their worst, but it has been proved repeatedly that the ball can travel faster than the man. (Ask any forward.) What's more, the forwards are limited by the *length* (in distance) of the line-out.

The length of the line-out

The line-out begins five metres from touch and ends fifteen metres from touch. No line-out player is allowed to stand more than fifteen metres from touch. This means that the actual line of players can never be more than ten metres long.

However, the side throwing in has some influence on the length of the line-out, because it has the privilege of deciding how many players may take part in the line-out. If it chooses to have fewer than usual, its opponents cannot exceed that number. Suppose the team throwing in opts for a three-man line-out. The other team must not have more than three men in that line-out. But those three are not obliged to stand opposite their opponents; they can place themselves wherever they wish, right up to the fifteen-metre mark.

But not beyond it. Occasionally a flanker will absentmindedly wander a yard or so beyond the mark. If the referee doesn't notice this, you can be sure the opposing half-backs will. If they get the ball, that yard or so will give the flanker an unfair start when he pressures the No. 10. Back-markers who drift infield before the line-out has ended are offside. They should be penalised.

When the line-out begins

The instant the ball leaves the hands of the player throwing it in, the line-out has begun and large gentlemen with hands like dinnerplates can start launching themselves upwards. And until the line-out ends, all line-out players must stay inside the fifteen-metre mark. (There is one exception to this: a *long throw-in* over the tail of the line-out; but that's not really a line-out at all. We get to long throw-ins a bit later.)

Even when the ball has left the hands of the player throwing it in, that doesn't give the line-out men a free hand. They must keep that metre-wide space between the lines unless they're actually jumping for the ball, until the ball has touched a player or the ground. This strikes me as a pretty broad exception, because everyone in the line-out *can* jump for the ball, if they want to. But according to law, that one-metre gap should survive until the ball has touched someone or something.

When the line-out ends

The line-out ends when one of four things happens:
1 The ball leaves the line-out.
2 A player with the ball leaves the line-out.
3 The ball is thrown beyond the last man in the line-out.
4 A ruck or maul has formed, and the *whole* of the ruck or maul moves beyond the line-of-touch.

When any one of those things has happened, the line-out is over and line-out offside is a thing of the past. In the case of the first three, the ball is in open play and anyone can go anywhere. In the case of the fourth – where a ruck or maul has formed – the offside law for rucks or mauls applies (obviously). So the back-lines can immediately move up to the tail-ends of the ruck or maul.

Notice that the line-out comes to an end, not when a ruck or maul forms, but when that ruck or maul has completely moved away from the line-of-touch (that's the imaginary line running through the middle of the line-out). A ruck or maul in a line-out is still a line-out, and so the back-lines must stay ten metres behind it. What's more, any line-out player who does not join the ruck or maul must retire to its offside line, which runs through its tail-end, and stay there.

Thus a line-out that develops into a ruck or maul presents the line-out players with three separate and distinct offside lines in quick succession. The first line, before the ball has been thrown in, is the line-of-touch. The second line, after the ball has been thrown in and touched something or someone, runs through the ball itself. If a ruck or maul forms the third line runs through the tail of the ruck or maul. All three can happen in the space of a few seconds, so line-out players need to keep their wits about them.

When the ruck or maul gives a convulsive shudder and lurches clear of the line-out – all of it, not just most of it – then the line-out has ended and the ruck/maul is promoted to Grade A status, with its own offside lines, luncheon vouchers, pension schemes, and so on.

And *that* is the moment when the back-line can, without fear of savage reprisals, nip smartly forward. It pays to know just when you can make that move without risking a penalty kick between your uprights. That's why I'm telling you all this.

Incidentally, the referee can end a line-out if he decides the ball has become unplayable. The game restarts with a scrum.

Where the ball-thrower can go. Also the scrum-half

While all this crucial decision-making is going on, what of the man who threw the ball in? He has done his bit – thrown it to number three in the line-out, Big Bert, only Bert wasn't quite ready so the other side caught it – and now he's watching rather anxiously, wondering what he can do to help.

After he has thrown in the ball there are only four things which the thrower (and his opposite number) can do, legally, until the line-out's over:

1 Stay where he is, between the line-out and the touch-line.
2 Get stuck into the line-out.
3 Nip round the side and play scrum-half, provided nobody else is doing it.
4 Get ten metres back.

If either of the scrum-halves sees a gap in the line-out, he can flit into it and take the ball, just as long as he doesn't go barging into or obstructing an opponent.

Once the ball's been thrown in, what most hookers do is lurk in the space between touch and the front of the line-out. That's fine, as long as they stay behind the ball. Occasionally, however, a hooker wanders forward, just a couple of paces but it's enough. Enough to what? Display his presence and thereby persuade the opposing scrum-half to forget about attacking down the touch-line. So bang goes one option. The hooker's offside, he's influencing play, he ought to be penalised. So should flankers who sometimes work a similar racket at the back of the line-out, taking a little walk across the offside line in order to discourage the scrum-half from attacking around the tail. Bang goes another option. Scandalous.

Peeling-off

The original idea of peeling-off was to let a player leave the line-out so that he could catch the ball when it was knocked or passed back by a team-mate. He can still do that, but he can also do a lot more. The old law said that a player peeling-off had to stay near the line-out and keep moving parallel to it. That is now history. The new law says a player who peels off can go up to ten metres behind the line-of-touch, if he wants to. Up to, but not beyond. That ten-metre line marks the offside line for his backs, and line-out players cannot join them until the line-out ends.

Nevertheless, an area 10 metres deep gives a lot of room for peeling-off players to operate in, and this has an interesting effect on the job of the scrum-half. Under the old law, there could be only one scrum-half at a line-out. Now, with any line-out player given

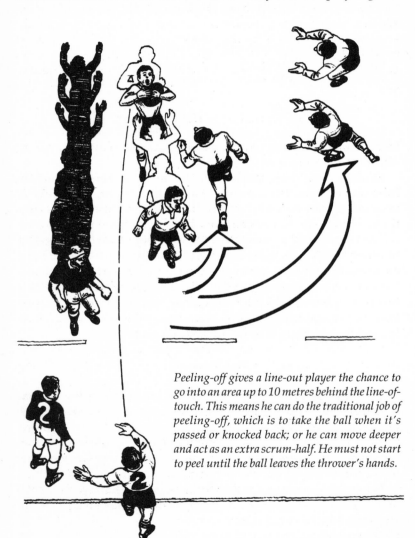

Peeling-off gives a line-out player the chance to go into an area up to 10 metres behind the line-of-touch. This means he can do the traditional job of peeling-off, which is to take the ball when it's passed or knocked back; or he can move deeper and act as an extra scrum-half. He must not start to peel until the ball leaves the thrower's hands.

carte blanche to peel off and roam in the scrum-half's patch, several players can do his job. The only restriction is that a player must not begin to peel off until the ball has left the thrower's hands.

This change in the law has some other tactical implications. When a team gets a line-out near its opponents' goal line, catch-and-maul is often their routine attack. Now that the line-out must be at least five metres from the goal line, the defending team can pack that area with players who have peeled off in readiness to counter the maul.

Line-out offside round-up

Here, then, is a quick wrap-up of the various ways you can be offside at a line out.

Offside at the front of the line-out. The line-out begins five metres from touch. If you stand nearer to touch than that, you are offside (except the relevant throwers-in). However, once the ball has been thrown beyond you, you can move into that space at the front.

Stepping out of line. Each line of forwards must leave a clear space one metre wide down the middle until the ball is thrown in. If you move into this space before the ball is thrown in, you're offside.

Overstepping the ball. Once the ball has been thrown in, the offside line runs through the ball. If you get in front of it, you're offside. However, if you got there because you were genuinely jumping for the ball, you'll be given a chance to get back onside.

Offside at the back of the line-out. Until the line-out ends, the furthest player in a line-out must not be more than fifteen metres from touch, or he will be offside.

Peeling-off too soon or too deep. If you peel off before the ball has been thrown in, or if you peel off and move or stand too far from the line-out, you are offside.

Not ten metres back. If you're not taking part in the line-out you must stay ten metres behind it. If you don't get back far enough, or if you advance too soon, you're offside.

I fancy I hear ugly mutterings from the back of the hall. Evidently there are those who feel that rugby, far from being the simple sport I promised, has developed into something bloody diabolical, so can they have their money back?

Stick with it, lads. Rugby *is* a simple game, even including line-out offside.

The thing about the line-out is that whilst there are no end of complicated ways of getting *offside*, there is only one, very simple way to stay *onside*. Master that, and you're home and dry.

The line-out has a simple shape. It starts here and it stops there, and between these ends are two straight, single lines. Stay in line until the ball arrives, and keep behind the ball until the line-out ends and you won't go far wrong.

You can always find trouble if you go looking for it; but in that case don't blame the laws for making life difficult. It's really your option.

Keeping what's left of your nose clean

There are a couple of other things which the laws would rather you didn't do in a line-out. Most of them can be summed up in these two commandments:

1 Until the ball is thrown in, don't touch anyone.
2 After the ball is thrown in, don't touch an opponent unless he has the ball, or unless a ruck or maul has formed.

Don't barge

If there is a clear space down the middle you shouldn't be touching an opponent. Most barging takes place when players are jumping for the ball and one player is more concerned with putting his shoulder into his opponent than getting his hands on the ball. This is illegal, and can even be dangerous: a player jumping at full stretch is very vulnerable to a bash in the ribs. (Even a sly nudge can unbalance him.) Line-out bargers are bad news. Good refs nobble them fast.

Don't obstruct

You've seen it; I've seen it; we've all seen it, and not a few of us have done it. The ball is thrown in, it bounces about, someone taps it back and it lands on the deck. The scrum-half goes after it, the opposing forwards *try* to go after it, and a wall of arms holds them back. This is obstruction. You must not hold or push or deliberately obstruct an opponent who hasn't got the ball. The urge to protect your winnings is strong. It is tempting to fling out an arm and hold your opponent back, and it is easy, and it is illegal.

This is true of all parts of the game, of course. It's just that obstruction seems more natural in a line-out. Players who wouldn't think of grabbing an opponent to keep him from tackling someone in open play will feel that they are being quite noble by holding off an opponent who has designs on their scrum-half.

There is, I suppose, a bit of a difference. A line-out by its very nature presents a wall of brawn between one lot of forwards and their opponents' scrum-half, and the brawn has every right to arrange itself in such a way that nobody can get through. But what it hasn't got a right to do is to grab, barge, or deliberately obstruct any opponent who would otherwise have got through. You're entitled to *be* in his way but not to *get* in his way.

Protecting the winnings — but it's obstruction. In any part of the game it is illegal to obstruct an opponent who hasn't got the ball — and that goes for line-outs too.

Don't use your outside arm only

You must not use your outside arm alone to catch or deflect the ball. Use both of your arms, or just the inner arm. (If both hands are above your head you can use either hand to play the ball.) Why? Read on.

Don't lever yourself up on an opponent

When this happens, the arm that the line-out player uses in order to lever himself up (and his opponent down) is the inside arm, because it is nearer his opponent's shoulder. Now you know why outer-arm catching is illegal. The laws reckon that, if the inner arm isn't reaching up for the ball, who knows what dirty work it might get up to?

Don't jump or support before the ball is thrown

You must not jump before the ball has left the hands of the thrower-in. Similarly, you must not support the jumper - or even grip him below the waist - until the ball is on its way. Once the ball is thrown, he can jump and you can help him. (If you support him up, then you must help him come down again.) Don't hold him below his shorts if you're behind, or below his thighs if you're in front.

Don't ankle-tap the jumper

If, as your opponents' ace jumper launches himself into space, it occurs to you to stay down at ground level, wait for his feet to come up to you, and then remove them, you're both in trouble. He may be badly injured and you will certainly be heavily penalised. Tackling or pulling the feet of a jumper while he's in the air is dangerous play.

Don't block the throw-in

The throw-in must travel at least five metres from touch, which is why a line-out player must not be less than five metres from touch.

Support versus levering. Any line-out player jumping for the ball must get off the deck by his own efforts. Once he's airborne, a team-mate can help him stay up. That's legal. But if a player levers himself up on an opponent, that's a penalty kick. Levering means playing the man without the ball, which is foul play. What's more, the levering jumper is using only his outside arm to win the ball. That too is illegal.

Not surprisingly, if he stands less than five metres, and if he blocks the throw-in, he'll get penalised.

The too-short throw-in

The short throw-in to the front man in the line-out is a thing you see fairly often, and if players knew how risky it was they would turn grey. Pseudo-scientific research has shown that as often as nine times out of ten, the ball doesn't travel the minimum of five metres.

When this is the result of tired blood on the part of the gent throwing it in, the referee may give him a pitying glance and let the other team have a go. But when the problem is the greed and impetuosity of a front marker in the line-out who can't wait for the ball to come to him and who invades the five-metre strip in order to get it first, that's different. That's a free kick to his opponents.

Blocking the throw. At a line-out the throw-in must travel at least five metres, and nobody must stop this. Here a line-out player is standing less than five metres from the touch line and blocking the throw-in, so he's in trouble two ways. Penalty: Free kick.

Rare and unusual line-outs

Not every line-out has all the stirring pageantry and solemn ritual described above. Some are short, scarcely as long as they are wide. Some are full-length, yet they never receive the ball because it goes clean over them. Both kinds are perfectly legal.

Short line-out

The minimum number of players in a line-out is two from each side, and if the side throwing the ball in decides that a two-man line is a good idea, their opponents have no choice but to go along with them.

If, however, the side throwing in already *has* seven men in the line-out, they cannot decide then to pull five of them out and leave two; it's too late for that. The decision must be made *before* these players formed up in the line-out. Once they're in they must stay there until the line-out's over.

Opponents of the side throwing the ball in are given a bit of leeway, though. Since they don't know how many men the other side is going to put into its line, they've got to prepare for the worst. Then, if it turns out to be a short line, the referee will give them a reasonable amount of time to withdraw the extra players before the ball is thrown in.

For instance, if Blues kick the ball into touch close to Whites' goal-line, and get ready for an orthodox, seven-man line-out, Whites might decide to form a short, two-man line and hold the other five in readiness in their in-goal. In that case, Blues would be given time to pull out five of *their* forwards, before Whites go ahead and throw the ball in.

Long throw-in

The invisible line-of-touch stretches – in theory – right across the field, and if you've got a man who can throw it that far there's nothing to stop him hurling the ball right past the line-out and into the wide open spaces – as long as it pitches on the line-of-touch.

As soon as the ball leaves his hands, any player in the line-out or out of it – forward, scrum-half or back – can run out to catch this long throw-in. The backs can run forward, and the forwards or scrum-half can run beyond the 15-metre mark. But if they anticipate a long throw-in which doesn't then take place – if the ball is not in fact thrown to them or beyond them – they're offside.

Throwing in straight is the crucial part of the line-out. Any discussion of long throw-ins is so much wasted breath when the player throwing the ball in has an effective range of about fifteen metres, and that only on days of flat calm. Show me a long throw-in where the ball has travelled more than twenty metres, and I'll show you a seven-to-four chance that it didn't go straight. Seven-to-four? Make it eight-to-three.

Penalties for line-out offences

As with scrums, so with line-outs. Faults and follies are penalised *either* by a free kick *or* by a penalty kick. Free-kick offences are mostly technical errors, whereas penalty kicks get handed out for serious crimes.

For example, a free kick is given for 'spacing' offences – where a player fails to leave a metre-wide gap between the lines, or he stands less than five metres or more than fifteen metres from touch when the line-out forms; for delaying or dummying the throw-in; for a 'numbers' offence – having too many players in the line; for levering on a team-mate's shoulder; for hoisting a team-mate; for using only the outside arm to catch the ball; or for peeling-off too soon or too deep.

By contrast, it's a penalty kick if you barge an opponent, or lever yourself up by using him as a support; or if you get yourself offside in any of the various ways I've already described; or if you hold or shoulder or obstruct an opponent who hasn't got the ball.

Touch judges

There are two of these officials, one for each touch-line, and their job is to help the referee by following play up and down and signalling (with a small flag provided for the purpose) whenever the ball goes into touch, or touch-in-goal. In the case of a high kick, this may involve some fast geometrical calculation between the ears: what matters is where the ball crosses the line, not where it comes to earth.

The touch-judge also signals which side is entitled to throw the ball in, so he has to decide who last touched the ball. If the kick was made outside the kicker's 22, the touch-judge has to decide whether or not it went directly into touch, and locate the throw-in accordingly – although the referee can over-rule him. It's for the referee to decide whether or not a player was outside his 22, and exactly where the throw-in should take place.

It's important that the touch-judge should flourish his flag the very moment the ball goes into touch. Often the referee is watching for this signal because, what with all the dust and steam, he can't actually see the ball.

Once the referee has whistled for touch, the touch-judge should stand at the appropriate spot, still keeping his flag up so that everyone can see him, and point to whichever side is to throw the ball in. Having done this, he should keep on doing it and above all *stay where he is* until the ball has been thrown in. If the players line up in the wrong place, the touch-judge should hold his ground, perhaps flaring the nostrils a little. What he should not do is feebly shuffle sideways. Just because they've got it wrong, there's no need for him to get it wrong, too.

If the wrong team throws the ball in, or if the man who throws it in steps in the field-of-play, or if a replacement ball or a twice-handled ball is used at a quick throw-in, the touch judge should keep his flag up as a signal to the referee – who can always overrule him and let play go on.

The touch-judges also help the referee when kicks at goal are being taken – penalty kicks or conversions. (For penalty kicks, where the kicker can decide whether or not to go for goal, the referee usually signals the touch-judges to come round behind the posts, using a sweeping gesture rather like a druid loosening up before a big sunrise.) One touch-judge stands at or behind each goal post; if the ball goes over the bar he raises his flag.

If the ball goes directly over the top of the post he doesn't raise his flag. The posts are considered to soar heavenwards indefinitely. If the ball went over one it must have hit it.

You might think that this is a lot of needless fuss about a rather dreary part of the game, and you would be completely wrong. Anyone who has played in a game where one touch-judge was eleven and always gave the ball to the home team because his big brother was playing on that wing, and the other touch-judge was eighty-three and never got closer than forty yards to the action all afternoon, knows that good touch-judging is worth having.

It's the responsibility of the team captains to produce touch-judges, and the traditional arrangement is for the teams to provide one each. Or so it should be. In a great many clubs, the tradition is to forget all about it until the referee asks, and then shout vaguely in the direction of the crowd of drinkers outside the clubhouse. The results are usually disastrous, but that doesn't stop the players complaining bitterly about unfair or inaccurate decisions. But then, nothing will.

Many people don't realise that the touch-judges come under the control of the referee just as the players do. If a touch-judge turns out to be clueless or crooked, the referee can ask for him to be replaced; and if the touch-judge goes completely bananas the referee can order him off the playing enclosure and report him to the Union for misconduct. It's not just an academic point. I've come across touch-judges who became quite crazed and began beating visiting players over the head with their flags. I even knew one touch-judge who, while his team were preparing to take a kick at goal, used to toss up little handfuls of grass to help the kicker gauge the wind-strength. He was quite surprised when the referee (me) told him to stop.

Most touch-judges aren't like that. The higher up the game you go the better they are, until at top matches the touch-judges will be highly qualified referees who are good enough to take over the whistle if the appointed referee gets injured. In these matches the touch-judges have been given extra powers: if they see dangerous play or misconduct they must signal the fact to the referee. The touch-judge does this by raising his flag to the horizontal and pointing it infield. That signal does not stop the game; but at the next stoppage the referee goes over to the touch-judge, finds out what happened, and takes action accordingly. You may also see the touch judge talking into the top of his flag-handle. This is where the microphone is installed. The referee and touch judges are often miked-up so that they can talk to each other. Players know this, of course. It helps to keep them honest. Occasionally the radio link fails, but the players don't know that, and they remain honest.

Readers write

H.G. of Vancouver writes: Every line-out I ever see, the two separate lines vanish the instant the ball gets thrown in. They all just merge into a mob.

D.R. I hear what you say.

* * *

T.T. of Gloucester writes: I agree that a line-out jumper must not use his outside arm alone to get the ball, but there's an exception you didn't mention.

D.R. Yes? What's that?

T.T. We've got a one-armed lock forward. Half the time, when he's jumping, he has no inside arm.

D.R. Astonishing.

* * *

B.A. of Ely writes: If the ball-carrier, or the ball, moves into the 5-metre gap between line out and touch, has the line-out ended?

D.R. Glad you asked. The answer is yes.

* * *

L.R.N. of Johannesburg writes: What's so terrible about jumping and lifting before the throw-in? Get the jumper up in the air, where the thrower can see the guy!

D.R. I've got a better idea. Let's all build human pyramids, and forget the rugby.

* * *

B.D. of Orrell writes: I've calculated that, at any line-out, a maximum of ninety-three separate offences can take place.

D.R. You missed a couple.

* * *

J.Y. of Tokyo writes: Up until 1946, you could choose to take a scrum instead of a line-out.

D.R. Stick around. Who knows? That day may return.

* * *

S.G. of Wolverhampton writes: What's all this I keep on hearing about the Team of Three?

D.R. It's not in the laws, but it's worth knowing about. The three are the referee and his touch judges, and at the top level of games – where touch judges are very competent – they work as a team.

S.G. Doing what?

D.R. The touch judge can signal Dangerous Play or Misconduct, of course, but he can spot lesser offences too – for instance at the line-out – and keep the referee informed. He also helps by indicating when a quick throw-in is allowable or not. The Team of Three gives the referee two extra pairs of eyes.

12
Scoring

The aim of the game is to score points. The best way to do this is by scoring tries.

Naturally, any team should have at least one man who can kick penalty goals from all parts of the field-of-play and adjoining counties. Nevertheless, a try can bring you a maximum of seven points. Any other score is worth only three. The moral is obvious.

Try

You score a try by being the first to ground the ball in your opponents' in-goal, and this is worth five points. You don't have to carry the ball across the line: you can chase someone else's kick or pass, and fall on it, or you can kick it ahead yourself and follow up and score. In fact the only thing you must be sure of is *grounding the ball* – which is not necessarily the same as touching it down, or touching it when it's on the ground. For instance, picking up the ball in the in-goal is not grounding it (so you can pick it up and run towards the posts if you want to improve the chances of conversion).

Grounding the ball

You can ground the ball in one of three ways. If you are holding it you can simply touch it to the ground. Some people think that it's necessary to press down, but it's not. They are thinking of the second method: if the ball is already on the ground, you must press down on it with your hands or arms (one is enough). Alternatively, if the ball is already on the ground you can fall on it so that it's under

The meaning of grounding. You score a try by grounding the ball in the in-goal. There are three ways of grounding the ball: (a) hold it and touch the ground with it; (b) press down on it when it's on the ground; (c) fall on it so that it's under your front anywhere between waist and neck.

the front of your body anywhere from the waist to the neck. Note that in this way you don't have to lay a finger on the ball. You can ground a ball, and score a try, simply by diving on top of it and hitting it with your shoulder, chest or stomach – provided you get there first.

On the other hand, if you *are* holding the ball, make quite sure that the referee has seen you touch it down. Occasionally you will see a player race fifty yards, swerving out of seven or eight tackles, beat the full-back with almost contemptuous ease, stroll over the line between the posts, and deposit the ball without so much as breaking stride. The sad thing is that he hasn't actually *touched the ball down*: he got within an inch or two of the turf and then gracefully let go, like a goose demonstrating the laying of a golden egg. And if the referee was paying close attention, then he won't have blown for a try.

It pays to let everyone see that you have actually grounded the ball; and any player who is so pleased with his brilliant approach work that he neglects this finishing touch is asking for trouble. It's not that the referee is being bloody-minded, it's just that he has no alternative. He can't say to himself, 'Stone me, that feller deserves a try after a run like that, even though he didn't really score one,' can he? He must do what the laws say.

Personally, if I had galloped fifty yards with the ball – well, let's be realistic: if I had lumbered ten yard with the ball and gone over the goal line, I would slam it down good and hard. And if I didn't hear the whistle I'd keep leaning on the ball until either the referee blew or I woke up and realized I'd only crossed the enemy 22.

Some players believe that an attacker who drops the ball when he has crossed the goal line cannot score a try. They are wrong. Dropping the ball is not an offence unless it's thrown or knocked forward. If it falls straight down, and the attacker then grounds it, that's a try. Why not?

Not seen. If you were the referee, would you give a try here? Bear in mind that a basic principle of refereeing is: Never guess. If you didn't see it, you can't give it. Sometimes even the best of referees can't see the ball because so many players are in the way. A try is not a try unless the referee can see it being scored.

Where are the lines?

The goal line is part of the in-goal, so you can score a try by grounding the ball on the goal line. The goal posts are also part of the in-goal, and if you have grounded the ball so that it is touching your opponents' goal post, you've scored. Whether or not the referee will agree with you is another matter, and there is no doubt that it's safer to get the ball right inside the in-goal.

The touch-in-goal lines and the dead-ball line are not in the in-goal, so you can't score on them. The corner flag, since we're picking so many nits, is part of touch-in-goal, but the flag – the actual cloth – is not; it's nowhere; it doesn't exist, in law.

Pushover try

A scrum can score a try. If one team shoves so hard that they push their opponents back over their goal-line and then ground the ball, it's a try. The cardinal sin of handling in the scrum doesn't apply,

Tackled and reaching out to score. If you get tackled so near to your opponents' goal line that you can immediately reach out and ground the ball on or over the line, that's a try. This is true even if the ball has already touched the ground.

Momentum try. If you get tackled short of your opponents' goal line, but your momentum is so great that it takes you into the in-goal and you ground the ball, that's a try. If you crawl to the goal line, it's not.

for the glaringly obvious reason that there is no scrum once it has crossed the goal line; a scrum can take place only in the field-of-play, and if the ball in the scrum touches or crosses the goal line the scrum has ended. If the *defenders* take the ball into their in-goal during a pushover and they ground it, this is considered a touchdown and leads to a five-metre scrum.

Sliding over to score

If you get tackled when you're hurtling for the line, but your hurtle is so momentous that it carries you over and you ground the ball, that is a try, even if the ball has already touched the field-of-play on the way. It's all a question of momentum. Your thrust has to be so irresistible that it carries you into the in-goal.

Reaching out to score

You can even reach out and score, even when you've been tackled short of the line and brought to a full stop. I should warn you that there are strong differences of opinion about this. The problem is combining parts of two separate laws.

The try law says that a tackled player can score a try if he's tackled in such a position that he 'can immediately reach out and ground the ball on or over' his opponents' goal line. It adds that he 'must not infringe the tackle law', but it helpfully points out that this law says a tackled player 'may place the ball on the ground in any direction provided it is done immediately'.

Now, nobody complains when a tackled player turns and places the ball at arm's length behind him. And since the tackle law lets him place it 'in any direction', common sense says that, if the line is within his reach, he's entitled to reach out and score, provided he acts immediately.

For years there has been a myth that any tackled player reaching out to score is guilty of 'second movement' which ruins his chances. Clearly, the laws say differently. A tackled player must not crawl or struggle to the line, because that's not immediate action. But if his arms can reach the line at once, without a struggle, he can score a try.

Scoring from touch

If the ball is in the enemy's in-goal and you are in touch or touch-in-goal, you can fall on it and score. If you pick it up, of course, you're an idiot.

Penalty try

If a defender does something unfair or illegal which, in the referee's opinion, prevents a *probable* try, then he will award a penalty try. If he thinks the foul play probably prevented a try being scored in a better place, he'll award a penalty try. The interesting word here is 'probably'. The referee doesn't have to be absolutely convinced that a try would inevitably have been scored; he just has to feel sure that the attacking side had a healthy odds-on chance. With that in mind, he can award a penalty try for an offence in mid-field just as much as for one inside the defenders' 22. A penalty try is always given between the posts. Contrary to an ancient myth, the defenders *can* charge the kick at goal.

Converting a try

Scoring a try gives a team the right to attempt to convert it into a goal (that's why it's called a 'try') by taking a kick at goal. A conversion is worth a further two points. The kick is taken exactly in front of the spot where the try was scored: anywhere on a line through the place of score, parallel with the touch-line. If the try was scored between the posts, it's a short, easy kick from right in front. If the try was scored in the corner, it's a long, hard kick from near touch. The kick can be a place-kick or a drop-kick. (But see Seven-a-Side Variations at the end of this book.) Anyone on the scoring side may take the kick, and he can have a placer to hold the ball if he wants. All the rest of his team must get behind the ball, and all their opponents must be behind the goal line until the kicker begins his run-up or offers to kick. They can then charge or jump and try to deflect the ball, but even if they touch it and it goes over the bar, the goal is good.

Conversion kick. This is taken opposite the place where the try was scored. Defenders must stay behind their goal line until the kicker starts his run-up. Then they can charge, wave or jump – but not shout. Contrary to myth, you can charge the conversion kick after a penalty try.

What they must not do is shout as they charge. If they do, or if they offend in any other way – charge too soon, for instance – the referee can allow the same kicker to take a second kick without any charge. If, despite the defenders' wrongdoing, the first kick goes over, then the referee lets it stand and chalks up two points to the forces of righteousness.

Should any of the kicker's team be crazy enough to be in front of the ball when kicked, the kick doesn't count. (Until recently, the same was true if a team-mate held the ball and the ball didn't touch the ground before it got kicked out of the placer's hands. The ball wasn't grounded, so it wasn't considered a proper kick. Nowadays, with plastic kicking tees, the ball is never grounded; so that little bit of law has been quietly dropped.)

It's not uncommon for the ball to fall over before the kicker has started his run. If it does, the referee should give him permission to tee it up again. If it falls over *after* he's started his run, he must carry on with his kick. This means that if it not only falls over but also rolls away, he may end up kicking it from a spot which is some little distance from the line through the place where the try was scored; nevertheless it's a goal if he gets the ball over the crossbar. On the other hand, if the ball falls over and rolls into touch, that's the end: no second kick allowed.

Get on with it

The laws make it clear that all kicks, including conversions, must be taken without delay. Until recently, that provoked a certain amount of discussion about how unreasonable a delay was, and referees sometimes got impatient with kickers who took great pains over tee-ing up the ball, paced backwards, and then seemed to fall into a trance. Well, the lawmakers have now simplified the ceremony. They have given the goal-kicker a maximum of one minute. It begins when he indicates that he intends to kick at goal. If sixty seconds pass and he hasn't taken the kick, then he never will. It's disallowed.

You'd think a minute was ample time to tee the ball up and take a hopeful pot at goal. Usually it is. The trouble is that many teams are so stunned by success that they leave the ball lying and forget all about the kick. By the time they've got hold of a kicker, and he has got hold of the ball, the first minute has about eight seconds left. That, of course, is entirely their fault. If the referee calls a halt to proceedings and heads for the centre of the field, they might wake up next time.

It's not compulsory to take the full minute, or anywhere near it. Plenty of world-class kickers have proved they can kick goals without a long-drawn-out preparation. Some don't even take a run-up; they achieve length and accuracy with just two strides. Some don't place the ball; they drop-kick it. And if the try was scored between the posts, why not? It saves a lot of time. Incidentally, the one-minute-maximum law means that time taken up in goal-kicking is no longer 'time lost', so it is never added on to playing time.

If you think that all this stopwatching is a bit superfluous, it isn't. There is a good reason for keeping a tight rein on these delays. Kicks at goal can easily total fifteen or even twenty minutes, which means up to one quarter of playing time. Check out a few games for yourself if you don't believe me.

It's not essential to waste any time at all after you've scored a try, of course. The conversion attempt is optional; you needn't take it if you don't want to. This has happened – usually right at the end of a game when the scoring side needed more than two points to win, and preferred to use the remaining time in an attempt to score another try. It has been known to succeed, too.

Penalty goal

Apart from tries and conversions, you can score points in two other ways: by a penalty goal or a dropped goal. Each is worth three points.

A penalty goal must be either a place kick or a drop kick in the field-of-play, and of course the ball has to go over the opponents' crossbar. (You can read all about penalty kicks in the chapter on Kicks.)

During a kick at goal, defenders must stand still, hands by their sides, from the start of the kicker's run until he kicks the ball. If they misbehave while the penalty kick is being taken but the ball goes over just the same, the referee will give a goal. If it doesn't go over, he can award a second kick ten metres further forward. And if he thinks that the ball would *probably* have gone over if a defender hadn't illegally got in its way, he can even award a goal without the ball crossing the bar at all.

The time limit for penalty kicks at goal is the same as that for conversion attempts: one minute is the maximum, starting when the player indicates that he's going to kick at goal. If he fails to kick in time, the referee orders a scrum, opponents' put in.

Dropped goal

You can score a dropped goal (three points) any time the game is going on, except from a free kick or at a kick-off or drop-out. All you have to do is drop-kick the ball from the field-of-play over your opponents' cross-bar. Even if an opponent touches the ball (or *vice versa*) before it goes over, it is still a goal. This applies to all kicks at goal. But if you drop-kick for goal and the ball touches one of your *own* players before going over, it's no goal – not because he may have diverted it but because he must have been, at the very least, accidentally offside.

A dropped goal need not be the slick, well-oiled action you normally associate with international half-backs. All that is required is a drop kick that sneaks over the bar; and a drop kick is simply a ball that has been dropped and kicked after the first bounce. If you get tackled in the enemy 22, drop the ball in a blind panic, lash out and kick it on the first bounce, and accidentally send it flying between the posts, that's worth three points. Crummy points, but they all count.

Odds and Sods

Blown back; hitting the woodwork

If the ball goes over the cross-bar and the wind blows it back, a goal is scored. (This ruling was made in 1885, so blowing back probably happened for the first time in 1884. The winter of '84 was terribly windy, I remember.) If the ball hits a goal post, or both goal posts, or the cross-bar, or all three, and then goes over the bar, a goal is scored. If the ball goes directly over the top of a goal post it's not a goal; but you knew that already.

No goal from a free kick

And not just from a free kick. If a player tap-kicks a free kick and passes to a team-mate, *that* player cannot score a dropped goal, either. In fact, the team given a free kick can't score a dropped goal until after an opponent has played the ball, or after an opponent has made a tackle, or after the ball is dead. In other words, the team can't score a dropped goal until it's lost and regained possession.

Illegally deflected but still a goal

At all types of kick at goal – conversion, penalty goal or dropped goal – if the referee reckons that the ball would *probably* have gone over if a defender hadn't illegally touched it, he can award a goal even though the ball never reached its target. Hard to imagine a defender getting his hands on a penalty kick in full flight, but he might be able to do it to a conversion kick or a dropped kick. Suppose, for instance, that after a scrum a fly-half attempts a drop kick at goal and an opposing flanker – miles offside – bats the ball away. If the referee reckons the drop kick would probably have been successful, he gives a dropped goal.

The archives of my society – the Bristol Referees Society, probably the best in the world – contain a report of a penalty kick at goal during which a defender leaped so high that he managed to reach over the cross-bar and punch the ball back into the field-of-play. Intentional knock-on, of course. The referee, without hesitation, awarded the goal. A fine leap, nevertheless.

A kick at goal can also be *legally* deflected. It has been known for a player to hook his kick so ferociously that the ball set off towards a corner flag. The player turned away in disgust, and so failed to see the ball connect with a defender's head and ricochet over the cross-bar. Not a great goal, but a goal all the same.

No dummying the kick

If a player pretends to take a conversion kick but in fact doesn't, so that defenders charge too soon, the referee will allow them to go on charging. Same applies to free kicks and penalty kicks not taken at goal. If you dummy the kick in order to con your opponents and win another penalty, the referee will let play continue and you'll have to take the consequences.

Use the same ball

For a conversion kick or a penalty kick at goal, the kicker must use the ball that was in play. He can tee it up on sand or sawdust or a plastic tee if he likes.

Charge! (But do it quietly)

A defender must not charge a penalty kick. He can charge a conversion kick; as soon as the kicker begins his run or starts to kick, a defender can charge or jump or both. If the kicker is slow enough and the defender is fast enough, the defender might even charge down the kick, or at least take the kicker's eye off the ball. What defenders must not do is shout (or whistle, or sing).

Readers write

V.J. of Aberavon writes: Last Saturday, I kicked the ball over the goal-line, me and an opponent both dived for it, and I definitely got my hand to it first, but the bloody ref wouldn't give me the try.

D.R. Did you press down on the ball?

V.J. I definitely touched it first.

D.R. When you're not holding the ball – no downward pressure, no try.

V.J. You bloody refs are all alike.

D.R. I certainly hope so. And another thing: if the referee couldn't see you ground the ball, perhaps because other players were diving on it, he can't give the try.

V.J. That's scandalous.

D.R. That's life.

* * *

N.J.S. of Buenos Aires writes: I know the goal-posts are in the in-goal, but what about the protective post pads? Can you score a try against a post pad? Some are very thick.

D.R. They are still part of the goalposts. So the answer's yes.

* * *

W.W of West Hartlepool writes: I understand the momentum try, where you take the tackler with you. How about a sort of skate-over try, where the ball-carrier hasn't been tackled and he dives on to a big wet patch of mud that's short of the in-goal, so as to skid over the goal-line?

D.R. What's the advantage?

W.W. Makes it very hard for a tackler to stop him.

D.R. So what's your point?

W.W. Well, the tackle law says a player who goes to ground with the ball must immediately get up or let go of it, doesn't it?

D.R. True. But this skid-over happens in a flash, doesn't it?

W.W. How long is a flash? You'd be surprised how far some players can slide. It rains a lot up here.

* * *

G.D.L. of London writes: What you said about a player tackled just short of the line and reaching out to score, that's nothing new. There was a big debate about it at a meeting of the London Society of Referees in 1920.

D.R. What did they decide?

G.D.L. They said it was a try. By a majority vote.

D.R. Nothing changes.

* * *

C.J. of St. Ives writes: Just before the kick-off, our goal-posts got blown skew-whiff by the wind, so they looked like a letter H leaning sideways.

D.R. Italic.

C.J. If you say so. Anyway, I took a kick at goal and if the posts had been upright I'd have scored. But they weren't, and I didn't, so we lost.

D.R. That's tragic.

* * *

L.G. of Coventry writes: What's all the fuss about the rush of penalty tries? An attacking team takes a tapped penalty on their opponents' 5-metre line, they get nowhere because defenders simply stay offside and block the attack, the ref penalises this with another kick in exactly the same place – or a third, fourth, or fifth kick. He's wasting his breath!

D.R. Let's look at the law. A penalty try isn't an easy decision. Would the attackers *probably* have scored, but for foul play? Remember, offside is not foul play.

L.G. No, but intentionally offending is. So is repeatedly offending. They're professional fouls. If players won't respect the ref's big stick, they force him to reach for an even bigger stick. Otherwise he may as well go home.

D.R. You're right. The International Board "fully supports referees in the strict and uniform enforcement of the Laws as to repeated infringement". In senior matches, the IB says the referee "should always apply a strict standard". It says that "on the third occasion a caution must be given". It says that if he's unsure as to the balance of probability, he should give the benefit of the doubt to the non-offending team and award the penalty try.

13
Kicks

Kick-off

The game starts, and re-starts after half-time, with a place kick at the centre of the half-way line. After every score, play re-starts with a drop-kick taken on or behind the centre spot.

Who kicks off?

A toss-up before the match decides who kicks off. The winner can *either* choose which end he wants to defend *or* take the kick-off. If he prefers to choose ends, his opponents take the kick-off; if he wants the kick-off, his opponents choose ends.

Naturally, after half-time, when they change ends, the other side kicks off; and after a score it is always the side which has been scored against that kicks off.

It may come as a surprise to some people to learn that, strictly according to law, the captains actually perform the toss. I once refereed in Ireland, and the two captains gave me a very peculiar look when I offered them a coin before the match. Apparently it was the custom in those parts for the referee to spin the coin. Several interested spectators told me afterwards that, knowing those two fellahs, I was a lucky man to see my cash again.

What makes a good kick-off?

First, it must be in the right place: the centre of the half-way line for a place kick; on or just behind the centre for a drop-kick.

Second, it must be the right type of kick.

Third, the opposing team must stand at least ten metres from the half-way line.

Fourth, they must not charge until the ball has been kicked. Failing any of these conditions – if the kicker makes the wrong sort of kick, or the right kick in the wrong place; or if his opponents stand too near or charge too soon – the referee will order the kick to be taken again.

Fifth, the kicker's team must all be behind the ball. If the referee sees any of the kicker's team in front of the ball at the moment of kick-off, he orders a scrum at the centre.

Sixth, the ball must reach the ten metres line (a line ten metres from the half-way line and parallel to it) unless an opponent plays it first, in which case the game goes on. If it doesn't go far enough, the opponents can *either* have it kicked off again *or* take a scrum at

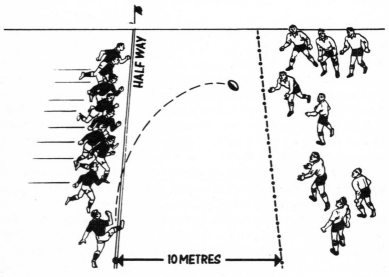

Kick-off from the centre. To start the match, and to restart it after half-time, the kick-off is a place kick from the centre spot. To restart play after a score, the kick-off is a drop kick from or behind the centre. The kicker's team must be behind the ball when kicked, and their opponents must be at least ten metres away. The ball should reach the ten-metre line and land in the field-of-play. If it fails to go ten metres but an opponent plays it first, then play goes on.

the centre. If it goes ten metres and the wind blows it back, play continues.

Seventh, the ball should land in the field-of-play. If it doesn't, what happens next depends on where it does land.

If the ball is kicked directly into touch, the other team has a three-way choice: either to have another kick-off, or to take a scrum at the centre, or to accept the kick and all that goes with it (which means a throw-in on the halfway line). If the ball is blown behind the halfway line and goes directly into touch, the throw-in is where it went into touch.

If the ball is kicked into the in-goal without touching a player on the way, the other team has a very different choice. They can either play on, or ground the ball, or make it dead by putting it into touch-in-goal or over the dead-ball line. Of course, it might go dead of its own accord, if it's travelling fast enough.

If they don't play on, they have yet another choice: either to have the ball kicked-off again, or to take a scrum at the centre. (They get the same choice if the kick-off sends the ball clean over the in-goal without even bouncing in it.)

Once a team has played on, they can't change their mind, ground the ball and ask for a scrum at the centre. When a defender runs with the ball or passes it, his team has played on. There's no going back.

This all makes sense. The purpose of the kick-off is to start the game in such a way that both sides have a fair chance of getting to the ball and doing something with it. By making one team stand back, and making the other team kick the ball to them, the laws create a situation in which anything could happen, and usually does.

If you're wondering what lies behind the option of a scrum-back at the centre after a kick-off that was grounded in the in-goal, I'll tell you. Not long ago, a kind of sleeping sickness had infected the game. The kick-off always went deep into the in-goal, the defending team always grounded the ball, and (under the old law) they restarted play with a 22 drop-out, which was what their opponents wanted. This dreary exchange guaranteed that, three seconds after the game began, the game stopped. The whole thing was a monumental yawn, until the lawmakers stepped in and put a sock in it. Now, any team that kicks off too deep finds itself rapidly back where it started; so it doesn't.

Drop-out

Apart from the special case I've just described, if the ball crosses a goal line and is made dead there, play restarts *either* with a five-metre scrum *or* with a drop-out, depending on several things which you can read all about in the chapter on the in-goal.

A drop-out is a drop-kick by the defending side, taken anywhere on or behind their 22-metre line. This line separates the two teams.

Up to this point, a drop-out is very like a kick-off: if the kicker makes the wrong sort of kick, or kicks from the wrong place, or if his opponents charge over the line too soon, the referee will whistle and order the kick to be taken again. And if any of the kicker's team is in front of the ball when it's kicked, the referee will order a scrum at the centre of the line. However, if they are in front of the ball because the kick was taken quickly, the referee will not stop play –

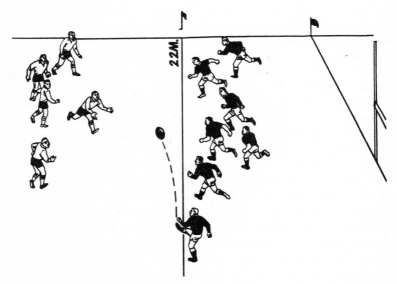

The 22 drop-out. The kick must be a drop-kick. It can be taken anywhere on or behind the 22-metre line. The kicker's team must be behind the ball when kicked, and their opponents must be on the other side of the line. The ball should cross the line and land in the field-of-play. Penalty for delay: free kick.

provided they keep retiring and stay out of the game until put onside by a team-mate.

Like the kick-off, a drop-out must go far enough but not too far. The ball must cross the 22-metre line; if it doesn't, the other team can either have the ball dropped out again or take a scrum at the centre of the line. (If the ball crosses the line and the wind blows it back, play goes on.) The ball should pitch inside the field-of-play. If it doesn't, the other side can either have another drop-out, or a scrum at the centre of the line, or accept the kick (which means taking a throw-in where the ball went into touch). All this, of course, follows the pattern of the kick-off.

Penalty kick

A penalty kick is a kick given to one side because the other side has done something seriously wrong.

The side that has been penalised has to (a) hand over the ball, and (b) clear off quickly. Temporarily, the game becomes very one-sided. That is the penalty for doing things that are penalised with penalty kicks.

As soon as the referee has given your opponents a penalty kick, you must at once run – not walk, but run – to a line ten metres behind the mark for the kick, or to your own goal line, whichever is the nearer. You can go further if you want to; but you must, if you can, give the other side at least ten metres of green grass in which to do their stuff. I don't know what you did to deserve all this, but let it be a lesson to you.

If you don't get back ten metres, or if you don't move fast enough, or if you deliberately put the ball out of your opponents' reach, or if you backchat, the referee will penalise you again by awarding a second penalty kick, ten metres in front of the first. (This second kick replaces the first. It must not be taken until the referee has made the mark for it – a slight pause which gives the penalised team time to retire.) And if you keep asking for trouble, he can shunt you back, ten metres at a time, until the mark is only five metres from your goal line.

That is the closest a penalty kick can be to the opponents' goal-line: five metres. When the offence takes place *less* than five metres

10 METRES

Beating retreat. Part of the penalty of a penalty kick is that you have to give the other team a clear ten metres in which to do what they like with the ball. As soon as the referee gives them a penalty kick, you must run ten metres from the mark towards your own goal line, or to that line if it's nearer.

from the line, the mark for the kick is always given on the five-metre line. This is to prevent the kind of situation where, with only inches separating the penalty kicker from the line, sheer brawn is bound to score.

So the situation is this. You have given them the ball, the foreground and the initiative. Can things get worse? Yes, they can.

Kick taken quickly

You, as the guilty team, must retreat immediately, but your opponents need not wait for you to do so. They can take a quick kick and attack. Even if some of their players are in front of the ball, the kicker is free to do his stuff. As long as they don't get involved in play, and they do their best to get onside, the game can carry on at high speed.

The scene at a quickly taken penalty kick may look thoroughly confused. You and your penalised team-mates are scrambling back ten metres. Some of your opponents are scrambling in the opposite direction, to get behind the ball. Simultaneously, the kicker – reckoning that the best time to attack is when you are completely disorganised – takes a tapped penalty and accelerates forward. You

Penalty kick taken quickly: two-way traffic. A player can take a quick penalty even though some team-mates are offside, provided they are trying to get back onside. Meanwhile, their opponents must retire 10 metres from the mark, fast. In the picture, the White No. 9 takes a quick tapped penalty and runs ahead. Black opponents, retiring 10 metres and running in the same direction, cannot touch him. White players (1 and 3), running in the opposite direction to get onside, are also out of the game. Thus, briefly, the White No. 9 is surrounded by friends and enemies who can do nothing except run away from each other. However, the Black No. 6 has retired 10 metres and can now make a tackle.

may find yourself running alongside him, heading for your own goal line yet unable to lay a finger on him.

This is because, even *after* the penalty kick is taken, you must keep retiring until you have covered ten metres or reached your goal line. The taking of the penalty kick does not put everybody back into the game. There is a terrible temptation to stop and see what's going on, because after all they *are* the enemy, and they *are* up to something. Resist it. The first thing you must do is retire ten metres. Your opponents may be launching the most dangerous attack, but there's nothing you can do about it until you've put yourself back into the game by retiring ten metres or to your own goal line – *with one exception*. If, while you are straining every nerve to retire ten metres and so on, a team-mate who was a least ten metres from the mark for the kick runs in front of you, this brings you back into the game. You can stop retiring and get stuck in again.

But it's worth understanding the full implications of this bit of law. For instance: suppose that when your team is penalised you are 15 metres nearer your opponents' goal line. This means you must retire a total of 25 metres (or to your own goal line) before you can rejoin the game – unless, of course, a team-mate runs forward and puts you onside. Meanwhile your opponents are on the attack. Several may have handled the ball by the time you catch up. You're keen to tackle. Don't do it. Don't do anything, until you've done what the law requires.

Penalty round-up

A penalty kick can be of any kind – place, drop or punt – and any player can take it. The kicker can use a placer to hold the ball, if he wants. He must not place-kick for touch. The kick must be made either on or behind the mark, which the referee indicates with a delicate bash from his heel. Pay attention to that mark, and be sure you make your kick somewhere on a line through it. If the referee makes his mark *here*, and you gallop up, all a-twitter with impatience, and take the kick *there*, five metres to the right, he'll blow up, recall the ball, and give a scrum, opponents' put-in.

You can take a penalty kick anywhere behind the mark, on a line through it and parallel with the touch-lines. This allows you to adjust the angle to improve your chances of a kick at goal. You can even go as far back as your own in-goal if you want to (I can't see what good it would do). If you take a penalty kick inside your in-goal and the ball goes into touch-in-goal or over the dead-ball line, the referee orders a five-metre scrum, attacking team's put-in.

Apart from this, you're free to kick the ball in any direction, and any player – including the kicker – can play it next. Mind you, a penalty kick must be a *kick*. Bouncing the ball on your knee is not a kick. Tapping it on your toe is not a kick. Knocking it with your heel is not a kick. A kick is only a kick if you hit the ball with your foot, or your leg below the knee, hard enough to send it out of your hands (if you're holding it) or away from the mark (if it's on the ground). It doesn't have to go far but it must go somewhere. More important, the referee must see that it has gone somewhere. If you turn your back on the referee and fumble with the ball, don't be surprised if he calls play back and orders a scrum; he's not clairvoyant, you know. Do the obvious thing: let him *watch* you taking the penalty kick. Then he can see what's happened.

Penalty kick at goal

Once you've let the referee know that you're going to take a penalty kick at goal, you're committed to it. You must go for goal; if you try anything else the referee will disallow the kick and give a scrum. And there are more ways of letting the referee know than spitting on the ball and mumbling something about having a bash. If you start placing the ball as if for a kick at goal, squinting at the uprights, tossing little bits of grass into the wind, and so on, this says irrevocably that you are going for goal, and it's no good whispering huskily to him that really you're not. He may even ask you what you plan to do; he has the right.

The reason is simple. If you are taking a kick at goal, he will send the touch-judges around behind the posts. If you're not, he'll leave them where they are more use. What he *won't* stand for is sending the touch-judges behind the posts and then seeing you kick the ball into touch.

If you don't let the referee know that you intend to kick at goal, and then you take a drop kick and it goes over, this is a goal. It just

Penalty kick at goal. This can be taken anywhere on a line through the mark for the kick, so the kicker can go back to improve his angle. Defenders must retire at least ten metres from the mark (or to their goal line if it's nearer) and they must stand still, arms by their sides, while the kick is being taken.

means that you've done it without benefit of touch-judges.

As with kick-offs and drop-outs and conversions, all the kicker's team (except the placer, if one is used) must be behind the ball when it's kicked. Otherwise the referee will give a scrum at the mark.

You are not obliged to accept a penalty kick, by the way. You can have a scrum at the mark, if you'd rather. Up to you.

Drop kick

You make a drop kick by letting the ball fall to the ground from your hands and kicking it on the first rebound. The only times when you *must* drop-kick the ball are when making a drop-out, when making a kick-off after a score, and when attempting a dropped goal. Otherwise you might as well punt.

In the early days of the game, most kicks were drop kicks. As late as the 1860s spectators booed punting; but the ball was a slightly different shape then. The oval leather case was filled with an inflated pig's bladder, and this usually made the ends well rounded. The ball was more suited to place-kicking and drop-kicking than today's relatively pointed ball, which is shaped for handling as well as kicking. Of course, a hundred years ago many people thought there was far too much handling in rugby too.

Free kick

There is only one sort of free kick, but there are two reasons for giving it. *Either* it's a kick awarded to one team because of an offence by the other team, *or* it's a kick which a player earns by making a fair-catch, or 'Mark!'.

A free kick can be a place, punt or drop, but you cannot place-kick to touch with a free kick. You cannot score a goal from a free kick. If you prefer, you can take a scrum instead of a free kick.

Free kick from a fair-catch, or 'Mark!'

A fair catch gives you a chance to stop the game temporarily in order to protect yourself when you're catching the ball from an opponent's kick.

Mark! or Fair-Catch. To claim a fair-catch, you must do three things, all at once – catch the ball cleanly; be in or behind your 22; and shout 'Mark!' Get it right and the referee will award you a free kick.

To make a fair catch you must do three things, all at the same time:

1 Catch the ball cleanly, direct from an opponent's kick (but not including a kick-off).
2 Be in your 22-metre area or your in-goal.
3 Shout 'Mark!'

This feat isn't easy, especially when the ball is coming out of the sun and the earth is trembling beneath the pounding hooves of hungry opponents. The usual time to make a fair-catch is when your team is in deep trouble and you need a break, so by definition you're under pressure. Nevertheless, you must bring off all three parts perfectly, and all together. If you catch the ball and then drop it, or if you knock-on and make a second catch, or if you're outside your 22, or if you shout the magic word too late – it's no good. The referee won't whistle, and it's no use giving him that long, reproachful stare.

Robinson's First Law of Rugby says that, when a law is changed, it always takes at least ten years for the old version to fade away. Long ago, when you claimed a fair-catch you had to make a mark with your heel as you shouted 'Mark!' Occasionally today you can see veteran players still denting the turf in that old-fashioned way as they field a kick. More recently, the fair-catch law was changed so that the player need not have both feet on the ground at the crucial moment. Now even that has been abolished. Now he can jump and claim a fair-catch while he's off the ground entirely. And he is reckoned to be inside his 22 even if he has only one foot on the 22-metre line or behind it.

You can make a fair-catch on the run and when you've done it you shouldn't hang around. Your opponents won't wait for the whistle, and neither should you. Beat it fast, while your legs still function. If the referee allows your fair-catch you haven't lost anything, and if he doesn't, then you're going to have to do something in a hurry anyway.

You can make a fair-catch in your own in-goal, and you can make one after the ball has bounced off a goal post or cross-bar.

Making a fair-catch entitles you to a free kick. Only the player who made the fair-catch can take the free kick. If he's injured there's a scrum at the mark instead, with his team putting in the ball. And if he made his fair-catch in his in-goal, the scrum goes down five metres from the goal-line, opposite the mark.

Free kick following an offence

Unlike the 'fair-catch' free kick, this free kick can be awarded anywhere in the field-of-play and it can be taken by any player in the team.

The free kick: full description

A free kick has a lot in common with a penalty kick. A free kick must be taken at the mark or anywhere behind it on a line through the mark, parallel with touch. If the kick has been awarded for an offence within five metres of the opponents' goal-line, the mark is made five metres out from that goal-line. The kick must be taken without undue delay. All the kicker's team must be behind the ball (except a placer to hold a place kick). The kick must noticeably move the ball, either out of the kicker's hands or away from the mark on the ground. The kicker is free to kick the ball in any direction and he can play it again if he wishes.

The big difference between a free kick and a penalty kick lies in its scoring power (none) and in the fact that the opposing side is allowed to charge it.

A team awarded a free kick cannot score a dropped goal until after an opponent has played the ball, or after an opponent has made a tackle, or after the ball is dead. A lot to remember.

As soon as a free kick is awarded, the other team must immediately run until they are ten metres behind the mark or they have reached their own goal line – just as for a penalty kick. They must keep running, even after the free kick has been taken, until they've covered ten metres or until an onside team-mate runs in front of them. And – just as with a penalty kick – a team awarded a free kick need not wait until all its players are behind the ball. If the kick is taken so quickly that some team-mates are offside, they won't be penalised as long as they take no part in the game and they retire at once. This is all very familiar.

Unlike a penalty kick, however, a free kick can be charged, and even charged down. Once the other team has retreated ten metres, their beady little eyes will be fixed on the kicker and their feet will be pawing the ground, just itching for him to make a move. The instant the kicker starts his run or offers to kick, they can hurl themselves at him. He can't afford to waver or feint and then draw back. Once he's made a move his opponents will be after him, and if he hesitates they may well succeed in preventing him from taking the kick altogether. That means a scrum at the mark, their put-in.

Now that you see what a difference a good charge can make, you'll understand why the laws insist that the kicker makes a definite kick, moving the ball unmistakeably out of his hands or along the ground, even if it only goes a matter of inches; and why rubbing the ball on the toecap is not enough. The other team must be able to tell when they're entitled to charge.

There's no doubt about the start of the kicker's run; but if the kicker takes a tapped kick, it must be a clear and visible signal to everyone, including the enemy. (The same is true of the penalty kick. Although the other team must not move *until* a penalty kick has been taken, they're free to rush in all directions *as soon as* it's taken, so it's essential that they should know exactly when that moment is.)

If the other team fails to get back ten metres quickly enough, or if they charge too soon, the referee will cancel the free kick and give a second free kick, ten metres forward (not to be taken until he's made the mark). Any player may take this kick. And if they do something gormless like throwing the ball over the hedge, he might well regard that as misconduct and award a penalty kick.

Readers write

B.M. of Llanelli writes: I still reckon you should be able to kick a goal from a free kick.

D.R. Forget it. You're history.

* * *

P.Z. of Bucharest writes: This business about a team being free to take a quick penalty kick is all very well, but what if the ref wants to warn an opponent for his foul play? The ref's standing and talking, while they're off and running.

D.R. You're right. Yet another dilemma for the referee. It's a tough job.

14
The in-goal

The in-goal is the area behind the goal-line. It is bordered by the goal-line, which is part of the in-goal. If the ball lands on the goal line, play goes on (unless a try is scored). The rest of the in-goal is bordered by the touch-in-goal lines and the dead-ball line. They are not part of the in-goal. If the ball touches them, or anything or anyone beyond them, it's dead.

The great attraction of the in-goal is that it's the only place where you can score a try or make a touch-down. Apart from that – and the fact that scrums, rucks, mauls, line-outs and tackles can't take place there – the in-goal is just like the field-of-play. A knock-on in an in-goal is still a knock-on; a player who is offside in an in-goal can get into trouble just as easily as if he were in midfield. Nearly all the laws apply behind the goal-line just as they do in front of it.

But although the game is much the same, the consequences are not. The referee's decision varies according to which team did what, and where.

Drop-out

If an attacking player puts or takes the ball into his opponents' in-goal and it becomes dead there, the result is a drop-out.

This does not include the situation where an attacker knocks-on or throws-forward in the field-of-play so that the ball goes into the in-goal and it's made dead there. In that case, the referee orders a scrum where the knock-on or throw-forward happened.

It does include the situation where a defender's kick is charged down by an attacking player in the field-of-play and the ball goes into the in-goal.

What matters is the fact that an attacking player's action sent the ball into the in-goal. It makes no difference if the ball touched a defender before it crossed the goal line, provided he didn't try to play the ball.

So the drop-out law is simple. If an attacker – without breaking a law – sends the ball into his opponents' in-goal, and anyone makes it dead (not including a try), the defending team gets a drop-out. (Made dead in in-goal direct from a kick-off is different; see *kick-off*.)

What's more, if an attacker boots the ball into his opponents' in-goal and his kick makes it dead in touch-in-goal or over the dead-ball line, his opponents get a choice – either a drop-out, or a scrum where the ball was kicked. Reason? To discourage delaying tactics, and keep the ball in play.

For the purposes of this law, 'made dead' means a defender grounded the ball (touch-down) or any player put it into touch-in-goal or over the dead-ball line. It doesn't mean a try was scored.

Foiled pushover. Once the ball in a scrum reaches or crosses the goal line, the scrum has ended and anyone can ground the ball – including (as shown here) the defending scrum-half. Result: touch-down and (because the attacking team took the ball into the in-goal) a drop-out.

Five-metre scrum

This is a scrum on the defending team's five-metre line, and it's even simpler than the drop-out law, because a five-metre scrum is awarded on every other occasion when the ball is made dead in or beyond the in-goal. If the ball's dead and it's not a drop-out, it must be a five-metre scrum. Unless the attacking team infringed a law in some way, they always get the put-in.

To sum up: a ball made dead after an attacker put it into the in-goal (without offending) means a drop-out. A ball made dead after a defender put it into the in-goal means a five-metre scrum. Is that really all there is to it? Well, almost.

A five-metre scrum usually comes about because a defending player took or put the ball into his in-goal and couldn't get it out again, so he had to make it dead. (One foot on or behind the goal line puts him in-goal.) But the in-goal can be a hectic place. What happens if a player – either a defender or an attacker – has the ball in an in-goal, and his opponents have such a grip of him that he can't ground it? He's what's known as 'held up in the in-goal' and the referee orders a five-metre scrum, attackers' put-in. Same applies if the referee can't decide which team first grounded the ball, as sometimes happens when opposing players dive on it. And in both these cases, it makes no difference which team originally took the ball into the in-goal: it's always a five-metre scrum, and it's always the attackers' put-in.

What happens when a scrum or a ruck gets pushed into an in-goal and a defender grounds the ball? Well, it depends. If the defending team was in possession at the time – that is, the ball was in their half of the scrum or ruck as it got rumbled over the goal line – then a five-metre scrum is formed. But if the attacking team was in possession but a defender managed to poach a touch-down first, the outcome is a drop-out. I've seen it happen. The attacking team bust a gut in an effort to get a pushover try, and just as their No. 8 dribbled the ball onto the goal line, the opposing scrum-half dived in and whacked the ball with his hand. Smart play, and well worth the drop-out it earned.

Lastly, an oddity. If a defending team takes a free kick or a penalty kick in their in-goal, and they cock it up so that the ball is made dead before it can cross the goal line, the consequence is a five-metre scrum, attacking team's put-in.

Errors in the in-goal

You can knock-on or throw-forward in an in-goal just as easily as in the field-of-play. If the referee's any good, he'll wait for a second or two before he blows up, in case the other team can take advantage of your mistake. If there's no advantage, he'll give a five-metre scrum, opposite the place where you went wrong. And if you're an attacking player, this is the one case where the defending team gets the put-in at a five-metre scrum.

You can be offside in an in-goal. Easily. After all, the space may be up to 22 metres deep: plenty of room for you to stray in front of a team-mate who has the ball or who has just kicked it, and then to interfere with play. In fact, most of the offences that happen in the field-of-play can also happen in the in-goal. Not the tackle offences, nor the scrum/ruck/maul offences, because those events are confined to the field-of-play. But the Foul Play law certainly applies to the in-goal. Punching, charging, kicking, tripping and any other kind of dangerous or unfair play will get you penalised, and – as usual – the referee can warn a player or send him off. The referee can always award a penalty try if he thinks that foul play prevented a probable try; equally, he can disallow a try if he thinks foul play by an attacker contributed to it.

So any action (foul play, offside, whatever) that deserves a free kick or a penalty kick if it happens in the field-of-play gets just the same treatment when it's done in an in-goal – with one big difference. The mark for a free kick or a penalty kick can never be in an in-goal. The mark must always be in the field-of-play. Where exactly, depends on whether the ball was in play or out of play at the time of the crime.

For any offence in an in-goal while the ball is in play, the kick is awarded on the five-metre line. If an attacker was guilty, the defending team gets the kick and probably boots the ball into touch. If a defender was guilty, the attacking team gets the kick. As they can take the ball back from the mark, they might well attempt a penalty goal.

Misconduct while the ball is out of play is different. Dirty work in an in-goal when the ball is dead – I leave the grubby details to your steamy imagination – results in a penalty kick being awarded where the ball would next have been brought into play. That could be on the five-metre line (instead of a five-metre scrum), or on the 22 (instead of a drop-out), or at the centre spot (after a try). So it's conceivably possible for a team to score a try, then commit misconduct in the in-goal, then attempt the conversion kick, and *then* have to face a penalty kick by their opponents from the centre spot.

There's one exception. It applies to the offence of intentionally obstructing an opponent in the in-goal when he's just kicked the ball. I think we can safely assume that this opponent is a defender. His team can choose to take a penalty kick *either* on their five-metre line *or* where the ball landed. If it came down in or near touch, leave it to the ref to sort out.

Fine tuning

A five-metre scrum is always awarded opposite the place where the knock-on or throw-forward happened or where the ball was made dead. The scrum must be at least five metres from a touch line. The attacking team always puts in the ball, unless they made the knock-on or throw-forward.

When a free kick or penalty kick is awarded on the five-metre line, the mark for the kick is opposite the place of the offence. When the kick is awarded instead of a drop-out, it can be taken anywhere on the 22-metre line. When it's awarded on the centre spot it's taken on the centre spot, which is so obvious that I wonder why I bother.

Last word

There can be no rucks or mauls in the in-goal, remember. This is one of the few laws which don't apply there. Another is the tackle, legally speaking. Tackles – as the law defines them – cannot happen in an in-goal, which is not to say that you can't grab an opponent who has the ball there. You can, and as there are no mauls, legally speaking, in the in-goal, other defenders can converge from all sides to help hold him up. Result: stalemate, which the referee breaks with his famous five-metre scrum.

Readers write

M.M. of Essex writes: Someone told me that when Romania played Wales, in September 1994, Wales scored ten points without a Romanian player touching the ball. How?

D.R. Simple. Try plus conversion plus penalty goal equals ten points. Immediately after a Welsh player scored a try, a Romanian player fell on him and jabbed him in the back with his elbow. That's misconduct while the ball is out of play, so the kick was awarded where the game would have restarted, and Wales kicked the penalty from the halfway line.

* * *

B.R. of Sydney writes: I've been thinking about what you said to V.J. of Aberavon at the end of the chapter on scoring. Several players dive on the ball, the referees can't see who grounded it, so he can't give the try, you said.

D.R. Correct. Good refs never guess.

B.R. But you never said what he does next.

D.R. You're right, I didn't. It's a 5-metre scrum. Any time the referee has doubts about grounding in the in-goal, it's always a 5-metre scrum, attacking team's put-in.

15

Advantage

The Advantage Law is the best law in the book, because it lets you ignore all the others for the good of the game. It goes like this.

When one side breaks a law, and the other side gains an advantage from this, the referee lets the game go on.

For example: if a player knocks on but an opponent intercepts the ball and makes good use of it, the referee will gladly forget about the knock-on. And the advantage gained doesn't have to be territorial; it can be tactical. Take the same example again: if the opponent who snapped up the knock-on found himself about to be tackled, he obviously couldn't hope to make much ground, so territorial advantage is out. On the other hand, he might have an unmarked team-mate outside him, just waiting to take a pass; in which case there would be a good chance of tactical advantage.

Now, perhaps, you see why people are always urging you to play to the whistle. It isn't just that the referee might have missed the knock-on (which you saw so clearly and slowed down because of). It's far more likely that he saw the knock-on *and waited to see if it gave any advantage to the other side.* For the referee, as we have discovered already, is not clairvoyant; the only way he can find out if you are smart enough to exploit your opponents' mistakes is by giving you the chance.

Therefore, he must let play go on for a couple of seconds after the infringement, before he can decide whether or not an advantage has been gained. If you hesitate about grabbing an opportunity because you think the whistle *should* have gone, you defeat the whole purpose of the advantage law, which is to *keep the game going.* Let the referee look after the mistakes; your job is to get the ball and score. The referee will do all he can to leave these opportunities open to you, but only you can take advantage of them.

And if it turns out that you don't in fact get any advantage from whatever it was, he'll bring back play and award you the scrum or the kick. So you can't lose.

The advantage law covers ninety-nine per cent of the game. Virtually every time your opponents go wrong, you can profit from it. Advantage covers scrums, rucks, mauls, line-outs, knock-ons, forward passes, free kicks, tackles, drop-outs, in-goal play, and all kinds and conditions of offside. There are a million ways you can use advantage, and the referee will be looking for them all.

Exceptions. Only five parts of the game are *not* covered by advantage. They are:

1 When the ball or a player carrying it touches the referee.
2 When a scrum is wheeled through more than 90 degrees.
3 When a scrum collapses.
4 When a player in a scrum is lifted off his feet or forced upwards out of the scrum.

Territorial advantage: gain in ground. This little scenario happens all the time. The Black player gets a pass, knocks it on, and an opponent smartly boots the ball past him. This is territorial advantage. The referee lets play go on. If Whites get no advantage (for instance, if another Black catches the kick-ahead) the referee orders a scrum where the knock-on happened.

5 When the ball comes out of either end of the tunnel at a scrum
   without having been played.

That last item raises several interesting points which I've already
kicked around in the chapter on scrums, so I shan't repeat them
here. I just want to add the obvious fact that although advantage
may not always apply to the way the ball comes out of the tunnel, it
certainly does apply to the way it goes into the tunnel. If the scrum-
half, in a fit of absentmindedness, puts the ball in crookedly under
the opposing hooker's feet, the referee should let him get on with it.

The same thing applies to line-outs. The thrower is supposed to
throw the ball in straight, but if his unstraight throw favours his
opponents, why stop the game?

*Tactical advantage: good possession. At a scrum near Whites' goal line, Blacks win
the ball. A White flanker (No. 6) breaks too soon and is caught offside. However,
Blacks have good possession and they're in a good position to take tactical
advantage, so the referee lets play go on. If Blacks' attack comes to nothing, he goes
back and penalises the White flanker. So Blacks can't lose. Note that the ball is still
in the scrum. The Black scrum-half is waiting for it to come out before he grabs it.*

And if, at a drop-out, the ball goes backwards instead of forwards and the other side is waiting for it when it comes down, good luck to them. Also full advantage.

Consider a scrum near the posts. As the attacking side heels the ball a defending flanker is caught offside. Should the referee immediately blow up? Not necessarily. The attacking team might get a try and convert it: seven points, against three for a penalty goal. So, while making it clear that he has seen the offside offence, the referee can let the attack develop. If it fails, he can still award the penalty kick for offside.

One of the biggest idiots in rugby is the player who keeps reminding the referee when something has gone wrong. He thinks he sees a knock-on, so he shouts 'Knock-on!'. This is stupid, because:

1 the referee, being human, resents being told what to do, and
2 he's playing advantage and trying *not* to stop the game, while this pessimist has never heard of advantage and spends his afternoon *looking* for reasons to stop the game.

The advantage law is a splendid idea. It makes playing a pleasure and refereeing an art. It is beautifully simple: when in doubt, play on! As Milton* once said, 'Advantage is the oil that greases the gears of the game,' and he should know. In rugby, as in life, one man's grief is another man's gravy.

* Cedric McGregor Milton, famed Manx referee.

Readers write

P.R.A. of Middlesex writes: The law says: 'If advantage is being played following an infringement by one team and then the other team commit an infringement, the referee blows the whistle and applies the sanction associated with the first infringement.' What the hell does that mean?

D.R. At first glance, it suggests that a second infringement *always* means the whistle goes and the teams *always* return to where the first offence happened.

P.R.A. And what does a second glance say?

D.R. Well, let's look again at those opening words: `If advantage is being played...'. Now, suppose the referee is no longer playing advantage. Suppose he reckons the team has gained all the benefit it deserves, and life is too short for him to go on running about with his arm stuck out, signalling advantage. In that case, we're back to normal play again, aren't we? If there's a second infringement, the referee isn't always obliged to blow his whistle and return to the first offence, because he stopped playing advantage some time ago.

P.R.A. So what's next?

D.R. Well, if the other team can gain advantage from the second infringement, the referee lets play go on.

P.R.A. That's advantage after advantage, then?

D.R. Yes. Many of the world's best referees are willing to play advantage once, twice or even three times in a continuous sequence, provided each advantage is real and no foul play is involved.

P.R.A. And if advantage doesn't follow the second infringement, what then?

D.R. The referee should use his commonsense. Consider this scenario. Reds versus Blues. Reds are attacking, bang in front of Blues' goal, when they knock-on. Advantage is played. Blues grab the ball and run it the length of the field. Now Blues knock-on. Question: should the referee return to the first infringement and award a scrum where Reds knocked-on - now nearly 100 metres away - and give Blues the put-in? Or would that be like giving Blues two bites at the cherry?

P.R.A. What's the answer?

D.R. The law tells us when advantage begins, but not when it ends. That's for the referee to decide. One of the charms of the lawbook is its flexibility, and this is a case in point.

16
Loose ends

What you can't wear

The law about what you can and cannot wear has been considerably tightened up. Some padding is allowed. You can wear shoulder pads provided they cover only the shoulder and the collarbone, and are no thicker than one centimetre when uncompressed (including any straps or containers). Same applies to scrumcaps. One centimetre is three-eighths of an inch. All shoulder pads, scrumcaps and (for women players) chest pads must carry the authorised mark of the International Rugby Board to prove that they conform. This is a circle with 'iRB' in white on a blue background and 'APPROVED CLOTHING' in green around the edge.

You can wear elasticated supports (like cycling shorts) but they must be washable. Padded shorts are banned. So is any bloodstained clothing. You can wear bandages or dressings to cover an injury; tape for support or to prevent an injury; shinpads and ankle supports (which must be under a sock); mitts (but not gloves). There's an obvious ban on buckles, clips, rings, zippers, and the like; and a general ban on any item (apart from shoulder pads and scrumcaps) more than half a centimetre thick, and made of a hard material. (What does 'hard' mean? It means a density of more than 45kg per cubic metre. I bet you're sorry you asked.) So any clothing more than half a centimetre (three-sixteenths of an inch) thick is banned. A player must not wear a 'communication device' (such as a radio link).

Studs must be of regulation size, carry the kite mark, and not have sharp edges. A single stud in the toe of the boot is illegal.

(Moulded-rubber-studded boots are allowed.) Finally there's a catch-all bit of law that says the referee can ban any item of clothing if he thinks it's liable to injure any player. And if, before the match, the referee tells a player something's illegal, and then finds he's wearing it on the field of play, that's an offence under the law of Unfair Play, and he gets sent off.

How long is a match?

Maximum playing time in a match is 80 minutes. Internationals and other top matches always last 80 minutes. Lower down the game there's no set time, and the two teams can decide how long they want to play. Failing that, the referee decides. There's no minimum time, but play must be split into halves, and after half-time the teams must change ends. Players and officials may leave the field at half-time, if they wish. The half-time interval is ten minutes at the most, and if both teams dislike standing about in the pouring rain they can scrub round the interval and kick off as soon as they've sucked their bits of orange; or sooner.

Some games may go on after the end of the second half: these are drawn matches in a knock-out competition for which the Union has authorised extra time to be played if necessary. Extra time must not be played in Under-19 matches. On the other hand some matches may stop before the end of the second half: the referee has power to call a halt at any time if he believes that the match cannot be completed (because of fog, say, or a blizzard) or if he reckons it would be dangerous to carry on playing.

Leaving and entering the field

Except at half-time, you (or your team) cannot leave the playing enclosure to change jerseys – unless a jersey's become blood-stained, in which case it *must* be changed. If you want to leave the field-of-play for any reason, you must get the referee's permission. Similarly, you must not come back until he allows it, which he will do only when the ball is dead. A friend of mine was refereeing a fairly non-vintage match with more than its fair share of thud and blunder, when two large players began fighting. They lurched over

the touch line, still swinging haymakers, but he ignored them and
let play continue. When they realised that nobody was paying any
attention, they gradually stopped fighting and turned towards the
field-of-play. He told them to stay where they were. They had
left the playing enclosure without his permission, he said, and
according to law they must not return until he gave them
permission to do so, which certainly wasn't going to happen in a
hurry. Five minutes later he let them come back. From then on, he
said, it was a much better game. He bent the law a little. However,
he certainly made it fit the needs of the moment.

Throughout a match – and that includes half-time – nobody is
allowed on the playing area unless the referee says so. If he lets anyone
come onto the field it's only briefly. As soon as they've done what they
came to do – treat an injury, for example – they go off again. At half-
time, if a team decides not to go off, its coach can come on and tell
them what's going wrong. Then he, too, disappears.

When does the match end?

Unlike soccer – where, believe it or not, the final whistle can blow
while the ball is in mid-air, *en route* from boot to goal – each half of a
game of rugby can end only when the ball is dead. Even then, the
game may not be over. If time runs out after the referee has awarded
a scrum, a line-out, a try, a penalty kick or a free kick, then play goes
on until the ball next becomes dead. Normal playing time is up, but
the scrum or line-out takes place, or the scoring team tries to convert
the try, or the penalty or free kick is taken. And in the case of the set-
piece restarts or the last two kicks, play may well go on for some
time, especially if *another* penalty or free kick is awarded. The losing
team might even score, and win. Stranger things have happened.

How many players?

You can have any number of players up to a maximum of fifteen in
each team. Fifteen is the customary number, and seems about right for
this sort of game; but if you can't raise that many, it's perfectly legal to
play with fewer, as countless Sevens Tournaments have proved.

Fifteen is an extraordinarily difficult number to count up to, involving as it does both hands and one foot; so it sometimes happens during a game that one team, finding itself constantly outnumbered, starts adding up its opponents and reaches the figure sixteen. If this occurs they're entitled to inform the referee, who will make the opposing captain get rid of one man; but he won't alter the score. Most referees check the teams before the kick-off anyway, and reduce the numbers if they're over the limit.

However, the referee is not obliged to do anything if a team has *fewer* than fifteen players – and it's amazing how many sides spend the first ten minutes of the match wondering why there's such a big hole in their defence, until they realise that their inside-centre is watching the women's hockey, two pitches away.

What if the ball touches the referee?

1 *In the playing area.* This includes the in-goals. If the ball – or a player carrying it – touches the referee, and neither team gains an advantage from this, he lets play go on.
2 *In the field-of-play.* If the ball or a ball-carrier touches the referee and he thinks one team *has* gained an advantage, he orders a scrum on the spot. The team of the player who last had the ball puts it in.
3 *In the in-goal.* If the ball held by a player, or a player with the ball, touches the referee in an in-goal, he whistles up immediately. If an attacking player had the ball, he awards a try at that place. If a defending player had the ball, he awards a touch-down.
4 *Ball touches non-player in an in-goal.* If the ball (not held by a player) touches the referee, a touch judge or a spectator in an in-goal, the referee whistles up at once and uses his judgement to decide what would have happened next – either a try (if he thought an attacking player would probably have scored) or a touch-down (if he thought the ball would probably have gone dead or a defending player would probably have got a touch-down).

This is commonsense. Rugby is a fast-moving game. Occasionally the ball or the ball-carrier will touch the referee. As long as neither team benefits, there's no reason to stop play. But a loose ball in the in-goal: that's different.

Injury time and other delays

If you are injured, you are allowed up to one minute to recover. After that you must either get on or get off, always assuming that you *can* get off. If you can't, the referee will allow whatever time it takes to load you on to the stretcher. But for walking wounded, one minute each is the maximum delay. This time is always made up in the half when it was lost. If the referee has to stop play because of an injury, he restarts it with a scrum. The team last in possession of the ball gets the put-in.

Injury time is a privilege, not a right. The referee is not obliged to halt proceedings just because someone isn't feeling very well, and in any case he certainly won't interrupt play for injury if he thinks the damage is minor. What he will do is let the casualty lie in the mud, moaning piteously and twitching, while the action continues all around.

If somebody who's medically trained is available, the referee may let him or her come onto the field and treat a minor injury while play continues. When the ball is dead the referee will go over and look at the player, who has usually staged a miraculous recovery by then.

Referees take no risks in this area, especially in junior rugby; but they soon get to know the difference between a dislocated shoulder and the aftermath of ten pints of lager and a double vindaloo. I was refereeing a Sunday-morning match when a player got tackled, not very hard, and lay on his back, making peculiar noises. I waved play on. The rest of his team protested angrily. They claimed he was badly hurt. Eventually the ball went dead, and I went back and asked him what was wrong. 'Hangover,' he croaked. Then he threw up on his captain's boots and crawled off the field. I suppose it might have been a heart attack. But if the referee treated every winded player as if he were dying, the match would never end.

Furthermore, if the referee has reason to believe that a player's injury is bogus, that he's not really hurt at all, he can order him to be dumped outside the playing area so that everyone else can get on with the game.

The referee also allows time for a player to change or repair his shorts, jersey or boots if they are badly torn or damaged, and he allows time for a player to re-tie his bootlaces. He allows time for replacement and substitution of a player, and for a touch judge to report foul play.

Any such playing time lost is made up in the same half of the match. Other delays (lost balls, goal posts blown down, straying cattle on the pitch) are best left to the referee's judgement. I remember a game where three minutes were added on for pushing the ambulance out of the mud. They couldn't leave it where it was: the bloke inside was bleeding all over the floor. Besides, the back wheels were right across the touch-in-goal line.

Bleeding wounds

A player who has an open or a bleeding wound must go off. He can't come back until it's been patched up or stitched up so that it's no longer leaking gore, and also covered up. Don't be fooled by that word 'wound'. A nose that's pouring blood is a bleeding wound, even though there's no broken skin to be seen.

Replacements and substitutes

A replacement is not the same as a substitute. A player can be replaced only for injury, and if that's no worse than a bleeding wound which can be treated and covered, then he can return to the game. There's nothing to stop a player coming on as a replacement more than once in a match; but he can come on as a substitute only once. A player can be substituted for any reason. Once that's done, he's off for good – with one small exception. A player who's been substituted may replace a blood injury, or an injured or Sin-Binned or sent-off front-row player, if no suitable replacement is available.

If you find all this confusing, you're not alone. The fact is that each one of those players in tracksuits sitting on the bench is capable of being used either as a replacement or as a substitute. Indeed, he could be a temporary replacement (for a blood injury) and later a permanent substitute (for any reason at all). What's more, if he got a blood injury while playing as a substitute, he could be temporarily replaced, get patched up, and return to the action.

There is a lot of coming and going in modern rugby; so much so that in top matches the referee has the help of what's called a 'fourth official' to monitor and control changes in personnel.

Temporary versus permanent

Since all substitution is permanent while some replacement is temporary and some isn't, it's useful to know exactly how the system works. After all, a team might want its key player back in the game, even if he has lost some blood.

The only player who may be temporarily replaced – meaning that if he returns, his replacement leaves the field – is one with an open or bleeding wound. This is the only kind of injury which gets such special treatment. For instance, if a player twists an ankle (no broken skin, no blood), he can be replaced – but it must be a permanent replacement. His ankle might feel fine after a while. Tough luck. He can't come back.

There's a reason for this discrimination. A bleeding player has no choice. The referee orders him to go and get treatment. Other players with other injuries can decide for themselves whether to stay or go; and if a suffering player reckons the internal damage (no blood, remember) is so great that he needs replacing, then the laws reckon he's not fit to play again in that match.

Note that you can replace a replacement. If he too gets injured, you can bring on yet another player. It makes no difference to the status of the original bleeding player. If he can get repaired, he can return.

There's an interesting historical sidelight on the question of replacement. It involves the meaning of the word 'match'. A match was so-called because it was reckoned that the teams were matched: they were alike enough to make a good contest. In the early days of rugby they used to solve the whole problem of replacement by adopting what you might call 'reverse substitution'. Whenever an injured man had to go off, the captain of the *other* team sent off one of his men. This restored the balance and made it a true match once more. There have been worse ideas.

Concussion and other headaches

Normally, the best person to decide whether or not an injured player should go off is that player himself. Sometimes, however, the player cannot make that decision – for instance, if he's been concussed. If someone medically qualified advises that it would be dangerous for that player to stay in the game, or if the injury is obviously serious, the referee has the power to make him go off either for running repairs or for good. (And if he has been concussed, the International Board has laid down that he should not play or train for at least three weeks, and then only if a neurological examination has cleared him.)

At the very top level (such as international matches or matches involving a national representative team) the tricky question of whether or not a player is badly hurt has been taken out of the referee's hands. At that level, a doctor decides whether or not the injury is so bad that the player should not continue. Note that the question is not how *fit* the player is, but how damaging his injury is. The point of the replacement-for-injury law is to protect an injured player from aggravating the damage by playing on because he doesn't want to leave his team a man short. At all the top matches, the referee will get the advice of a doctor when a player is hurt. The first priority of the referee is the player's safety. If he thinks someone might be badly hurt, he'll stop play immediately – even if a team may be about to score a try.

The Cardiff Scenario

If a replacement for a blood injury gets sent off for Foul Play, that's bad news for the bleeding player. He can't return. He suffers for his team-mate's folly. But there's an interesting twist to the tale. A few years ago, in the middle of a Wales-England match, a Welsh prop got sent off. No other Welsh player on the field was competent to move into the front-row. In those days, rugby had replacements for injury but not substitutes. For a horrible moment it looked as if an international match would proceed with uncontested scrums. (The referee must order these when, for whatever reason, a team can't provide enough front-row players. There's no shoving, no contest for the ball, and the team putting it in must win it. Very tame stuff, which the Cardiff crowd would not have enjoyed.) The captains did some fast thinking, and agreed with the referee that another Welsh forward should also leave the field so that a 'substitute' front-row player could come on. This scenario is now enshrined in law.

How many on the bench?

For international matches, a Union can nominate up to seven players as replacements/substitutes. For all other matches, the Union with jurisdiction has responsibility for deciding how many may be nominated. Bearing in mind the Cardiff Scenario and the need to avoid uncontested scrums, the laws make certain conditions. A team that nominates 16, 17, or 18 players for a match must include at least four who can play in the front row. If the team nominates 19, 20, 21 or 22 players, at least five must be front-row players. And no matter how many get nominated, a team may substitute no more than two front-row players and no more than five in other positions.

How many in a team?

Here's a clue. The answer is not fifteen.

When replacement/substitution arrived in a big way, the lawmakers changed the definition of a 'team'. It now means the players out there on the field (maximum fifteen) plus all the replacements/substitutes waiting to take part. And the referee's authority covers *all* these players, whether they are on or off the park. If a replacement/substitute who is still in his tracksuit does anything that would be unacceptable on the field-of-play, the referee can penalise his team with a penalty kick on the 15-metre line. Or more. I've never heard of a replacement/substitute getting sent off before he even came on, but there's a first time for everything.

The slippery slope

Without replacement, a good game can be knocked sideways if a key player has to depart injured. In that respect, replacement is a good thing; but let nobody kid himself that it has not created new problems while it solved old ones. For a start it means having players who will probably not play and who will certainly not play the full match. Other sports – basketball, soccer, American football – stand as grim warnings of what can happen when replacement/substitution gets out of hand. Rugby has started to slide down that slippery slope.

Which raises a central question. Who's in charge? The lawmakers settled for the passive tense: *substitutes may be made.* That's fine on paper, but the game isn't played on paper; and nowhere in the lawbook does it define the role of the coach or manager or whoever it is who thinks it's time to pull off the scrum-half and send on a substitute. What gives him the right to interfere with play? Presumably the answer is: the agreement of the players. But what if the scrum-half thinks he's playing a blinder and refuses to leave? What then? Don't say it couldn't happen. In rugby, anything can happen, and I guarantee that this will happen, sooner or later.

'If there's no fun in it, there's no future in it'

I didn't say that; the All Black Chris Laidlaw said it. He was talking about rugby, and he was right. One reason the game has not only survived for over a hundred years but also spread and flourished throughout the world, is that underrated word, fun. Outsiders may find it hard to believe that hundreds of thousands of rugby players spend their Saturday afternoons bringing each other down with a sickening thud simply because they enjoy it, but it's a fact. The game is no longer entirely amateur, but that doesn't mean it's entirely professional. Rugby is now an open game, like golf or tennis. You can play it for money (if you're good enough), or you can play it just for the satisfaction of doing so – and that's what 99% of all players will go on doing. The spirit that fuels rugby is fun.

Appendix A: Under-19 variations

Like all laws, these come from the International Rugby Board. They apply world-wide to the 15-a-side game when played at Under-19 level (U19), meaning a player is under the age of 19.

Time: 35 minutes each way. Play in any U19 match must not last longer than 70 minutes. Even in a knock-out competition, extra time must not be played.

Replacement and substitution. This follows the same lines as in the laws governing the senior game, except that a player who has been substituted may replace an injured player. If a team nominates 22 players, at least 6 must be able to play in the front row in order to provide replacements for each prop and the hooker. If a team nominates more than 22 players, at least 3 must be able to play in the lock position.

Scrum

Front rows meeting. For safety's sake, each prop shall touch his opponent's upper arm and then pause before the front rows meet. The sequence should be: crouch, touch, pause, engage.

Wheeling. A team must not intentionally wheel a scrum. If an unintentional wheel passes 45 degrees, the referee orders another scrum. Penalty: Penalty kick.

Maximum shove: 1.5m. A team in a scrum must not shove it more than 1.5 metres forward. Penalty: Free kick.

Must release ball. Once a team has heeled the ball and they control it at the base, they must not keep it in the scrum. Penalty: Free kick.

Scrum formation must be 3-4-1, with the No. 8 packing between the two locks and binding on them. However, if a complete team is not available, or if a player gets sent off or goes off because of injury, a scrum can have fewer than eight players per team. When that happens, the scrum formations are as follows:

- If a team lacks one player, both teams must use a 3–4 formation (no No. 8).
- If a team lacks two players, both teams must use a 3–2–1 formation (no flankers).
- If a team lacks three players, both teams must use a 3–2 formation (front five only).

Even so, each team must always have at least five players in a scrum.

Uncontested scrums. If a team cannot field suitably trained players for any of the front five positions (prop, hooker, lock), the referee must order uncontested scrums. In these, there is no shoving, the teams do not compete for the ball, and the team putting it in must win it.

Appendix B: Seven-a-side variations

Made by the International Rugby Board to standardise play worldwide.

Maximum numbers. Each team has no more than seven players on the field. Three players from each team form a scrum. They must remain bound until it ends.

Replacement and substitution. This follows the same lines as the 15-a-side game. A team can nominate no more than three replacements/substitutes. Up to three players may be replaced or substituted. A player who has been substituted cannot return to that match except to replace a bleeding player.

Maximum playing time is 14 minutes, with a one-minute interval at half-time, except for the final of a competition, which lasts no longer than 20 minutes, with a two-minute interval. Play is divided into halves.

Extra time: sudden death. When a match is drawn and extra time is needed, the captains must toss a coin for the right to kick off or choose ends. Extra time is played in periods of five minutes. After each period, the teams change ends without an interval. The one that scores first is immediately declared the winner and the match ends.

Conversion kick must be a drop kick, which the kicker can take even if team-mates are still in front of him. As soon as a try is scored, the team scored against go immediately to the area of their own 10-metre line.

After a score, the scoring team re-starts, with a drop kick from the centre. If this fails to reach the 10-metre line (unless first touched by an opponent) or if it goes directly into touch, their opponents are awarded a free kick at the centre.

No place kicks, except to start the match and re-start it after half-time. Any penalty kick cannot be a place kick.

In-goal judges. These act as extra touch judges, one in each goal area. They help the referee in decisions on tries and touch-downs. They signal when the ball or the ball-carrier has gone into touch-in-goal. When a conversion kick or a penalty kick at goal is being taken, the in-goal judge stands at or behind one goal post, while a touch judge stands at or behind the other. They signal if the kick is successful. Finally, if the match organiser authorises it, the in-goal judges may signal foul play in the in-goal.

Sin Bin. A player who has been yellow-carded for foul play leaves the field for a period of two minutes playing time.

Apart from these variations, all the Laws of the Game apply.

Index

KU-323-421

Pocket Rough Guide

Las Vegas

written and researched by

GREG WARD

Contents

INTRODUCTION TO

Las Vegas

A dazzling oasis where forty million people a year let their hair down, Las Vegas has made a fine art of indulging its visitors' every appetite. From its ever-changing architecture to cascading chocolate fountains, adrenaline-pumping zip-lines and jaw-dropping stage shows, everything is built to thrill; as soon as the novelty wears off, it's blown up and replaced with something bigger and better. Not only does the city hold almost all of the world's largest hotels, but that's pretty much all it holds; it's these extraordinary creations that everyone comes to see.

ELVIS IMPERSONATOR, FREMONT STREET

Best places to get a view of the Strip

Although towering hotel blocks jostle for position along the Strip, there are surprisingly few places that offer non-guests a panoramic view of the whole thing. Possibilities include the summit of the Stratosphere (but that's a little far north and not quite aligned with the Strip), and the Voodoo Rooftop Nightclub at the Rio, off to one side. So the winner is – the observation platform at the top of Paris's **Eiffel Tower** (see p.57), perfectly poised to look north and south along the Strip's busiest stretch, as well as west, and down, to the fountains of Bellagio.

Each hotel is a neighbourhood in its own right, measuring as much as a mile end to end; crammed full of state-of-the-art clubs, restaurants, spas and swimming pools; and centring on what makes the whole thing possible – an action-packed casino where tourists and tycoons alike are gripped by the roll of the dice and the turn of the card.

Even if its entire urban area covers 136 square miles, most visitors see no more than two short, and very different, linear stretches. Downtown, the original centre, now amounts to four brief (roofed-over) blocks of Fremont Street, while the Strip begins a couple of miles south, just beyond the city limits, and runs for four miles southwest. It's the Strip where the real action is, a visual feast where each mega-casino vies to out-do the next with some

outlandish theme, be it an Egyptian pyramid (Luxor), a Roman extravaganza (Caesars Palace), a fairytale castle (Excalibur) or a European city (Paris and Venice).

In 1940, Las Vegas was home to just eight thousand people. It owes its extraordinary growth to its constant willingness to adapt; far from remaining kitsch and old-fashioned, it's forever reinventing itself. Entrepreneurs race to spot the latest shift in who has the money and what they want to spend it on. A few years ago the casinos realized that gamblers were happy to pay premium prices for good food; top chefs now run gourmet restaurants in venues like Bellagio and the Cosmopolitan. More recently, demand from younger visitors has prompted casinos like Wynn Las Vegas to open high-tech nightclubs to match those of Miami and LA.

NEW YORK–NEW YORK

The reputation Las Vegas still enjoys, of being a quasi-legal adult playground where (almost) anything goes, dates back to its early years when most of its first generation of luxury resorts were cut-throat rivals controlled by the Mob. In those days illegal profits could easily be "skimmed" off and respectable investors steered clear. Then, as now, visitors loved to imagine that they were rubbing shoulders with gangsters. Standing well back from the Strip, each casino was a labyrinth in which it was all but impossible to find an exit. During the 1980s, however, visitors started to explore on foot; mogul Steve Wynn cashed in by placing a flame-spouting volcano outside his new Mirage. As the casinos competed to lure in pedestrians, they filled in the daunting distances from the sidewalk, and between casinos.

With Las Vegas booming in the 1990s, gaming corporations bought up first individual casinos, and then each other. The Strip today is dominated by just two colossal conglomerates – MGM Resorts and Caesars Entertainment. Once you own the casino next door, there's no reason to make each a virtual prison; the Strip has therefore opened out, so that much of its central portion now consists of open-air terraces and pavilions housing bars and restaurants.

The city may have tamed its setting, but the magnificent wildernesses of the American West still lie on its doorstep. Dramatic parks like Red Rock Canyon and the Valley of Fire are just a short drive away, or you can fly to the Grand Canyon, and Utah's glorious Zion National Park makes a wonderful overnight getaway.

When to visit

Visitors flock to Las Vegas throughout the year, however the climate varies enormously. In July and August, the average daytime high exceeds 100°F (38°C), while in winter the thermometer regularly drops below freezing. Hotel swimming pools generally open between April and September only.

It's which day you visit that you should really take into account; accommodation can easily cost twice as much on Friday and Saturday as during the rest of the week.

LAS VEGAS AT A GLANCE

>> EATING

Las Vegas used to be a byword for bad food, with just the occasional mobster-dominated steakhouse or Italian restaurant to relieve the monotony of the pile–'em-high buffets. Those days have long gone. Every major Strip casino now holds half a dozen or more high-quality restaurants, many run by top chefs from all over the world. Prices have soared, to a typical minimum spend of $50 per head at big-name places, but so too have standards, and you could eat a great meal in a different restaurant every night in casinos such as Aria, Bellagio, Caesars Palace, the Cosmopolitan and the Venetian.

>> DRINKING

Every Las Vegas casino offers free drinks to gamblers. Sit at a slot machine or gaming table, and a cocktail waitress will find you and take your order; tips are expected. In addition, the casinos hold all kinds of bars and lounges; very few tourists venture further afield to drink. Along the Strip bars tend to be themed, as with the Irish pubs of New York–New York or the flamboyant lounges of Caesars Palace; downtown they're a bit more rough-and-ready. Note that the legal drinking age is 21 – you must carry ID to prove it.

>> NIGHTLIFE

The Strip is once more riding high as the entertainment epicentre of the world. While Elvis may have left the building, headliners like Elton John and Celine Dion attract thousands of big-spending fans night, after night and all the major touring acts pass through. Meanwhile the old-style feathers-and-sequins revues have been supplanted by a never-ending stream of jaw-droppingly lavish shows by the Cirque du Soleil, plus the likes of the postmodern Blue Men. A new generation of visitors has been responsible for the dramatic growth in the city's clubbing scene. Casinos like the Cosmopolitan, the Palms and Wynn Las Vegas now boast some of the world's most spectacular – and expensive – nightclubs and ultra-lounges.

>> SHOPPING

Shopping now ranks among the principal reasons that people visit Las Vegas. Downtown is all but devoid of shops, however, and while the workaday city holds its fair share of suburban malls, tourists do almost all of their shopping on the Strip itself. Their prime destination is the amazing Forum at Caesars Palace, followed by the Grand Canal Shoppes at the Venetian and Miracle Mile at Planet Hollywood. There are also a couple of stand-alone malls – Fashion Show opposite Wynn Las Vegas, which is the most useful for everyday purchases, and the very high-end Crystals in CityCenter.

OUR RECOMMENDATIONS FOR WHERE TO EAT, DRINK AND SHOP ARE LISTED AT THE END OF EACH CHAPTER.

Day One in Las Vegas

1 **Jean Philippe Patisserie, Bellagio** > p.51. Head to the back of Bellagio to enjoy a morning pick-me-up and pastries while admiring the world's largest chocolate fountain.

2 **Conservatory, Bellagio** > p.49. Part greenhouse, part camp and colourful fantasyland, Bellagio's indoor flower show must be seen to be believed.

3 **Eiffel Tower Experience** > p.57. Ride into the skies atop Las Vegas's own miniature version of Paris and look down on the rest of the Strip.

 **Lunch** > p.64. Enjoy a quintessentially French bistro meal, with a ringside seat on the Strip, at *Mon Ami Gabi* in Paris.

4 **The Forum Shops** > p.62. Marble statues, fountains and a false sky that cycles hourly between day and night; is it ancient Rome or simply Caesars Palace?

5 **Grand Canal Shoppes** > p.77. Operatic gondoliers ply the waters of the Grand Canal, serenading shoppers perusing the Venetian's upstairs, upmarket mall.

6 **V Bar, the Venetian** > p.82. Start your evening with a martini or cocktail in one of the Venetian's chic, sophisticated bars.

 **Dinner** > p.81. Pan-Asian food and lush red decor at *Wazuzu* in Wynn Las Vegas combine to offer a memorable dining experience.

7 **Love, the Mirage** > p.84. Las Vegas's favourite Canadian clowns, the Cirque du Soleil, join forces with the Beatles to stunning effect.

Day Two in Las Vegas

1 Il Fornaio, New York–New York > p.40. This New York-style Italian bakery is the perfect place to grab breakfast.

2 The Roller Coaster, New York–New York > p.36. Let's shake things up – loop around the Manhattan skyline in a little yellow cab, upside down, at 70mph.

3 Excalibur > p.34. If things haven't been kitsch enough yet, stroll through this bizarre Arthurian castle-casino.

4 Luxor > p.33. Things are getting weirder – enter an Egyptian pyramid through the paws of the Sphinx to see... artefacts recovered from the *Titanic*.

5 Shark Reef, Mandalay Bay > p.31. Watch crocodiles and sharks swim amid the ruins of a Mayan temple.

 Lunch > p.39. Break for a Mexican meal beside Mandalay Bay's wave pool, at the *Border Grill*.

6 CSI The Experience, MGM Grand > p.37. After lunch use your razor-sharp forensic skills to solve a murder.

7 Art collection, CityCenter > p.47. Standing aloof from the Strip, the sleek, modernist CityCenter district holds a surprising array of contemporary sculptures from the likes of Maya Lin, Henry Moore and Antony Gormley.

8 Crystals Retail Center > p.50. The flamboyant interior of Las Vegas's priciest mall is well worth seeing.

 Dinner > p.52. Dine on superb "new Italian" food in *Scarpetta*, overlooking Bellagio's fountains.

9 Jersey Boys > p.67. Las Vegas doesn't always get Broadway right, but this romp of a musical goes down a storm in Paris.

Classic Las Vegas

If you yearn for the days when casinos smelled of mobster menace and the Rat Pack ruled the Strip, the new, corporate-owned Las Vegas can sometimes feel too tasteful for comfort. Vestiges of the bad old days still survive, though, if you know where to look.

1 The Flamingo > p.60. Okay, so the Flamingo these days is more Donny Osmond than Bugsy Siegel, but the original Strip resort still holds plenty of classic kitsch, including its trademark pink flamingoes.

2 Caesars Palace > p.58. With its half-naked centurions and Cleopatras, Caesars is where the Strip first veered towards full-on fantasy fifty years ago – and it hasn't let up since.

Lunch > p.91. The all-you-can-eat buffet is one tradition Las Vegas will never let go; prices have risen on the Strip, but head downtown and you'll find amazing value, at the *Paradise Buffet* for example.

3 The Mob Museum > p.91. There's no better place to learn the seedy story of Las Vegas's shady past than at this gripping, gruesome new museum.

4 El Cortez > p.89. For the true Las Vegas experience, gamble in downtown's least-changed casino, with its hard-bitten characters and rock-bottom odds.

5 Fremont Street Experience > p.86. All bright lights and flashing neon, downtown's must-see block-spanning canopy is pure old-fashioned spectacle.

Dinner > p.92. Former mayor Oscar Goodman's steakhouse, *Oscar's Beef * Booze * Broads*, oozes unabashed love for downtown's long-lost heyday.

6 Jubilee! > p.67. With its cheesy sets and high-kicking showgirls, the city's last surviving tits'n'tassles revue, at Bally's on the Strip, is a hugely enjoyable throwback.

Budget Las Vegas

While Las Vegas is not the budget destination it used to be, it's still possible to visit on the cheap if you play your cards right (better still, don't play cards at all...).

1 Excalibur > p.116. Wake up in your "wide-screen" room at Excalibur – from $50 for a large suite, they're the Strip's best value.

2 Free monorails > p.126. Hop on the free monorail system to see Luxor and Mandalay Bay.

3 The Deuce > p.125. Ride the Deuce bus north from Mandalay Bay and enjoy the Strip in all its glory.

4 The Midway > p.74. Stop off at Circus Circus to watch free circus performances on the Midway stage.

Lunch > p.62. Head for Caesars Palace and buy a "Buffet of Buffets" pass, valid for 24 hours at all Caesars' properties. Start with the *Bacchanal Buffet*, which epitomizes decadent. Las Vegas excess.

5 Big Elvis > p.66. Cross the Strip to Harrah's for the best free show in town – this hunka-hunka love just keeps on burning all afternoon.

6 The volcano > p.69. Once darkness falls, take your place outside the Mirage and watch the gargantuan volcano just outside as it erupts.

7 Sirens of TI > p.69. Next door, the wild rock chicks who crew Treasure Island's pirate ships are locked in an eternal love-hate tussle with renegade buccaneers.

Dinner > p.62. Use your "Buffet of Buffets" pass again to sample the irresistible selection of all-French cuisine at *Le Village* in Paris.

8 Bellagio Fountains > p.49. The mesmerizing jets of this free water ballet make a suitably soothing end to the day.

11

NY
1936

ZUMANITY

Big sights

1 The Venetian Festooned with dazzling frescos and echoing to the song of costumed gondoliers, the opulent Venetian is loved by kids, clubbers and culture vultures alike. **> p.71**

2 Bellagio Las Vegas at its most luxurious, an Italianate marble extravaganza with its own eight-acre lake. > **p.48**

4 Hoover Dam A mighty wall of concrete holding back the Colorado River – the architectural showpiece that made Las Vegas possible. > **p.106**

3 Fremont Street Experience Where else has the sheer chutzpah to roof over four entire city blocks just so they can project multicoloured snakes and aliens onto the ceiling? > **p.86**

5 Caesars Palace This huge and ever-playful casino is a city in itself – and an ancient Roman one at that. > **p.58**

Shows

1 Kà For sheer spectacle and breathtaking stunts, the most jaw-dropping Cirque show in town. **> p.43**

2 Terry Fator
Old-fashioned family entertainment, taken to another dimension thanks to ventriloquist Fator's uncanny singing skills. > **p.85**

3 Blue Man Group A
bizarre but compelling blend of performance art, slapstick and high-octane rock. > **p.53**

4 Love
Cirque meets the Beatles, in a double whammy of music and performance. > **p.84**

5 Jubilee!
The last of the great chorus-line, ostrich-feather Las Vegas revues – catch it while you can. > **p.67**

Restaurants

1 Bouchon, the Venetian The menu at Thomas Keller's French bistro is every bit as special as the setting, on an elegant upper-storey patio. > **p.78**

2 Mon Ami Gabi, Paris The perfect venue for an al fresco French lunch, on a sidewalk patio beneath Paris's Eiffel Tower. **> p.64**

3 Beijing Noodle no. 9, Caesars Dazzling futuristic decor makes this mid-priced pan-Asian diner a truly memorable experience. **> p.63**

4 Scarpetta, Cosmopolitan Watch the Bellagio fountains as you savour Scott Conant's wonderful contemporary take on Italian cuisine. **> p.52**

5 Jean Philippe Patisserie, Bellagio Pastries and drinks to die for, given an extra air of indulgence by the extraordinary, swirling chocolate fountain. **> p.51**

Offbeat exhibits

1 Titanic: The Artifact Exhibition The world's only permanent display of *Titanic* artefacts, including a huge and very eerie chunk of the ship herself, upstairs in the Luxor pyramid. **> p.33**

2 The Mob Museum
Downtown's prestigious new museum tells the story of the men who made Las Vegas – and the men who arrested them. **> p.90**

3 Secret Garden and Dolphin Habitat Siegfried and Roy are long gone from the Mirage, but their famed white tigers (and lions) are still prowling the gardens. **> p.69**

4 The Mob Attraction Visitors to this Tropicana attraction receive a personal invitation to help out the Mob; it's up to you whether you make it out in one piece. **> p.35**

5 CSI: The Experience A hugely enjoyable interactive adventure, in which visitors can try their wits to solve a mysterious recent murder. **> p.37**

Shopping

1 Miracle Mile Shops With larger stores, and more of them, the best Strip mall for leisurely browsing and shopping around. > **p.62**

2 Grand Canal Shoppes As much for souvenir hunters and sightseers as serious shoppers, the Venetian's Grand Canal is a great place for window-shopping. > **p.77**

3 Fashion Show The one Strip mall not linked to a casino offers large department stores as well as designer boutiques, across from Wynn Las Vegas. > **p.77**

4 The Forum Shops America's most profitable shopping mall, stuffed inside the faux Roman pomp of Caesars Palace – though the price tags are real enough. > **p.62**

5 Town Square At the far southern end of the Strip, this locals' favourite is not so much a mall as an outdoor shopping neighbourhood. > **p.38**

BEST OF LAS VEGAS

23

Thrill rides

1 The Roller Coaster Climb aboard a tiny yellow taxi-cab and loop the loop around New York–New York. > **p.36**

2 Dig This! If you've always wanted to drive a bulldozer, or play basketball with a giant digger, this is where your dreams come true. > **p.94**

4 Stratosphere Thrill Rides The craziest thrill rides of all – spin off the Stratosphere strapped to a lurching bench or simply jump off the edge. > **p.76**

3 Slotzilla Ziplines are the new big thing in Las Vegas; this one lets you slide the length of the Fremont Street Experience. > **p.87**

5 Helicopter flights There's no better way to see the Strip at night than swooping above it in a chopper. > **p.132**

The deserts

1 Zion National Park You can drive to Utah's magnificent red-rock park in little more than two hours to enjoy dramatic scenery and breathtaking hikes. **> p.110**

2 Valley of Fire Lurid desert scenery, bizarre rock formations and supremely remote hiking. > **p.107**

3 Grand Canyon South Rim
Seeing Arizona's world-famous wonder makes a fabulous weekend road trip, but you can also fly there and back in a day. > **p.109**

4 Red Rock Canyon Las Vegas's great escape; hike and bike amid stunning red-rock sandscapes just twenty miles from the Strip. > **p.104**

5 Grand Canyon West Venture out onto the Skywalk or take a helicopter ride down to the Colorado River; the West Rim is a pricey day-trip by air, but you won't forget the adventure. > **p.108**

PLACES

The South Strip

For seven decades huge casinos have pushed ever further south along Las Vegas Boulevard, and what constitutes the South Strip has been repeatedly redefined. One thing has remained constant, however: entrepreneurs love to build lavish, eye-catching properties here because they're the first to be seen by drivers arriving from southern California. The current generation thus includes a scale model of Manhattan, New York–New York; the vast MGM Grand; a fantasy castle, Excalibur; an Egyptian pyramid, Luxor; and what's currently the true start of the Strip, the gleaming tropical paradise of Mandalay Bay. Thanks to successive buy-outs and mergers, all these five are now owned by MGM Resorts and run as a cohesive unit. The exception, the ageing Tropicana, has not surprisingly struggled to keep up.

MANDALAY BAY

3950 Las Vegas Blvd S ☎ 702 632 7777, ⓦ www.mandalaybay.com. MAP P.32, POCKET MAP B7

The southernmost mega-casino on the Strip, **Mandalay Bay**, consists of two golden skyscrapers that tower over a sprawling complex covering a greater area than any other single property in Las Vegas. Linked to Luxor (see p.33) and Excalibur (p.34) by a stand-alone outdoor **monorail** as well as indoor walkways, it belongs to the same owners, MGM Resorts. It was built in 1999 to provide a more sophisticated alternative to what were then its more overtly child-oriented neighbours, and apart from the **Shark Reef** aquarium (see p.31) offers little to lure in casual sightseers.

MANDALAY BAY

"Welcome to Fabulous Las Vegas"

Familiar no doubt from every Las Vegas movie or TV show you've ever seen, the "Welcome to Fabulous Las Vegas" sign is an obligatory photo-op for every visitor, just over half a mile south of Mandalay Bay. To minimize the risk of accidents, only cars heading south, away from the city, can access the narrow patch in between the north- and southbound carriageways of the Strip. Don't try walking this far, least of all in summer.

Beyond a certain vague tropical theming, there's no significance to the name "Mandalay". Instead Mandalay Bay's strongest selling point is its nightlife, with a high-end array of restaurants, bars, clubs and music venues. When this book went to press, the casino was about to open the first-ever Cirque du Soleil nightclub (see p.42) and to unveil a new permanent Cirque show based on the music of Michael Jackson. To keep its young, affluent guests on site during the day as well, there's also an impressively landscaped network of pools and artificial beaches that includes a wave pool and the "toptional" **Moorea Beach Club**.

Being further south of the Strip's centre of gravity than anyone would choose to walk, Mandalay Bay can feel a little stranded. Forced to work hard to attract and keep visitors, however, it has continued to prosper through the recession. Inevitably, some of its restaurants have lost their original buzz, while the Mandalay Place mall holds little to lure shoppers based elsewhere. For a night out, though, or a weekend in a self-contained luxury resort, Mandalay Bay can still match the best Las Vegas has to offer.

Incidentally, the *Four Seasons* hotel is right here too – its rooms occupy the top five floors of Mandalay Bay's original tower.

SHARK REEF

Mandalay Bay, 3950 Las Vegas Blvd ☎ 702 632 4555, ⓦ www.sharkreef.com. Daily 10am–10pm. Ages 13 and over $18, ages 5–12 $12. MAP P32, POCKET MAP B8

In keeping with Las Vegas's emphasis on immediate thrills, the **Shark Reef** aquarium focuses almost exclusively on dangerous marine predators, prowling through tanks designed to resemble a decaying ancient temple that's sinking into the sea. The species on show – largely chosen for their scary teeth and deadly stings – include giant crocodiles and Komodo dragons as well, of course, as enormous sharks. Separate eerily illuminated cylindrical tanks are filled with menacing-looking jellyfish.

Shark Reef is located right at the back of Mandalay Bay; to reach it, you have to walk along several hundred yards of internal corridors, beyond the two convention centres.

SHARK REEF

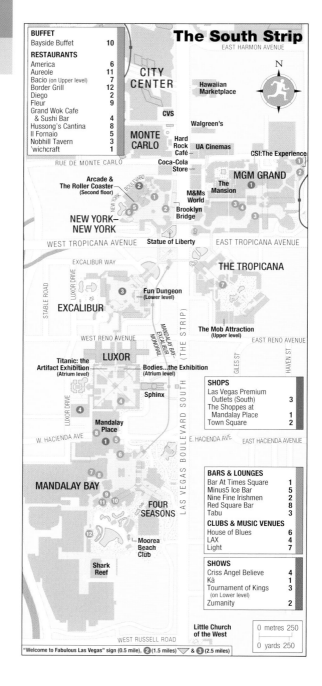

The South Strip

BUFFET	
Bayside Buffet	10

RESTAURANTS	
America	6
Aureole	11
Bacio (on Upper level)	7
Border Grill	12
Diego	2
Fleur	9
Grand Wok Cafe & Sushi Bar	4
Hussong's Cantina	8
Il Fornaio	5
Nobhill Tavern	3
'wichcraft	1

SHOPS	
Las Vegas Premium Outlets (South)	3
The Shoppes at Mandalay Place	1
Town Square	2

BARS & LOUNGES	
Bar At Times Square	1
Minus5 Ice Bar	5
Nine Fine Irishmen	2
Red Square Bar	8
Tabu	3

CLUBS & MUSIC VENUES	
House of Blues	6
LAX	4
Light	7

SHOWS	
Criss Angel Believe	4
Kà	1
Tournament of Kings (on Lower level)	3
Zumanity	2

EAST HARMON AVENUE
N
CITY CENTER
Hawaiian Marketplace
CVS
Walgreen's
MONTE CARLO
Hard Rock Café
UA Cinemas
CSI:The Experience
Coca-Cola Store
MGM GRAND
RUE DE MONTE CARLO
The Mansion
Arcade & The Roller Coaster (Second floor)
M&Ms World
NEW YORK–NEW YORK
Brooklyn Bridge
WEST TROPICANA AVENUE
Statue of Liberty
EAST TROPICANA AVENUE
EXCALIBUR WAY
THE TROPICANA
EXCALIBUR DRIVE
STABLE ROAD
LUXOR DRIVE
Fun Dungeon (Lower level)
EXCALIBUR
MANDALAY BAY–EXCALIBUR MONORAIL
The Mob Attraction (Upper level)
WEST RENO AVENUE
EAST RENO AVENUE
GILES ST
HAVEN ST
(THE STRIP)
LUXOR
Titanic: the Artifact Exhibition (Atrium level)
Bodies...the Exhibition (Atrium level)
Sphinx
LUXOR DRIVE
LAS VEGAS BOULEVARD SOUTH
Mandalay Place
W. HACIENDA AVE
E. HACIENDA AVE
EAST HACIENDA AVENUE
MANDALAY BAY
FOUR SEASONS
Moorea Beach Club
Shark Reef
Little Church of the West
WEST RUSSELL ROAD

"Welcome to Fabulous Las Vegas" sign (0.5 mile), **2** (1.5 miles) **3** (2.5 miles)

0 metres	250
0 yards	250

LUXOR

3900 Las Vegas Blvd S ☎ 702 262 4444,
🌐 www.luxor.com. MAP P.32, POCKET MAP B6

The huge **Luxor** pyramid, with
its sloping, monolithic walls of
black shiny glass, was built in
1993 as the follow-up to the
much more fanciful Excalibur
(see p.34) next door.
Originally it was filled to
bursting with ancient
Egyptian motifs, holding not
only a replica of King Tut's
tomb but even an indoor
River Nile. Then, when Las
Vegas (and owners MGM
Resorts in particular) decided
to gear itself less towards kids
and more towards adults,
much of Luxor's archeological
theming was stripped away.
Nothing can mask the fact it's
a colossal pyramid, though,
and Luxor today seems to be
in an odd sort of limbo,
embarrassed about its
Egyptian past but unable to
find an alternative identity.

Visitors who venture this far
down the Strip – especially those
arriving on the **Mandalay
Bay–Excalibur monorail** – still
congregate outside to take
photos of the enormous Sphinx
that straddles the main driveway.
Immediately inside the main
doors, there's also a re-creation
of the facade of the Egyptian
temple of Abu Simbel. Beyond
that, however, there's little to
distinguish the main casino
floor. In the absence of
noteworthy restaurants or shops,
Luxor is best known for its bars
and clubs, including an outpost
of LA stalwart *LAX* (see p.42).

Immediately upstairs, the
so-called Atrium Level, is
home to two permanent
exhibitions – **Bodies** (see p.34)
and **Titanic** – as well as a small
food court. It's also the best
vantage point from which to
admire the pyramid's

LUXOR

cavernous interior; only guests
can access the higher levels.

As this book went to press,
plans were under way for a
new **zipline** attraction to be
added to Luxor.

TITANIC: THE ARTIFACT EXHIBITION

Atrium Level, Luxor, 3900 Las Vegas Blvd S
☎ 702 492 3960 🌐 www.rmstitanic.net. Daily
10am–10pm. $32, ages 4–12 $24, over-64s
$30; audio guides $6 extra. MAP P.32,
POCKET MAP A5

In an enclosed building
upstairs in Luxor, **Titanic: The
Artifact Exhibition** is the
world's only permanent
exhibition of items salvaged
from the *Titanic*. Displays that
also include mock-ups of the
fabled Grand Staircase tell the
full story of the great ship, from
construction to destruction.
Each visitor receives a
"boarding pass" named for a
specific passenger; you find out
whether he or she survived as
you leave.

Prize artefacts include the
actual wheel at which the
helmsman tried and failed to
steer clear of the iceberg on
April 14, 1912, and the
enormous Big Piece, which
detached from the C Deck.

BODIES...THE EXHIBITION

Atrium Level, Luxor, 3900 Las Vegas Blvd S ☎ 702 262 4400, ⓦ www.bodiestheexhibition .com. Daily 10am–10pm, last admission 9pm. $32, under-14s $23; audio guides $6 extra. MAP P.32, POCKET MAP A5

You might expect **Bodies...the Exhibition** to be a gory horror show. In fact, despite the advertising images of goggle-eyed corpses, it provides a surprisingly serious museum-quality experience. You have to keep reminding yourself that what look like brightly coloured mannequins really are dead bodies that have been "plastinated" for permanent display. Some are posed as though in life, playing sports in perpetuity, others have been dissected to show particular features of their anatomy. Certain sections, like that in which an entire circulatory system, down to the tiniest capillary, has been teased out and dyed in different colours, have an astonishing beauty; the sight of fatally diseased organs displayed alongside healthy counterparts are much more sobering. Even if you've wandered in for a quick laugh, you may leave determined to change your life around – not that Las Vegas is necessarily the best place to start.

EXCALIBUR

3850 Las Vegas Blvd S ☎ 702 597 7777, ⓦ www.excalibur.com. MAP P.32, POCKET MAP B4

Built in 1990, **Excalibur** remains the most visible reminder of the era when Las Vegas briefly re-invented itself as a vast children's playground. With its multicoloured turrets and ring of clunky battlements it doesn't so much look like a castle, as like a child's drawing of a castle – and to be more specific still, a drawing of Walt Disney's version of Sleeping Beauty's castle. Only a nit-picker would mention that the original Excalibur was a sword, not a castle.

These days, Excalibur is less child-oriented than it used to be. Its primary function for owners MGM seems to be as a kind of gateway to draw visitors towards the southern end of the Strip, complementing the free **monorail** to Luxor (see p.33) and Mandalay Bay (p.30), prominent outside, with an easy indoor walkway to those properties further back.

As Excalibur generally offers some of the Strip's least expensive hotel rooms, it caters largely to low-budget tour groups and families. That can result in a slightly jarring clash between its remaining child-friendly Arthurian theming, and blue-collar adult entertainment such as *Dick's Last Resort* bar and the *Thunder From Down Under* male stripper revue. Its lowest level is occupied by the **Fun Dungeon**, a jumble of fairground stalls and arcade games.

Much of the upstairs, officially known as the Castle Walk Level, is taken up by a huge **food court**, which includes a massive *Krispy Kreme* doughnut bakery. It's also home to the frankly poor *Round Table Buffet* and assorted souvenir "shoppes".

THE TROPICANA

THE TROPICANA

3801 Las Vegas Blvd S ☎ 702 739 2222, ⓦ www.troplv.com. MAP P.32, POCKET MAP C4

Built in 1957, standing proudly aloof a mile south of the Strip, the **Tropicana** swiftly became a byword for luxury. It was also renowned from the start as being in the pocket of the Mob, and spent twenty years under investigation for skimming, money laundering and other Mafia-related skullduggery.

Although it's now poised at the country's busiest cross-roads, the Tropicana has long struggled to compete with its mighty MGM-owned neighbours – Excalibur (p.34), the MGM Grand (p.37) and New York–New York (p.36). Barely rescued from bankruptcy in 2008, it was given a $125-million makeover intended to restore its tropical-playground image.

While it's looking much crisper and brighter than before, the Tropicana still can't match the latest Strip giants. Hopes that it would blossom as a nightlife destination have failed to materialize, and it holds little to draw in shoppers, diners or sightseers apart from **The Mob**

Attraction (see below). Instead it remains slightly apart, with its strongest feature being an extensive pool complex that's open to guests only.

THE MOB ATTRACTION

Tropicana, 3801 Las Vegas Blvd S ☎ 702 739 2662, ⓦ www.mobattraction.com. Mon–Sat 10am–9pm, last admission 8pm. $28, ages 6–11 $18. MAP P.32, POCKET MAP D4

Part theme park, part museum, **The Mob Attraction**, towards the back of the Tropicana (see p.35) beyond the pool, plays on the casino's legendary involvement with the Mafia. Costumed mobsters invite each visitor to run errands and earn their trust. From there it's all too easy to slide into fully fledged criminality; watch out, because if things go wrong you're liable to wind up "whacked". The individual attention, the enthusiasm of the actors and the sheer detail go a long way towards justifying the hefty admission fee.

There's also a substantial museum section, chronicling the careers of notorious underworld figures like Bugsy Siegel and Sam Giancana, and holding assorted treasures that belonged to them or their families.

NEW YORK–NEW YORK

3790 Las Vegas Blvd S ☎ 702 740 6969,
Ⓦ www.newyorknewyork.com. MAP P.32,
POCKET MAP C3

The first, and arguably the best,
of Las Vegas's modern breed of
replica "cities", **New York–New
York** opened in 1997. Its
exterior consists of a squeezed-
up, half-sized rendition of the
Manhattan skyline as it looked
in the 1950s. The interior,
which makes no attempt to
correspond to the specific
"buildings" outside, holds a
smaller than average casino,
plus a dining and nightlife
district intended to evoke
Greenwich Village.

Despite the broad Brooklyn
Bridge that stretches along the
Strip sidewalk, and the Empire
State and Chrysler buildings
etched against the Nevada sky,
the most iconic feature of the
facade is the **Statue of Liberty**,
facing the intersection with
Tropicana Avenue. Unlike the
other elements here it's actually
twice the height of the real-life
statue. The area immediately in
front, modelled on New York
Harbor, still holds memorials
to the tragedy of September 11.

New York–New York has lost
much of its original playful
theming in recent years.

Sightseers once stepped off the
Strip to find themselves in
Central Park at night, with owls
peeping down from the trees.
Things are more serious these
days, enlivened here and there
with stylish Art Deco motifs.

New York–New York isn't
served by any monorail, but
pedestrians pass through one
corner en route between the
pedestrian bridges to Excalibur
and the MGM Grand. Perhaps
to tempt them to stay, the areas
nearest the Strip hold an
abundance of bars, pubs and
food outlets. Much of the
second floor is taken up by the
Arcade, a rather ramshackle
assortment of sideshows, games
and kids' attractions.

THE ROLLER COASTER

New York–New York, 3790 Las Vegas Blvd S
☎ 702 740 6969, Ⓦ www.newyorknewyork
.com. Mon–Thurs & Sun 11am–11pm, Fri & Sat
10.30am–midnight. $14 first ride, $25 for an
all-day Scream Pass. MAP P.32, POCKET MAP B3

From the moment you catch a
glimpse of New York–New York
(see p.36), you'll almost certainly
also see – and hear – the tiny
little yellow cabs that loop and
race around its skyscraper
towers. Formerly known as the
Manhattan Express (now for
obvious reasons re-renamed

The Roller Coaster), it operates from a replica subway station on the casino's upper floor. Speeding at 67mph, plunging over 200ft and rolling like a jet fighter, it's a serious thrill ride no theme-park fan should miss.

MGM GRAND

3799 Las Vegas Blvd S ☎ 702 891 7777, ⓦ www.mgmgrand.com. MAP P.32, POCKET MAP C3

The enormous **MGM Grand** casino has been through many changes since it opened in 1993. Back then, it attracted huge publicity as the largest hotel in the world and the first to incorporate its own theme park. It was also the location of the legendary boxing fight when Mike Tyson bit Evander Holyfield's ear in 1997.

These days, however, the MGM Grand keeps a lower profile, and it would be hard to say quite what identity it's aiming for any more. All traces of the theme park have long since vanished, while only the general preponderance of green now recalls the property's initial *Wizard of Oz* theme. With its original 5005 rooms boosted by the addition of the three all-suite *Signature* towers, it's surpassed in size only by the Venetian-Palazzo combination. Only in Las Vegas could such a behemoth seem to blend into the background.

One reason for this may be that with so many guests on site, the MGM Grand simply doesn't need to lure visitors in. It still boasts a fabulous array of dining and entertainment options, which includes the stunning Cirque de Soleil show *Kà*, and the *Joel Robuchon Restaurant*, where the $425 Degustation Menu is said to be the most expensive prix-fixe menu in the world.

As this book went to press, MGM Resorts were embarking on a massive overhaul of the Grand that has so far seen more old things disappear than new ones emerge. Casualties have included the live lions previously displayed in a glass enclosure just off the Strip, and the veteran *Studio 54* nightclub.

CSI: THE EXPERIENCE

MGM Grand, 3799 Las Vegas Blvd S ☎ 702 891 7006, ⓦ www.csiexhibit.com. Daily 9am–9pm, last admission 7.30pm. Ages 12 and over $28, $26 for repeat visits on same day, ages 4–11 $21/$20. MAP P.32, POCKET MAP E2

Set well back from the MGM Grand's Strip entrance, **CSI: The Experience** is perhaps the most enjoyable family attraction in Las Vegas. Trading on the worldwide success of the CSI TV franchise, it enables participants to investigate, and almost certainly solve, fictional murder mysteries.

Each ticket entitles you to solve one of three possible cases, taking roughly an hour to examine the murder scene, test out various hypotheses in the lab, and come up with a solution. Assistants are on hand to help, though you don't interact with any actors.

CSI: THE EXPERIENCE

Shops

LAS VEGAS PREMIUM OUTLETS (SOUTH)

7400 Las Vegas Blvd S ☎ 702 896 5599,
Ⓦ www.lasvegasoutletcenter.com. Mon–Sat
10am–9pm, Sun 10am–8pm. MAP P.32 & P.95,
POCKET MAP C9

The sort of mall you might
find beside the highway on the
outskirts of any town in
America, Las Vegas Premium
Outlets (South), 3 miles south
of Mandalay Bay, offers
no-frills, no-nonsense
shopping at Banana Republic,
Gap, Nike and the like. For
visitors with the use of a car,
it's not a bad option for picking
up everyday items to take back
home. There's a basic fast food
court but no restaurants.

LAS VEGAS PREMIUM OUTLETS (SOUTH)

THE SHOPPES AT MANDALAY PLACE

Mandalay Bay, 3930 Las Vegas Blvd S ☎ 702
632 7777, Ⓦ www.mandalaybay.com. Mon–
Thurs & Sun 10am–11pm, Fri & Sat 10am–
midnight. MAP P.32, POCKET MAP B6

Arranged along the indoor
hallway that connects
Mandalay Bay with Luxor – a
fair walk from the centre of
either, and from the monorail

too – The Shoppes at Mandalay
Place does not rank among Las
Vegas's premier shopping malls.
Instead, it's a rather haphazard
mix of big names such as
Urban Outfitters, Nike Golf
and Frederick's of Hollywood,
with smart boutiques, galleries
and novelty stores, plus several
bars and restaurants.

TOWN SQUARE

6605 Las Vegas Blvd S ☎ 702 269 5001,
Ⓦ www.mytownsquarelasvegas.com. Mon–
Thurs 10am–9pm, Fri & Sat 10am–10pm, Sun
11am–8pm. MAP P.32 & P.95, POCKET MAP C9

Especially popular with locals
who prefer to steer clear of the
Strip, Town Square, 3 miles
south of Mandalay Bay, is a
rarity in Las Vegas, designed to
be experienced as an outdoor
"neighbourhood" rather than
an air-conditioned enclave.
Visitors from further afield may
be less enthused by its attempt
to evoke the feel of a "European
village". Big stores include Fry's
Electronics, a Whole Foods
supermarket and an Apple Store
that offers free wi-fi; there are
also some unremarkable
restaurants and a cinema.

Buffet

BAYSIDE BUFFET

Mandalay Bay, 3950 Las Vegas Blvd S
☎ 702 632 7402, Ⓦ www.mandalaybay.
com. Mon–Sat 7–11am $16, 11am–2.30pm $20,
4.45–10pm $30, Sun 7am–2.30pm $30 &
4.45–10pm $30; all-day pass $43. MAP P.32,
POCKET MAP B7

Mandalay Bay's buffet has a
much nicer setting than most
of its Las Vegas rivals,
overlooking the resort's pool
and open, when weather
permits, to breezes. Apart from
the wide range of desserts,
though, and the pre-cut deli
sandwiches at lunchtime, the
food is not all that amazing.

Restaurants

AMERICA

New York–New York, 3790 Las Vegas Blvd S ☎ 702 740 6969, ⓦ www.newyorknewyork .com. Daily 24hr. MAP P.32, POCKET MAP B3

While serious foodies will find nothing remarkable about this 24-hour diner, it's a great place to bring kids, or Las Vegas first-timers, thanks to the colossal, cartoon-like relief map of the USA that hangs from the ceiling. Serving signature dishes from all over the country, from Southern fried chicken ($14) to New York steak ($27), there's food to match every appetite.

AUREOLE

Mandalay Bay, 3950 Las Vegas Blvd S ☎ 702 632 7200, ⓦ www.aureolelv.com. Daily 5.30–10.30pm. MAP P.32, POCKET MAP B7

With its astonishing "wine tower", a 42ft vertical wine cellar that's accessed by flying, white-clad "wine angels", Chef Charlie Palmer's showcase restaurant is a real must-see. His contemporary American cooking is something special, best sampled on the set menus – $75 for three courses, $95 for seven ($10 extra in the smoochy Swan Court section).

BACIO

Tropicana, 3801 Las Vegas Blvd S ☎ 800 462 8767, ⓦ www.troplv.com/dining/bacio. Daily 5–10.30pm. MAP P.32, POCKET MAP C4

Carla Pellegrino's classic Italian diner has been a big hit at the revamped Tropicana, not least for its dazzling bright-white styling. The speciality veal chop costs over $40, but you can get half a roast chicken with Italian sausage for $22, and the early-evening "Happy Prefix" menu offers three courses with wine for $39. The one drawback can be occasionally slow service.

BORDER GRILL

Mandalay Bay, 3950 Las Vegas Blvd S ☎ 702 632 7200, ⓦ www.bordergrill.com. Mon–Thurs 11am–11pm, Fri 11am–11pm, Sat 10am–11pm, Sun 10am–10pm. MAP P.32, POCKET MAP B8

Serving light and zestful "modern Mexican" cuisine that's a perfect match for its sun-kissed indoor-outdoor setting, this poolside veteran serves lunchtime salads, tacos and *tortas* (flatbreads) for well under $20, and larger dinner plates like Yucatan pork for $24 or *mole* roasted chicken for $28. A three-course set dinner costs $42 and the hugely popular weekend brunch $30.

DIEGO

MGM Grand, 3799 Las Vegas Blvd S ☎ 702 891 3200, ⓦ www.mgmgrand.com. Wed, Thurs & Sun 5.30–10pm, Sat 5–10pm. MAP P.32, POCKET MAP E2

Top-quality Mexican restaurant, far back in the MGM Grand. Serves the expected array of enchiladas and *chile rellenos* for around $20, as well as *clasicos* including a rib-eye steak *carne asada* for $35 and *puerco pibil* (pork shank baked in banana leaves) for $24. With its hip nightclub decor, it's also popular as a bar.

FLEUR

Mandalay Bay, 3950 Las Vegas Blvd S ☎702 632 7200, ⓦwww.mandalaybay.com/dining/fleur. Daily 11am–10.30pm. MAP P.32, POCKET MAP B7

There's much more to Hubert Keller's modern tapas restaurant than its notorious $5000 foie gras burger. Its sumptuous menu features exquisite dishes from all over the world, including a fabulous steak tartare served with salty lavash bread ($12). Even the so-called "Large Plates" are pretty small, though, so it's no place to be counting your pennies. Parties of six or more can "order the menu" for $435.

GRAND WOK & SUSHI BAR

MGM Grand, 3799 Las Vegas Blvd S ⓦwww .mgmgrand.com. Mon–Thurs & Sun 11am–10pm, Fri & Sat 11am–1am. No reservations. MAP P.32, POCKET MAP D3

This pan-Asian restaurant is the kind of place you wish you could find everywhere in Las Vegas. The prices are low, the service fast, the decor fancy enough to make you feel you're somewhere special and they only take walk-ins. And the food? That's great too, drawing on Vietnamese, Thai, Chinese and Japanese. Dim sum and sushi plates cost around $12, and mains more like $20.

HUSSONG'S CANTINA

Mandalay Bay, 3930 Las Vegas Blvd S ☎702 632 6450, ⓦwww.hussongslasvegas.com. Daily 11am–11pm. MAP P.32, POCKET MAP B6

An outpost of the Mexican original that's said to have invented the margarita, *Hussong's* is as much a bar as a restaurant. Don't let that put you off the food, though – it's surprisingly good, with $15–20 flautas, fajitas and chimi-changas in case you're hungry for more than the $12 nachos. Don't miss the $6 plazero corn, dusted with cheese flakes.

IL FORNAIO

New York–New York, 3790 Las Vegas Blvd S ☎702 650 6500, ⓦwww.ilfornaio.com /nyny. Restaurant Mon–Thurs & Sun 7.30am–midnight, Fri & Sat 7.30am–1am; Panetteria daily 6am–6pm. MAP P.32, POCKET MAP B3

While *Il Fornaio* is open for decent Italian food pretty much round the clock, in-the-know locals love it best of all in the morning, when you can enjoy a wonderful sit-down breakfast or simply pop in to the separate deli/bakery next door for fresh breads and espresso coffee.

NOBHILL TAVERN

MGM Grand, 3799 Las Vegas Blvd S ☎702 891 7337, ⓦwww.mgmgrand.com. Tues–Sat 5pm–late. MAP P.32, POCKET MAP D3

In a nod to his San Francisco roots, top Las Vegas chef Michael Mina serves up substantial portions of good old-fashioned American standards at *Nobhill Tavern*. Prices are far from cheap, with pork belly or shrimp and grits at around $32, and steaks well over $40, but if you're in the mood to eat what you know you like, with no surprises, it's a fail-safe option.

IL FORNAIO

'WICHCRAFT

MGM Grand, 3799 Las Vegas Blvd S ☎ 702
891 3166, Ⓦ www.mgmgrand.com. Daily
10am–5pm. MAP P.32, POCKET MAP E2

An instant smash in Las Vegas
just as it was in New York, Tom
Colicchio's gourmet take on the
fast-food sandwich bar makes a
quick, high-quality option for
visitors way too busy for a
restaurant breakfast and lunch.
Whether it's steak and eggs on
ciabatta for $9, or gruyere on rye
for $7, it's all delicious.

Bars and lounges

BAR AT TIMES SQUARE

New York–New York, 3790 Las Vegas Blvd S
☎ 702 740 6466, Ⓦ www.newyorknewyork
.com. Daily 11am–2.30am, showtime
8pm–2am. Cover $10 standing, reserved
seating Mon–Thurs & Sun $15, Fri & Sat $25.
MAP P.32, POCKET MAP B3

If you like your nights out
sophisticated or edgy, steer
clear of this raucous sing-along bar alongside New
York–New York's main casino
floor; if you prefer to scream
along at the top of your voice
as two pianists go head-to-
head, playing whatever requests
spring to their tipsy audience's
mind, you're in the right place.

MINUS5 ICE BAR

Mandalay Bay, 3930 Las Vegas Blvd S ☎ 702
740 5800, Ⓦ www.minus5experience.com.
Mon–Thurs & Sun 11am–2am, Fri & Sat
11am–3am. Cover varies, typically $25 including
1 drink. MAP P.32, POCKET MAP B6

This funny, gimmicky Mandalay
Place bar is exactly what it says it
is – every single thing is made of
ice, from the walls to the glasses,
though at least the couches are
spread with deer skins.
Customers are loaned jackets,
gloves and boots to tolerate the
temperature – yes, it's minus 5.

MINUS ICE BAR

NINE FINE IRISHMEN

New York–New York, 3790 Las Vegas Blvd
S ☎ 702 740 6463, Ⓦ www.ninefineirishmen
.com. Daily 11am–2.45am. Cover $5 Wed &
Thurs, $10 Fri & Sat. MAP P.32, POCKET MAP C3

A genuine Irish pub, shipped
in pieces from Ireland,
celebrating Irish beer, food
and, in the evening, music and
dance too. A small patio out on
the Strip looks over "Brooklyn
Bridge". During the weekday
Happy Hour (Mon–Thurs
2–5pm), Guinness and other
beers cost $5 per pint.

RED SQUARE BAR

Mandalay Bay, 3950 Las Vegas Blvd S
☎ 702 632 7407. Mon–Thurs 4pm–1am, Fri
& Sat 4pm–2am, Sun 1pm–1am. MAP P.32,
POCKET MAP B7

Both a bar and a restaurant,
Red Square is designed to
evoke all things Russian – the
decadence of the Tsars, the
graphic style of the Commu-
nist era and the icy chill of the
steppes. Unless you have a real
penchant for caviar, the food
is a bit too expensive to be
worth it, but the bar is great,
with its solid-ice counter-top
and frozen vodka vault.

TABU

MGM Grand, 3799 Las Vegas Blvd S ☎ 702 891 7183. Mon, Thurs & Sun 10pm–4am, Fri & Sat 10pm–5am. Cover men $20, women $10. MAP P.32, POCKET MAP D3

While the first of Las Vegas's much trumpeted "ultra-lounges" has inevitably been surpassed by copy-cat newcomers, with its dressed-to-kill hostesses and sensational lighting it remains a great spot to kick off the night. Customers are encouraged to dance on the tables, but there's no proper dance floor.

Clubs and music venues

HOUSE OF BLUES

Mandalay Bay, 3950 Las Vegas Blvd S ☎ 702 632 7600, ⓦ www.hob.com. Mon–Thurs & Sun 8am–11pm, Fri & Sat 8am–midnight. MAP P.32, POCKET MAP B6

The national *House of Blues* music chain has recently revamped its Las Vegas outlet, in the heart of Mandalay Bay. While retaining its funky, voodoo-esque feel, the capacity has been reduced to a more intimate 1300. Individual concerts are interspersed with longer artist residencies; thus Carlos Santana has been signed up until at least 2014, with ticket prices from $89.

LAX

Luxor, 3900 Las Vegas Blvd S ☎ 702 262 4529, ⓦ www.laxthenightclub.com. Wed–Sat 10pm–4am. Cover men $30, women $20. MAP P.32, POCKET MAP B6

This offshoot of Hollywood's hot *LAX* nightclub can be a victim of its own success; the whole place, from the dramatic staircase to the long dance floor, gets way too crowded for comfort on big nights. If money is no object, skip the

HOUSE OF BLUES

queues by paying for VIP table service. If you're happy with the mainstream music choices it's up there with Las Vegas's best.

LIGHT

Mandalay Bay, 3950 Las Vegas Blvd S Contact details, hours and prices to be confirmed. MAP P.32, POCKET MAP R7

As this book went to press, Mandalay Bay was about to pull off a real coup – the opening of the first-ever Cirque du Soleil nightclub, designed to keep visitors to Cirque's new Michael Jackson show dancing all night. Precise details remain subject to change, but it was expected to hold over two thousand clubbers and feature a moving DJ booth that rises from the floor, as well as live Cirque performers.

Shows

CRISS ANGEL BELIEVE

Luxor, 3900 Las Vegas Blvd S ☎ 702 262 4400, ⓦ www.luxor.com. Tues–Sat 7.30pm & 9.30pm. $59–160. MAP P.32, POCKET MAP A6

Believe bears the Cirque brand, but beyond the odd animal costume it's no longer really targeted at Cirque fans. Instead it's a showcase for everything Angel does best, blending close-up trickery with mind-blowing illusions to become the city's most exciting magic show. See past the pyrotechnics and blaring heavy metal, and Angel is a surprisingly old-fashioned performer who wins over his audience night after night.

KÀ

MGM Grand, 3799 Las Vegas Blvd S ☎ 702 531 3826. Ⓦ www.ka.com. Tues–Sat 7pm & 9.30pm. $69–180. MAP P.32, POCKET MAP D2

There's more martial-arts musclery to the Cirque du Soleil's MGM Grand spectacular than to the company's more ethereal offerings; even sceptics are guaranteed to find the set-piece stunts enacted on its tilting, rotating stage absolutely jaw-dropping. Add in some extraordinary puppetry and sumptuous costumes, and while the twins-in-jeopardy storyline may leave you unmoved, *Kà* is certain to expand your horizons.

TOURNAMENT OF KINGS

Excalibur, 3850 Las Vegas Blvd S ☎ 702 597 7600. Ⓦ www.excalibur.com. Mon & Wed 6pm. Thurs–Sun 6pm & 8.30pm. $59 including dinner, $44.35 without. MAP P.32, POCKET MAP A4

Excalibur's swashbuckling swords-and-slapstick supper show plunges family audiences back to "the Olden Days" to participate in a medieval jousting contest, complete with villainous black knights and maidens in peril. If you'd rather eat chicken with your fingers than sit through Shakespeare, this is the show for you.

ZUMANITY

New York–New York, 3790 Las Vegas Blvd S ☎ 702 740 6815. Ⓦ www.zumanity.com. Fri–Tues 7.30pm & 10.30pm. $76–137.50 or $129 per person for a "duo sofa". All shows over-18s only. MAP P.32, POCKET MAP B3

Cirque rule the roost in Las Vegas these days and this show contains enough of their trademark flair for acrobatics to remind you why. However, while the concept – Cirque goes sexy – may pique your curiosity, the reality is disappointing. What's most surprising is how it undercuts the erotic potential of fit bodies performing astonishing feats with pratfalls and smut. At times, it looks amazing, but it's no substitute for Cirque at their peak.

Wedding chapel

LITTLE CHURCH OF THE WEST

4617 Las Vegas Blvd S ☎ 702 739 7971. Ⓦ www.littlechurchlv.com. Daily 8am–11pm. MAP P.32, POCKET MAP C9

Oddly enough, this cute little chapel really is old, at least by Las Vegas standards, having been built for the Last Frontier casino in 1942 and migrated down the Strip to its current location, half a mile south of Mandalay Bay. With its tranquil garden, it feels a world away from the big-casino chapels. Packages range from the $259 "Let's Elope" to the $2075 "Sealed With A Kiss".

LITTLE CHURCH OF THE WEST

CityCenter and around

When MGM Resorts opened the CityCenter complex, in 2009, the aim was to add a whole new neighbourhood to Las Vegas, giving the city a new kind of sleek, corporate architecture. By building a self-contained enclave set back from the Strip, they would vastly increase the value of what was previously unused land, and finally make it possible to expand east–west. A massive financial gamble, the project involved a huge new casino, Aria; a high-end shopping mall, Crystals; and several hotel-and-condo skyscrapers. A new neighbourhood has indeed appeared, at each end of which MGM have cannily integrated an older Strip-front casino – Monte Carlo to the south and Bellagio to the north. The one fly in the ointment is the brash new Cosmopolitan, cheekily added to the one tiny speck of Strip real estate that MGM didn't own.

MONTE CARLO

3770 Las Vegas Blvd S ☎702 730 7777, ⓦwww.montecarlo.com. MAP P.45, POCKET MAP C2

Named for Monaco's world-famous gambling destination, the low-profile **Monte Carlo** is one of Las Vegas's less showy casinos. It comes alive early each evening, however, when the **Blue Man Group** (see p.53), who appear nightly in its theatre, stage a heavily percussive free parade through the casino at 6.15pm.

The Monte Carlo's primary function is as the southern gateway to the CityCenter complex. An indoor-outdoor Mexican bar, *Diablo's Cantina*, lures pedestrians in off the Strip in the hope that they'll keep walking all the way back to Aria.

Although a futuristic **monorail** system connects the Monte Carlo to Bellagio by way of Aria, it's so far back from the Strip, at either end, that its only significance is as a free fun ride.

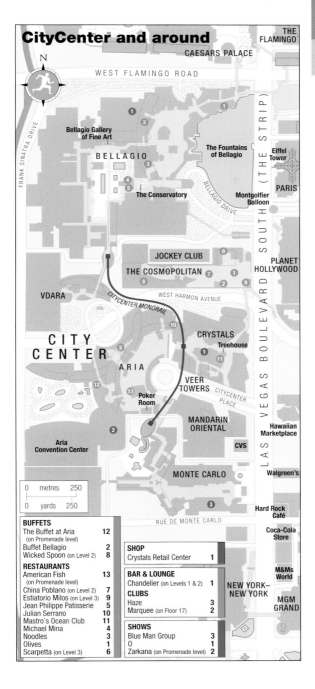

CityCenter and around

THE FLAMINGO

CAESARS PALACE

WEST FLAMINGO ROAD

N

Bellagio Gallery of Fine Art

BELLAGIO

The Fountains of Bellagio

Eiffel Tower

PARIS

The Conservatory

Montgolfier Balloon

JOCKEY CLUB

THE COSMOPOLITAN

PLANET HOLLYWOOD

VDARA

CITYCENTER MONORAIL

WEST HARMON AVENUE

CITY CENTER

CRYSTALS

Treehouse

ARIA

VEER TOWERS

CITYCENTER PLACE

Poker Room

MANDARIN ORIENTAL

CVS

Hawaiian Marketplace

Aria Convention Center

MONTE CARLO

Walgreen's

FRANK SINATRA DRIVE

LAS VEGAS BOULEVARD SOUTH (THE STRIP)

BELLAGIO DRIVE

| 0 | metres | 250 |
| 0 | yards | 250 |

RUE DE MONTE CARLO

Hard Rock Café

Coca-Cola Store

M&Ms World

NEW YORK–NEW YORK

MGM GRAND

BUFFETS	
The Buffet at Aria (on Promenade level)	12
Buffet Bellagio	2
Wicked Spoon (on Level 2)	8

RESTAURANTS	
American Fish (on Promenade level)	13
China Poblano (on Level 2)	7
Estiatorio Milos (on Level 3)	9
Jean Philippe Patisserie	5
Julian Serrano	10
Mastro's Ocean Club	11
Michael Mina	4
Noodles	3
Olives	1
Scarpetta (on Level 3)	6

SHOP	
Crystals Retail Center	1

BAR & LOUNGE	
Chandelier (on Levels 1 & 2)	1
CLUBS	
Haze	3
Marquee (on Floor 17)	2

SHOWS	
Blue Man Group	3
O	1
Zarkana (on Promenade level)	2

CRYSTALS

THE COSMOPOLITAN

3708 Las Vegas Blvd S ☎ 702 698 7000,
Ⓦ www.cosmopolitanlasvegas.com. MAP P.45,
POCKET MAP F9

At first glance, most Las Vegas visitors assume that the **Cosmopolitan**, facing Planet Hollywood (see p.54) across the Strip, is just one more piece of the modernist jigsaw puzzle that comprises CityCenter. It's not; it's an entirely separate luxury casino-hotel, stacked up vertically rather than sprawling horizontally, and impishly squeezed atop the former Jockey Club car park, slap in front of CityCenter, which MGM never managed to buy up.

Since opening in 2010, the Cosmopolitan has made itself very much at home in this prime spot, seducing locals and tourists alike with its glitzy architectural flourishes, high-profile **Marquee** nightclub (see p.53), excellent array of appealing restaurants just steps away from the Strip, and general evocation of glamorous days gone by. In the evenings especially, its buzzing public spaces tend to jostle with excited crowds.

The Cosmopolitan is a throwback to the old Las Vegas, when each casino was separately owned and run, acted like the rest of the city didn't exist, saw its business as being all about gambling and nightlife rather than shopping, and aimed to keep visitors on site by making it all but impossible to find the exits. Be warned that the Cosmopolitan also has the last laugh on CityCenter: while you might understandably assume that you could simply walk all the way through the building and reach Aria (see p.47), you can't – there's no pedestrian through route.

CRYSTALS

3720 Las Vegas Blvd S ☎ 702 590 9299,
Ⓦ www.crystalsatcitycenter.com. MAP P.45,
POCKET MAP B1 & F9

As the one public component of CityCenter to abut the Strip, **Crystals** certainly catches the eye. Designed by Daniel Libeskind, its jagged, colourful facade makes a contrast with the white walls and air-conditioned cool of its interior. Its primary role is as a (hugely expensive) shopping mall, the **Crystals Retail Center** (see p.50).

Purely as a spectacle, however, Crystals is well worth a quick walk-through. At one point, it was planned as an urban park, and it features some extravagant, playful wooden structures, including the intricate 70ft **Treehouse**, home to the stylish *Mastro's Ocean Club* restaurant (see p.51), as well as a pair of arching wooden "pods".

There's also plenty of water on show, including the swirling glass-encased **fountains** on the lower floor, and some dazzling **sculptures** of neon light.

ARIA

3730 Las Vegas Blvd S ☎702 590 7111, ⓦwww.arialasvegas.com. MAP P.45, POCKET MAP B1

Although the CityCenter "neighbourhood" is supposed to be easy to explore on foot, you're only likely to visit **Aria**, the casino at its heart, if you make a very deliberate effort to reach it. Pedestrians can get here outdoors by following its hot, exposed approach road 250 yards west from the Strip, or more comfortably indoors, via the Crystals mall or the much longer walkways through Bellagio (see p.48) and Monte Carlo (see p.44). A gleaming sci-fi **monorail** also connects Aria with both those properties, but the stations are so far back from the Strip that you gain very little by using it.

From the outside, with its sleek, curving skyscrapers, Aria looks more like a sophisticated big-city corporate HQ than a casino. The traffic circle in front of its main entrance holds a pulsating **fountain**, while to the left, more water cascades down a sleek, glistening black wall, 24ft tall.

Aria also identifies itself more with, say, Chicago than Las Vegas by eschewing billboards, video screens and neon in favour of prestigious contemporary **art**. Sculptors represented include Henry Moore, one of whose signature abstractions stands in the tiny gap between Aria and Crystals; Claes Oldenburg, responsible for the giant typewriter eraser near the Strip; Antony Gormley, whose *Feeling Material* hangs from the ceiling; and Maya Lin, whose 84ft silver casting of the Colorado River stretches above the check-in desks.

While Aria's dazzling modernism certainly makes a welcome contrast with traditional Las Vegas aesthetics, in the end, of course, it's all in the service of Mammon – and more specifically, gambling. There's plenty more cutting-edge design to admire as you walk through the casino proper – don't miss the **Poker Room** fringed by gigantic golden playing cards – but there's little reason to linger unless your intention is to gamble.

Both the upper and lower levels of Aria hold a fine roster of restaurants, bars and cafés, but there are very few shops. Devoid of slots and gaming tables, the upper level can feel cavernously empty unless the **Convention Center** is in full swing.

When Aria opened it was home to a Cirque du Soleil tribute show to Elvis Presley. Always an unlikely fit for such a forward-looking property, the show ended its run in 2012 and has been replaced by a more generic Cirque production, **Zarkana** (see p.53), which had already toured overseas.

ARIA

BELLAGIO

3600 Las Vegas Blvd S ☎ 702 693 7111, ⓦ www.bellagio.com. MAP P.45, POCKET MAP F7

Ranking high among Las Vegas's absolute must-see casinos, **Bellagio** proudly surveys the Strip across the graceful dancing fountains of its own broad, semicircular lake. This cream-coloured vision of Italian elegance was unveiled in 1998 as the final great flourish of the twentieth century's fastest-growing new city. It was the handiwork of legendary entrepreneur Steve Wynn, who spared no expense in his bid to follow his success with the Mirage (see p.68) by building the greatest hotel the world had ever seen. His original idea was to model it on a French Mediterranean beach and call it Beau Rivage; that changed after he visited the village of Bellagio, beside Lake Como in Italy.

Although Wynn himself is no longer at the helm – when MGM bought out his Mirage corporation in 2000, he took the money and ran down the street to start again – Bellagio is still going strong, racking up the highest turnover and biggest profits in the city. It's also larger than ever, having thrust a tentacle southwards to create an indoor walkway down to CityCenter. As Bellagio's northeast corner is just a few steps across a pedestrian bridge from Caesars Palace (see p.58), many sightseers use it as a corridor to stay out of the sun as they head south, creating a constant flow of visitors.

Almost all of Bellagio's Strip facade is taken up with waterfront restaurants, so once you're inside you won't see much of the lake. Similarly, its colonnaded pool area is only open to guests. Even so, the sheer opulence of the main casino floor is astounding, and several of the public areas should not be missed. In addition to the **Conservatory**, be sure to walk through the hotel lobby, where a vast chandelier of multi-coloured glass flowers, created by sculptor Dale Chihuly, swarms across the ceiling. And take a glance behind the check-in counter to see the Roman gardens accessible to employees only.

When Bellagio first opened, the management briefly attempted to impose a dress code and bar the children of non-guests. Las Vegas's democratic open-to-all traditions soon put paid to that policy, however, so there's

BELLAGIO

nothing snooty about the crowds you'll see window-shopping in the exclusive stores of the small Via Bellagio shopping arcade, or gasping at the menu prices for its magnificent but undeniably expensive restaurants. Other than the building itself, the two most popular attractions that bring in visitors from elsewhere are the **buffet** (see p.50) and Cirque du Soileil's long-running, breathtaking water spectacular, **O** (see p.53).

THE FOUNTAINS OF BELLAGIO

Bellagio, 3600 Las Vegas Blvd S. Mon–Fri 3–7pm every 30min, 7pm–midnight every 15min; Sat noon–7pm every 30min, 7pm–midnight every 15min; Sun 11am–2.30pm every 15min, 2.30–7pm every 30min, 7pm–midnight every 15min. Free. MAP P.45, POCKET MAP F7

Even when it's lying dormant, Bellagio's ice-blue eight-acre lake makes an impressive spectacle in the Nevada desert. When it erupts into a balletic extrava-ganza of jetting **fountains**, as it does from early morning/afternoon until midnight daily, it's the best free show in town. The sky-high spurts and streams are accompanied by booming music – mostly songs from Broadway shows and popular classics. For anyone other than diners in the expensive waterfront restaurants the best views are either from the Strip sidewalk (stake your place early), from the top of the Eiffel Tower in Paris (see p.57) or from the guest rooms in either Paris (see p.118) or the Cosmopolitan (see p.116).

THE CONSERVATORY

Bellagio, 3600 Las Vegas Blvd S. Open 24hr. Free. MAP P.45, POCKET MAP E8

Ever since Bellagio opened, its magnificent **Conservatory** has been considered one of the major sights of the city. A

THE CONSERVATORY

glassed-over courtyard ringed by galleries and restaurants, it's repeatedly transformed by a huge team of gardeners into extravagant themed shows that include bizarre whimsical props amid an extraordinary array of living plants. The five separate seasonal displays start with the Chinese New Year and then celebrate spring, summer, autumn and winter. During the week it takes to dismantle each show and prepare the next, there's nothing to see.

BELLAGIO GALLERY OF FINE ART

Bellagio, 3600 Las Vegas Blvd S ☎ 702 693 7871, ⓦ www.bellagio.com. Daily 10am–8pm. $15. MAP P.45, POCKET MAP E7

Originally home to Steve Wynn's own art collection, the **Bellagio Gallery of Fine Art** managed to survive Wynn's departure and continues to put on changing exhibitions that generally last for around six months. The entrance fee is high for such a small space though, and only worth paying for the better shows, such as the 2012–2013 display of twenty paintings by Claude Monet, which was curated in conjunction with the Museum of Fine Arts in Boston.

CRYSTALS RETAIL CENTER

Shop

CRYSTALS RETAIL CENTER

3720 Las Vegas Blvd S ☎ 702 590 5299, ⓦ www.crystalsatcitycenter.com. Mon–Thurs & Sun 10am–11pm, Fri & Sat 10am–midnight. MAP P.45, POCKET MAP F9

Pitched at Las Vegas's proverbial "whales"– high-rolling big spenders – the glitzy Crystals makes no bones about being very high-end indeed. With its sparkling white walls, and exquisite sculptural features, few dare stray into boutiques belonging to designers such as Paul Smith and Stella McCartney.

Buffets

THE BUFFET AT ARIA

Promenade Level, Aria, 3730 Las Vegas Blvd S ☎ 702 590 7111, ⓦ www.arialasvegas.com. Breakfast Mon–Fri 7–11am $17.25; lunch Mon–Fri 11am–4pm, Mon–Wed $21, Thurs & Fri $24; champagne brunch Sat & Sun 7am–4pm, $33; dinner daily 4–10pm, Mon–Thurs $31, Fri–Sun $39. MAP P.45, POCKET MAP A2

Choices at CityCenter's one buffet are more limited than elsewhere, but the food is a cut above. The sushi and Indian specialities are excellent and

the desserts are the best in town. Pay $6 extra for unlimited champagne or Bloody Marys. An entire lobster is served at your table during weekend dinners.

BUFFET BELLAGIO

Bellagio, 3600 Las Vegas Blvd S ☎ 702 791 7111, ⓦ www.bellagio.com. Breakfast Mon–Fri 7–11am $17; lunch Mon–Fri 11am–4pm $20; brunch Sat & Sun 7am–4pm $25 (or $31 with champagne); dinner daily 4–10pm, Mon–Thurs & Sun $30, Fri & Sat $37. MAP P.45, POCKET MAP E7

The first "gourmet buffet" in town sparked standards, and less happily prices, to rise all over Las Vegas. While no longer quite as exceptional, it still features an amazing array of food; even for breakfast you can have salmon smoked or baked and omelettes cooked to order, with fillings such as crabmeat.

WICKED SPOON

Level 2, Cosmopolitan, 3708 Las Vegas Blvd S ☎ 702 698 7000, ⓦ www.cosmo politanlasvegas.com. Brunch Mon–Fri 8am–2pm $22, Sat & Sun 8am–3pm $29; dinner Mon–Thurs & Sun 5–9pm, Fri & Sat 5–10pm $35. MAP P.45, POCKET MAP J6

Although the Cosmopolitan's buffet is hard to find, right at the back upstairs, plenty of visitors make their way here to enjoy a wide range of carefully prepared cuisines. Most are served as individual portions, though you can take as many as you like. There's no breakfast; fill up with a late-morning brunch instead.

Restaurants

AMERICAN FISH

Promenade Level, Aria, 3730 Las Vegas Blvd S ☎ 877 230 2742, ⓦ www.arialasvegas.com. Tues–Sun 5–10.30pm. MAP P.45, POCKET MAP A2

Much as it sounds, the emphasis at Michael Mina's sparkling, romantic Aria offering is on the riches of America's waters (including frog's legs). At $46 for a fillet of bass or $85 for the set menu, it's far from cheap, but the dishes are consistently sublime.

CHINA POBLANO

Level 2, Cosmopolitan, 3708 Las Vegas Blvd S ☎ 877 893 2003, ⓦ www.chinapoblano.com. Mon–Thurs 11.30am–11.30pm, Fri–Sun 10am–11.30pm. MAP P.45, POCKET MAP K6

The concept of combining Asia and Mexico goes back a long way – *china poblana* is the national dress of Mexico. Here, in what looks like a street café, it's Chinese and Mexican cuisines that are blended. Only a few dishes, like the $18 Huitlacoche noodles, literally mix the two, but picking and choosing you can make yourself an interesting, good-value meal.

ESTIATORIO MILOS

Level 3, Cosmopolitan, 3708 Las Vegas Blvd S ☎ 877 893 2003, ⓦ www.milos.ca/restaurants /las-vegas. Mon–Thurs 5.30–11.30pm, Fri 5.30pm–midnight, Sat noon–2.30pm & 5.30pm–midnight, Sun noon–2.30pm & 5.30–11pm. MAP P.45, POCKET MAP K7

Vast urns and exquisite statuettes adorn this beautiful Greek restaurant. For lunch there's a fantastic $20 set menu; in the evening diners are escorted to admire a tempting array of fresh fish, flown in daily from Athens. The one you choose will arrive at your table cooked to perfection, at a likely price of over $50 per person.

JEAN PHILIPPE PATISSERIE

Bellagio, 3600 Las Vegas Blvd S ⓦ www .jpchocolates.com. Mon–Thurs 7am–11pm, Fri–Sun 7am–midnight. No reservations. MAP P.45, POCKET MAP E8

It takes rare self-discipline to walk past Jean-Philippe Maury's extraordinary bakery without pausing to swoon at its central feature; the world's largest chocolate fountain swirls around the entire room, cascading through endless funnels and pipettes. The urge to stop for a $5 mug of hot chocolate, if not a pastry, is all but overwhelming.

JULIAN SERRANO

Casino Level. Aria, 3730 Las Vegas Blvd S ☎ 877 230 2742, ⓦ www.arialasvegas.com. Mon–Thurs & Sun 11.30am–11pm, Fri & Sat 11.30am–11.30pm. MAP P.45, POCKET MAP F9

One of Las Vegas's biggest hits of recent years, this beautiful tapas bar tastes even better than it looks. Most tapas cost $12–15 for a small portion; be sure to branch out and sample fabulous creations like the cocoa butter balls filled with chilled gazpacho. Larger mains include paella for two from $40.

MASTRO'S OCEAN CLUB

Crystals, 3720 Las Vegas Blvd S ☎ 702 798 7115, ⓦ www.mastrosrestaurants.com. Daily 5–11pm. MAP P.45, POCKET MAP B1

Even the new Las Vegas still has a penchant for a good old-fashioned steakhouse, though this one stands out from the crowd not so much for its heavy-duty $50-plus rib-eyes as its amazing setting; reserve early and you get to dine in the bowers of Crystals' whimsical wooden Treehouse.

JEAN PHILIPPE PATISSERIE

MICHAEL MINA

Bellagio, 3600 Las Vegas Blvd S ☎ 702 693 8665, Ⓦ www.michaelmina.net. Daily except Wed 5.30–10pm. MAP P.45, POCKET MAP E8

In his flagship restaurant adjoining Bellagio's Conservatory, Egyptian-born Michael Mina continues to reinvent his tried and tested classics. Starters like tuna tartare with mint cost up to $26, while mains range from $36 to the $55 filo-dusted Dover sole and Mina's signature lobster pot pie. The chef's tasting menu costs $98 (wine pairings $55 extra); there's a no-choice vegetarian menu for $68; and at 5.30pm or 6pm you can enjoy a $65 pre-theatre menu.

NOODLES

Bellagio, 3600 Las Vegas Blvd S ☎ 702 693 8131, Ⓦ www.bellagio.com. Daily 11am–2am. MAP P.45, POCKET MAP F8

Bellagio's casual, walk-ins only, pan-Asian diner, off the main casino floor behind the *Baccarat* bar, is well worth seeking out. Its intriguing decor looks great and the food, ranging from Thailand to Japan by way of China and Vietnam, is no disappointment. Noodle dishes are around $18 and at weekend lunchtimes dim sum typically cost around $9.

OLIVES

Bellagio, 3600 Las Vegas Blvd S Ⓦ www .bellagio.com. Daily 11am–2.45pm & 5–10.30pm. No reservations. MAP P.45, POCKET MAP F7

This elegant modern American restaurant offers an experience to savour. For a light meal, opt for an $18 flatbread topped perhaps with fig and prosciutto. Full mains tend to be pricier, with pasta dishes at over $40 and steaks over $50, but the succulent roasted chicken costs $22 at lunch, $29 for dinner.

SCARPETTA

Level 3, Cosmopolitan, 3708 Las Vegas Blvd S ☎ 877 893 2003, Ⓦ www.cosmo politanlasvegas.com. Daily 6–11pm. MAP P.45, POCKET MAP K7

Courtesy of "new Italian" chef Scott Conant, the food is even better than the view at *Scarpetta*, with huge panoramic windows overlooking the Bellagio fountains. *Le tout* Las Vegas has flocked to enjoy starters like his $18 tuna "susci", and mains including short rib and bone marrow agnolotti (stuffed pasta; $25). For the full works, go for the $110 set menu.

Bars and lounges

CHANDELIER

Cosmopolitan, 3708 Las Vegas Blvd S ☎ 702 698 7000, Ⓦ www.cosmopolitanlasvegas.com. Casino level open 24hr, other levels hours vary. MAP P.45, POCKET MAP K6 & F9

Beneath the dazzling, dangling canopy of the eponymous two-million-crystal chandelier, the Cosmopolitan's centrepiece bar soars through three separate levels. It's the middle floor where the actions is, with DJ music and a buzzy crowd.

SCARPETTA

than at Encore (see p.82), but attracts bigger-name DJs and celebs. Buying a wristband covers the whole weekend.

Shows

BLUE MAN GROUP

Monte Carlo, 3770 Las Vegas Blvd S ☎ 800 258 3626, ⓦ www.blueman.com. Mon, Tues & Sun 7pm, Wed–Sat 7pm & 10pm. $65–149. MAP P.45, POCKET MAP B2

The hilariously postmodern Blue Men are true Las Vegas favourites; kids love their craziness, adults their cleverness. Mute and lurid blue from head to toe, they combine paint-splashing, cereal-spewing clowning with pounding percussion, a relentless rock soundtrack and some amazing visual effects, to great success.

O

Bellagio, 3600 Las Vegas Blvd S ☎ 702 693 8866, ⓦ www.cirquedusoleil.com. Wed–Sun 7.30pm & 10pm. $98.50–155. MAP P.45, POCKET MAP E7

The real star of this phenomenal show is the theatre: it centres on a metal-mesh stage, any part of which can suddenly disappear beneath the performers' feet. That makes possible a dazzling array of death-defying leaps and heart-stopping plunges that create a show you'll never forget.

ZARKANA

Aria, 3730 Las Vegas Blvd S ☎ 855 927 5262, ⓦ www.cirquedusoleil.com. Mon, Tues & Fri–Sun 7pm & 9.30pm. $69–180. MAP P.45, POCKET MAP A2

To replace its ill-fated *Viva Elvis* tribute show, Cirque du Soleil opened its first show in Las Vegas that had previously toured the world. *Zarkana* tells the story of a magician searching for his lost love and lost art, with abundant acrobatics and a rock/electronica soundtrack.

CHANDELIER

Clubs

HAZE

Casino Level, Aria, 3730 Las Vegas Blvd S ☎ 702 792 7900, ⓦ www.lightgroup.com. Thurs–Sat 10.30pm–4am. Cover $20–40. MAP P.45, POCKET MAP E9

Even if the dance floor itself is smaller than you might expect, surrounded by tiers of lounge space and elaborate overhanging contraptions, there's a lot to like about Aria's showpiece nightclub. Run by the Light Group, it's especially strong on spectacular lighting effects and mind-blowing video screens.

MARQUEE

Level 1, Cosmopolitan, 3708 Las Vegas Blvd S ☎ 702 333 9000, ⓦ www.marqueelasvegas.com. Nightclub Mon, Thurs, Fri & Sat 10pm–4am; Dayclub daily 10am–7pm. Cover varies $20–80. MAP P.45, POCKET MAP K7

Marquee is a cutting-edge indoor-outdoor combination of a nightclub with a pool-centred "dayclub". It features a 50ft-high main floor, the Boombox, overlooking the Strip, and the Library, complete with pool tables. Add in drinks and you can expect to spend hundreds of dollars. The dayclub is smaller

The Central Strip

Long the scene of fierce inter-casino rivalries, the central portion of the Strip now feels much more like a pedestrian neighbourhood, where visitors stroll from one casino to the next thanks to new outdoor spaces like the Linq development adjoining the Flamingo and the Roman Plaza outside Caesars Palace. What's not obvious, however, is that all those casinos, from the block-spanning behemoth Caesars Palace to grizzled veterans like the Flamingo and Harrah's across the Strip, and newcomers like Paris and Planet Hollywood to the south, now belong to the same conglomerate; you'd never guess that it's Harrah's that rules the roost.

PLANET HOLLYWOOD

3667 Las Vegas Blvd S ☎ 702 785 5555,
🌐 www.planethollywoodresort.com. MAP P.55,
POCKET MAP G9

The only Strip giant saddled with a brand name not otherwise known for gambling, **Planet Hollywood** has struggled to establish a strong identity; it's not part of the dining chain or even an independent entity. The building itself opened in 2000 as a new version of the long-established Aladdin, where Elvis Presley married Priscilla in 1966. Planet Hollywood took it over in 2004, after the Aladdin went broke in the wake of 9/11, but they in turn soon floundered and sold out to Harrah's in 2010.

Planet Hollywood remains a second-tier property in Harrah's portfolio. As the Aladdin, it always seemed to be empty, thanks to the obvious design flaw that the door from the Strip was too hard to find – a problem now rectified by the simple expedient of erecting a huge sign reading "Casino Entrance". The main attraction within is the **Miracle Mile** mall (see p.56); the actual casino is relatively small, and with its loud music and flashing lights, largely targeted at "hip" younger visitors.

PLANET HOLLYWOOD

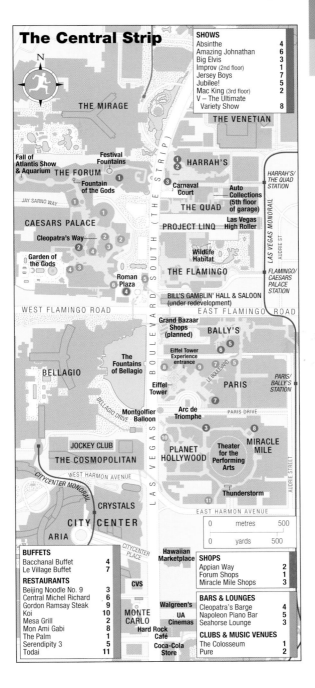

The Central Strip

THE MIRAGE

THE VENETIAN

Fall of Atlantis Show & Aquarium — THE FORUM

Festival Fountains

HARRAH'S

HARRAH'S/ THE QUAD STATION

Fountain of the Gods

Carnaval Court

Auto Collections (5th floor of garage)

THE QUAD

JAY SARNO WAY

CAESARS PALACE

PROJECT LINQ

Las Vegas High Roller

LAS VEGAS MONORAIL

AUDRIE ST

Cleopatra's Way

Garden of the Gods

Wildlife Habitat

THE FLAMINGO

FLAMINGO/ CAESARS PALACE STATION

Roman Plaza

BILL'S GAMBLIN' HALL & SALOON (under redevelopment)

WEST FLAMINGO ROAD

EAST FLAMINGO ROAD

Grand Bazaar Shops (planned)

BALLY'S

BELLAGIO

The Fountains of Bellagio

Eiffel Tower Experience entrance

PARIS/ BALLY'S STATION

Eiffel Tower

PARIS

AUDRIE STREET

Montgolfier Balloon

Arc de Triomphe

PARIS DRIVE

JOCKEY CLUB

THE COSMOPOLITAN

PLANET HOLLYWOOD

MIRACLE MILE

CITYCENTER MONORAIL

WEST HARMON AVENUE

Theater for the Performing Arts

CRYSTALS

Thunderstorm

CITY CENTER

EAST HARMON AVENUE

ARIA

| 0 | metres | 500 |
| 0 | yards | 500 |

CITYCENTER PLACE

Hawaiian Marketplace

CVS

MONTE CARLO

Walgreen's

UA Cinemas

Hard Rock Café

Coca-Cola Store

SHOWS

Absinthe	4
Amazing Johnathan	6
Big Elvis	3
Improv (2nd floor)	1
Jersey Boys	7
Jubilee!	5
Mac King (3rd floor)	2
V – The Ultimate Variety Show	8

BUFFETS

Bacchanal Buffet	4
Le Village Buffet	7

RESTAURANTS

Beijing Noodle No. 9	3
Central Michel Richard	6
Gordon Ramsay Steak	9
Koi	10
Mesa Grill	2
Mon Ami Gabi	8
The Palm	1
Serendipity 3	5
Todai	11

SHOPS

Appian Way	2
Forum Shops	1
Miracle Mile Shops	3

BARS & LOUNGES

Cleopatra's Barge	4
Napoleon Piano Bar	5
Seahorse Lounge	3

CLUBS & MUSIC VENUES

The Colosseum	1
Pure	2

MIRACLE MILE

Planet Hollywood, 3663 Las Vegas Blvd S
☎ 702 866 0703, ⊕ www.miraclemileshopslv
.com. MAP P.55, POCKET MAP G8

Coiled like an enormous snake around and through Planet Hollywood, the **Miracle Mile** mall is nonetheless an entirely separate operation. Built at the same time as the new Aladdin, in 2000, and still bearing traces of its original Arabian Nights theming, it was credited by some as being responsible for the Aladdin's financial failure; given the chance to stroll into a mall without having to walk through a casino en route, Strip sightseers simply ignored the Aladdin altogether. Besides a free **"thunderstorm" attraction**, the Miracle Mile holds a wide range of bars, restaurants and theatres to complement the clothing boutiques, shoe shops and galleries (see p.62).

PARIS

3655 Las Vegas Blvd S ☎ 877 603 4386,
⊕ www.parislasvegas.com. MAP P.55,
POCKET MAP G8

Designed by the architects previously responsible for New York–New York, and opened a few months before the millennium, **Paris** represented the final flourish of the Las Vegas craze for building entire miniature cities. Its exterior remains one of the Strip's most enjoyable spectacles, surmounted by a gigantic Eiffel Tower whose legs crash through the ceiling into the heart of the casino itself, and anchored by the Arc de Triomphe, the Opera and a Montgolfier hot-air balloon, which becomes a glowing landmark at night.

Although it's slightly misleading to think of Paris as a separate casino at all – it was originally built as an extension to Bally's (see p.57) next door, to which it's linked by a broad corridor at the back of the building – it was an immediate hit. With both of these properties now owned by Caesars Entertainment, the tail these days is clearly wagging the dog, and Bally's feels like a minor adjunct to Paris.

Pleasing Parisian touches such as the ironwork echoing the city's Metro stations still abound throughout the interior. From the excellent **buffet** to the pastry shops and bridal wear boutiques, the great majority of Paris's shops, restaurants and bars have

PARIS

some sort of French connection. Much of it is tongue-in-cheek, so even the more tenuous links, as in calling the sports bar the **Bar du Sports**, are just part of the fun. The one area where visitors have balked at the Gallic flavour has been entertainment; Paris has long since abandoned its hopes of staging all-French productions (like, say, *Phantom of the Opera* or *Les Miserables*) in favour of safer options like Barry Manilow and Engelbert Humperdinck.

BALLY'S

EIFFEL TOWER EXPERIENCE

Paris, 3655 Las Vegas Blvd S ☎ 888 727 4758, 🌐 www.parislasvegas.com. Daily 9.30am–12.30am. $10.50 daytime, $15.50 evening; $23 for both in same day. MAP P.55, POCKET MAP G8

Towering 540ft over the Strip, Las Vegas's version of the **Eiffel Tower** is half the height of the Seine-side original. It's not simply a half-sized replica, however; if it was, you wouldn't be able to squeeze into the elevators, for example. In addition, this one is made of steel not iron, and doesn't have a public staircase to the top.

Visitors can either dine in the luxury restaurant 100ft up, or buy a ticket inside Paris's main entrance for the **Eiffel Tower Experience** and ride all the way to the summit viewing platform. While it offers great views all day long, the prime time to come is in the evening; as its builders always cheekily intended, the Eiffel Tower makes the perfect vantage point for watching the Bellagio fountains.

BALLY'S

3645 Las Vegas Blvd S ☎ 877 603 4390, 🌐 www.ballyslasvegas.com. MAP P.55, POCKET MAP G7

These days, you could easily fail to notice **Bally's**, set well back from the Strip opposite Bellagio. When it opened in 1973, however, this was the MGM Grand, the biggest hotel in the world. Only after a terrible hotel fire killed 84 people here in 1980 was it bought and renamed by the gaming manufacturer Bally's, and a new MGM Grand constructed further south. Now owned by Caesars Entertainment, Bally's has become a humdrum casino that's mainly noteworthy for hosting the throwback revue show *Jubilee!* (see p.67).

Bally's was built in the era when casinos still needed huge Strip-front car parks. Legendary in Las Vegas lore as the landing site for Nicolas Cage and the parachuting Elvises in the 1992 movie *Honeymoon in Vegas*, and subsequently spanned by a network of neon-covered walkways, the former Bally's car park was due as this book went to press to become the site of an open-air "pop-up" shopping mall, the **Grand Bazaar Shops**, which may turn out to raise its profile considerably. Visit 🌐www.grandbazaarshops.com for the latest information on the project's development.

CAESARS PALACE

3570 Las Vegas Blvd S ☎866 227 5938,
Ⓦwww.caesarspalace.com. MAP P.55,
POCKET MAP F.6

Still a Las Vegas headliner in its own right, fifty years since it was built, **Caesars Palace** remains arguably the biggest name on the Strip. During the casino-building spree either side of the millennium, it slipped for a moment behind its newer rivals, to the point where Harrah's Entertainment were able to buy up control. Recognizing the prestige value of the name, however, they've not only reinvigorated Caesars and put it back on top, but changed their own name to Caesars Entertainment.

Caesars Palace was originally the creation of **Jay Sarno**, a hard-gambling associate of legendary Teamsters leader Jimmy Hoffa. Cobbled together for just $24 million, it was unveiled in 1966, complete with clerks dressed as Roman centurions and cocktail waitresses kitted out like Cleopatra. Sarno himself doubled his money and sold out in 1969; he moved on to build Circus Circus, and eventually died of a heart attack in a suite at Caesars in 1984.

As well as coming up with the Caesars Palace name, designed to appeal to American and European gamblers alike, Sarno also decreed that the one thing it will never have is an apostrophe – it does not belong to Caesar, it's filled by the thousands of Caesars who choose to visit it. His crucial legacy, however, was that he'd set Caesars up on an expanse of land – originally rented from Kirk Kerkorian, who remains a major Las Vegas player to this day – that has so far proved big enough to hold every

STATUE, CAESARS PALACE

enlargement architects have been able to imagine.

Pausing to admire Caesars Palace from the Strip is one of the great joys of visiting Las Vegas. White marble Classical statues are everywhere you look, from Julius Caesar forever hailing a cab on the main driveway to the Winged Victory of Samothrace guarding a row of gently cascading pools. Most impressive of all are the ornate fountains that surround the entrance to the Forum mall.

The central bulk of Caesars Palace is still proudly set back around 150 yards from the Strip; all that space between the casino and the Strip originally held an enormous car park. Once Las Vegas visitors began to arrive by plane not car, the gap became a deterrent to pedestrians. It was Caesars that pioneered the use of long moving walkways to haul them in – and naturally neglected to build corresponding outbound walkways to let them back out again. Bit by bit, the space has been built over. First, at the northern end, the vast **Forum** mall (see p.59) steadily extended until it reached all the way to the Strip; then the mighty **Colosseum** appeared alongside, in 2003; and more recently the **Roman Plaza** has burgeoned at the south, holding bars, restaurants and even, currently, a circus marquee, which is home to the *Absinthe* show (see p.66).

Inside, Caesars Palace bewilders most first-time visitors. Unlike newer Las Vegas properties, designed to be user-friendly and let you find what you're looking for, Caesars was laid out in the hope that gamblers might never be able to escape.

Making your way between the casino itself and the Forum is easy enough; the two simply meet on the casino floor. However, exploring the rest of Caesars Palace is less straightforward. A network of narrow and circuitous corridors lead to the older **Appian Way** mall, which offers the chance of a close-up inspection, from directly below, of Michaelangelo's naked *David*, and Cleopatra's Way, home to the Egyptian-themed *Cleopatra's Barge* nightclub (see p.65).

Much of the rest of the property, including the luxurious **Garden of the Gods** pool complex, based on the baths of Pompeii, is only open to registered guests.

THE FORUM

3500 Las Vegas Blvd S ☎702 893 6189, ⓦwww.forumshops.com. MAP P.55, POCKET MAP F5

By opening the **Forum** mall in 1992, Caesars Palace not only became the first Strip casino to turn both shopping and dining into major reasons to visit Las Vegas, it also created one of the city's most iconic attractions.

Though widely copied ever since, the Forum's domed false-sky ceiling still packs a mind-blowing punch. Designed to evoke the skyline of ancient Rome, it cycles hourly between the dazzling blue of "day" and the orange glow of "night".

Sadly, though, many of the kitschier elements of the Forum's earlier years, such as the animatronic "living statues" that adorned its centrepiece fountains, have been discarded in favour of ever more opulent and ornate decor. The most striking feature these days is the amazing convoluted spiral escalator at the Forum's main Strip entrance. Its separate moving pathways follow different trajectories, so you can never be sure they'll take you where you want to go.

The **Forum Shops** themselves still rank as Las Vegas's premier shopping spot (see p.62).

THE FORUM

THE FLAMINGO

3555 Las Vegas Blvd S ☎ 702 733 3111.
ⓦ www.flamingolasvegas.com. MAP P.55.
POCKET MAP G6

Now that it's just another glossy casino, shoulder to shoulder in the Strip's endless procession of identikit giants, it's all but impossible to picture **the Flamingo** in its original form. Whatever anyone may tell you, when it opened in 1946 it wasn't the very first Strip resort of them all. Standing alone in the desert, however, a mile south of its nearest neighbour, the Last Frontier, the Flamingo was an enticing hundred-room oasis that put Las Vegas on the map as a glamorous, even dangerous, getaway.

Not that the Flamingo was an immediate hit. So disastrously over budget that it was forced to close within a fortnight, its initial failure cost owner Benjamin "Bugsy" Siegel his life, when his fellow mobsters gunned him down the next

year. By then, however, the Flamingo was already going strong, and a wave of imitators was starting to appear.

With Bugsy a distant, sanitized memory, the Flamingo these days is much more Donny and Marie – long-term residents in its showroom – than Don Corleone. Its current owners, Caesars Entertainment, target it largely at older visitors, who remember Las Vegas as it used to be back in the 1980s, when the Flamingo was still the biggest hotel in the world, and before everything had to keep reinventing itself to suit the latest trend.

From its superb neon sign and the Strip-facing patio of *Jimmy Buffet's Margaritaville* at the front, to the real-life flamingoes and penguins in the free **Wildlife Habitat** and garden-set pool complex around the back, there's a lot to like about the Flamingo. It's also likely to be one of the main beneficiaries of the new Linq development (see box opposite); expect upgrades and improvements in the years to come.

THE QUAD

3535 Las Vegas Blvd S ☎ 702 731 3311.
ⓦ www.thequadlv.com. MAP P.55.
POCKET MAP G5

A major component of Project Linq (see box opposite) has been the revamping of the veteran Imperial Palace under a new name, **The Quad**. The building itself was not demolished, but totally "re-skinned", with its previous Japanese facade stripped away and its interior decor transformed. That process remained incomplete when this book went to press, so it was uncertain which if any of

Project Linq and the demise of the Imperial Palace

The biggest new construction project on the Strip this decade, and the first riposte from Caesars Entertainment since rivals MGM Resorts completed CityCenter in 2009, **Project Linq** is not, for once, a new casino. Instead it's a "retail, dining and entertainment district"; figuring Las Vegas has quite enough hotel rooms for the moment, Caesars have taken what was previously a narrow roadway between the Flamingo and the Imperial Palace, and turned it into a broader pedestrian corridor.

At the far end, away from the Strip, the 550ft-tall **Las Vegas High Roller** was promised but as yet uncompleted when this book went to press. Planned as the world's largest observation wheel, making it taller than the similar, 443ft London Eye, it was due to hold 28 see-through cabins carrying up to forty passengers each, for a projected fee of under $20 per ride. Spectacular long-range panoramas are promised, though intervening buildings will surely obstruct ground-level views of the Strip.

So far, the major casualty of the $550 million redevelopment has been the tiny **Bill's Gamblin' Hall & Saloon** (formerly the Barbary Coast), squeezed into a sandwich-sized slot where Flamingo Road meets the Strip. Closed at the time of writing, to allow construction of an enormous nightclub and pool complex on its rooftop, it was expected to reopen in 2014 with a new name and a new "boutique" identity.

the Imperial Palace's original features would survive. Prime among them were the **Auto Collections** – a remarkable array of vintage cars, most of which were for sale, on the fifth floor of the garage – and the section of the casino floor staffed by celebrity lookalike "dealertainers".

HARRAH'S

3475 Las Vegas Blvd S ☎ 702 369 5000, 🌐 www.harrahslasvegas.com. MAP P.55, POCKET MAP G5

Harrah's is the great unsung success story of the Strip. When all its rivals were going crazy for adding eye-catching, child-friendly gimmicks, constructing replica cities and enticing young hipsters to day-night pool parties, Harrah's just carried on giving their parents the same old, same old formula of cheap eats, plentiful slots and middle-of-the-road entertainment. And it did it all so well that one by one Harrah's swallowed all of its Central Strip rivals up. Then, having bought the lot, the Harrah's organization simply changed its name to Caesars Entertainment; it's as if it never happened.

For anyone under a certain age, Harrah's itself remains as boring as ever. Walk past on the Strip, and your attention may be captured by the performers on the open-air **Carnaval Court** stage, but step inside and you're in a soporific timewarp, where country superstar Toby Keith's *I Love This Bar & Grill!* is the biggest attraction. To be fair, Harrah's does put on some good-value daytime shows, including Mac King (see p.67) and Big Elvis (see p.66), but it's no place for thrill-seeking sightseers.

Shops

APPIAN WAY

Caesars Palace, 3570 Las Vegas Blvd S
☎ 702 731 7222, ⓦ www.caesarspalace.com.
Store hours vary. MAP P.55, POCKET MAP F6

Much smaller than the Forum,
the **Appian Way** is arrayed
along two corridors just off the
casino floor at Caesars Palace.
Centring on an 18ft marble
replica of Michaelangelo's
David, it includes Bernini
Couture, Gevril watches, and
an outlet selling Caesars' own
branded merchandise.

FORUM SHOPS

FORUM SHOPS

3500 Las Vegas Blvd S ☎ 702 893 6189,
ⓦ www.forumshops.com. Mon–Thurs & Sun
10am–11pm, Fri & Sat 10am–midnight. MAP
P.55, POCKET MAP F5

Still going strong after twenty
years, the Forum Shops is
foot-for-foot the country's most
successful mall. That's partly
because its big-name brands
tend to be squeezed into smaller
spaces than usual. While its two
main "streets" are hardly full of
surprises – expect to see an
Apple Store, Gap and H&M, for
example – they do offer a very
intense burst of shopping.

MIRACLE MILE SHOPS

Planet Hollywood, 3663 Las Vegas Blvd S
☎ 888 800 8264, ⓦ www.miraclemileshopslv
.com. Mon–Thurs & Sun 10am–11pm, Fri &
Sat 10am–midnight. MAP P.55, POCKET MAP G8

Give or take the odd fountain,
the largest casino mall, the
Miracle Mile Shops, could be
just about anywhere. Easily
entered straight from the Strip,
it really is a mile long; walk
from one end to the other and
you'll pass a huge range of
stores, from mall staples like
Urban Outfitters, American
Apparel, French Connection
and Gap to some
jaw-droppingly awful "art
galleries" and a couple of ABC
convenience stores.

Buffets

BACCHANAL BUFFET

Caesars Palace, 3570 Las Vegas Blvd S
☎ 702 731 7778, ⓦ www.caesarspalace.com.
Breakfast Mon–Fri 7–11am $20; lunch Mon–
Fri 11am–3pm $25; champagne brunch Sat &
Sun 7am–3pm $32; dinner Mon–Thurs & Sun
3–10pm $35, Fri & Sat 3–10pm $40. MAP P.55,
POCKET MAP F6

The Strip's latest gourmet
buffet – much the best at any
Caesars-owned property –
opened in 2012. It features five
hundred freshly-made items
daily, from sushi, dim sum
and pho soup to fresh oysters
and wood-fired pizzas,
prepared by chefs at nine
separate "show kitchens".

LE VILLAGE BUFFET

Paris, 3655 Las Vegas Blvd S ☎ 702 946
7000, ⓦ www.parislasvegas.com. Breakfast
Mon–Fri 7–11am $19, Sat & Sun 7–10am
$22; lunch Mon–Fri 11am–3.30pm $22;
champagne brunch Sat & Sun 10am–3.30pm
$31; dinner daily 3.30–10pm $31. MAP P.55,
POCKET MAP G7

Unique in focusing on a single
cuisine – or rather, on French
cuisine, from Brittany to

The Buffet of Buffets

Buffet fans should watch out for the **Buffet of Buffets pass**, sold at all the buffets in every Caesars-owned casino, which allows 24-hour unrestricted access to all those buffets for a total cost of $50. Use it to eat at, say, 8pm one night, 7pm the next, and you get two dinners into the bargain. Note, however, that each visit to the Bacchanal Buffet at Caesars Palace costs an additional $15.

Provence – *Le Village* offers the most satisfying meal of any casino buffet, You'll find a wider array elsewhere, but if you're partial to French meat or fish, or simply fancy a fresh baguette and all the cheese you can eat, in a playful themed setting, don't miss it.

Restaurants

BEIJING NOODLE NO. 9

Caesars Palace, 3570 Las Vegas Blvd S
☎877 346 4642, ⓦwww.caesarspalace.com.
Daily 11am–10.30pm. MAP P.55, POCKET MAP F6

Approached via aquariums that hold a thousand goldfish and resembling a pale, mysterious, underwater cavern, this Chinese noodle shop is one of Las Vegas's most enjoyable places to eat. Fortunately, the food matches the setting, though with dim sum buns and dumplings at around $12, and the (large) noodle dishes more like $20, so too do the prices.

CENTRAL MICHEL RICHARD

Caesars Palace, 3570 Las Vegas Blvd S
☎702 650 5921, ⓦwww.centrallv.com. Daily
24hr. MAP P.55, POCKET MAP F6

Serving far better food than you'd expect from a 24-hour diner, *Central Michel Richard* consists of a spacious outdoor patio alongside Caesars' main pedestrian entrance, an indoor dining room and a walk-up bar abutting the hotel lobby. Prices and dishes on its short bistro-style menu vary slightly around the clock; standouts include the $13 matzo onion soup, covered by a deep cheesy crust, and American standards like fried or rotisserie chicken for just over $20.

GORDON RAMSAY STEAK

Paris, 3655 Las Vegas Blvd S ☎702 946
7000, ⓦwww.parislasvegas.com. Daily
5–10.30pm. MAP P.55, POCKET MAP G7

For his first Las Vegas venture, perfectionist pottymouth Gordon Ramsay played it safe, opening a high-class steakhouse near Paris's main entrance – its tunnel approach represents the trip from France to England, incidentally. Diners select from a trolley laden with marbled, aged slabs of prime meat; a superbly cooked veal chop costs $50, a strip steak $63 and the $125 tasting menu includes Beef Wellington.

MON AMI GABI

KOI

Planet Hollywood, 3667 Las Vegas Blvd S
☎702 454 4555, ⓦwww.koirestaurant.com.
Mon–Thurs & Sun 5.30–10.30pm, Fri & Sat
5.30–11.30pm. MAP P.55, POCKET MAP G8
While not the celebrity
favourite it is in Hollywood,
this fancy restaurant serves
tasty Japanese food at what,
for Las Vegas, are reasonable
prices – especially considering
its views of Bellagio's
fountains. Sushi rolls, tuna
tartare or tempura shrimp
cost well under $20, mains
like steamed sea bass or
wasabi short ribs up to $30.

MESA GRILL

Caesars Palace, 3570 Las Vegas Blvd S
☎877 346 4642, ⓦwww.mesagrill.com.
Mon–Fri 11am–2.30pm & 5–11pm, Sat &
Sun 10.30am–3pm & 5–11pm. MAP P.55,
POCKET MAP F6
Contemporary Southwestern
chef Bobby Flay, who made
his name in New York, has
shown enough commitment to
his Las Vegas outlet, across
from the Colosseum entrance,
for it to become Caesars' most
dependable fine-dining
restaurant. Zestful, Mexican-
influenced favourites include

sixteen-spice chicken, which
costs $16 in a lunch salad,
more like $30 for dinner.

MON AMI GABI

Paris, 3655 Las Vegas Blvd S ☎702 944
4224, ⓦwww.monamigabi.com. Mon–Fri &
Sun 7am–11pm, Sat 7am–midnight. MAP P.55,
POCKET MAP G7
Among the first Las Vegas
restaurants to offer al fresco
dining, this exuberant
evocation of a Paris pavement
brasserie remains the city's
premier lunchtime pick. For a
real taste of France, you can't
beat a $13 *croque-madame*
(ham, cheese and egg
sandwich) for breakfast;
moules frites (mussels and
chips) for lunch ($22); or *steak
frites* for dinner ($25).

THE PALM

Forum Shops, Caesars Palace ☎702 732
7256, ⓦwww.thepalm.com. Daily
11.30am–11pm. MAP P.55, POCKET MAP F5
A veteran of the Forum scene,
this offshoot of the legendary
New York steakhouse offers a
stylish, surprisingly formal
escape from the shopping
mania outside. For lunch, $16
will buy you a salad, burger or
sandwich. In the evening,
classic Italian veal dishes cost
$32–34, and a prime, 24oz
rib-eye steak is $55.

SERENDIPITY 3

Caesars Palace, 3570 Las Vegas Blvd S ☎866
227 5938, ⓦwww.caesarspalace.com. Mon–
Thurs & Sun 8am–11pm, Fri & Sat 8am–
midnight. MAP P.55, POCKET MAP G6
There's nothing in the slightest
bit subtle about this larger-than-
life diner, set in and around a
columned pavilion in Caesars'
open-air Roman Plaza and open
to the Strip. It simply serves
unbelievably large portions of
irresistibly calorific Fifties-
style favourites, including
burgers the size of your head

and frozen hot chocolate you could swim in to cool off.

TODAI

Miracle Mile, Planet Hollywood, 3667 Las Vegas Blvd S ☎702 892 0021, ⓦwww.todai .com. Lunch Mon–Fri 11.30am–2.30pm $20, Sat & Sun 11.30am–2.30pm $22; dinner Mon–Thurs 5.30–9.30pm $32, Fri & Sat 5.30–10pm $34, Sun 5.30–9.30pm $34. MAP P.55, POCKET MAP G9

For fans of Japanese food, *Todai* is a dream come true – an all-you-can-eat buffet serving not just sushi and sashimi, but also all kinds of delicious noodles, soups, teriyaki meat and fried fish. Lunch costs $20 Mon–Fri and $22 Sat & Sun, while dinner is $32 Mon–Thurs and $34 Fri–Sun.

Bars and lounges

CLEOPATRA'S BARGE

Caesars Palace, 3570 Las Vegas Blvd S ☎702 967 4000, ⓦwww.caesarspalace.com. Daily 8.30pm–3am. MAP P.55, POCKET MAP F6

Caesars Palace was built just three years after Elizabeth Taylor's iconic performance as Cleopatra; centred on a floating replica of a Pharaonic barge, surrounded by gilded furniture and campy little nooks, this bar's been here ever since. A glorious reminder of Las Vegas's golden era, it's regularly transformed into the "Gossy Lounge" to stage performances by British crooner Matt Goss, of Bros fame.

NAPOLEON PIANO BAR

Paris, 3655 Las Vegas Blvd S ☎ 702 946 7000, ⓦwww.parislasvegas.com. Daily 4pm–2am; no cover charge. MAP P.55, POCKET MAP H7

Come in the early evening to this plush, dimly lit, bordello-red bar, poised halfway along the internal corridor that connects Paris to Bally's, and while there may be a lounge act on stage, like a vocal group or comedian, it feels like a sophisticated venue for champagne, cognac, cocktails or cigars. Between 9pm and 1am nightly, however, things turn much more raucous, as duelling pianists vie to belt out whatever the audience requests (and is prepared to tip for) – expect energetic, enthusiastic sing-along renditions of Bohemian Rhapsody and the like.

SEAHORSE LOUNGE

Caesars Palace, 3570 Las Vegas Blvd S ☎ 702 731 7110, ⓦwww.caesarspalace .com. Daily 8.30pm–3am. MAP P.55, POCKET MAP F6

Catch your breath after walking Caesars' endless hallways in this throwback of a lounge, open to the casino floor and kitted out with plush leopard-skin carpets, comfy armchairs and abundant nautical statues. The broad column at the main entrance, filled with 1700 gallons of seawater, holds live seahorses – Australian pot-bellied ones, no less.

SEAHORSE LOUNGE

Clubs and music venues

THE COLOSSEUM

Caesars Palace, 3570 Las Vegas Blvd S ☎866 227 5938, ⓦwww.thecolosseum.com. Showtimes and prices vary; Celine Dion typically ranges from $55–250. MAP P.55, POCKET MAP F5

Built in 2003 to house a long-term residency by Celine Dion, the 4000-seat Colosseum is the last great stronghold of the old-style Las Vegas headliner. Celine herself still returns frequently, while Elton John, Rod Stewart and Shania Twain also play regular extended engagements. Stars who appear for a night or two at a time have included Jerry Seinfeld, and even Leonard Cohen.

PURE

Caesars Palace, 3570 Las Vegas Blvd S ☎702 731 7873, ⓦwww.purethenightclub .com. Tues & Thurs–Sun 10pm–4am. Cover $20–50. MAP P.55, POCKET MAP F6

One of the few Strip nightclubs that genuinely lives up to the hype, *Pure* attracts huge, excited crowds night after night. Effectively this is actually three clubs in one, with each of its three main rooms having its own DJ and sound system. A glass elevator and elaborate twisting staircase climb to a massive Strip-view outdoor terrace on the top floor.

Shows

ABSINTHE

Caesars Palace, 3570 Las Vegas Blvd S ☎800 745 3000, ⓦwww.absinthevegas.com. Tues & Thurs–Sat 8pm & 10pm, Wed & Sun 8pm. $89–114. MAP P.55, POCKET MAP F6

Staged in the round, in a marquee on Caesars' outdoor Roman Plaza, this no-holds-barred circus-tinged burlesque show has taken Las Vegas by storm. Conceived as a crude and abrasive counterpoint to the fey whimsy of Cirque du Soleil, and eschewing PC in all its forms, it's more of a drunken night out than a traditional show, but it still charges Cirque-level prices.

AMAZING JOHNATHAN

Bally's, 3645 Las Vegas Blvd S ☎702 777 7767, ⓦwww.ballyslasvegas.com. Tues–Sat 10pm. $60 & $70. MAP P.55, POCKET MAP G7

As much comedian as magician, Amazing Johnathan brings a manic Looney-Tunes energy to his entertaining one-man, one-woman (in the shape of his sidekick Psychic Tania) show. Johnathan's colourful vocabulary and readiness to resort to violence when his tricks don't work out make it an evening for adults rather than kids, but it's all great entertainment.

BIG ELVIS

Piano Bar, Harrah's, 3475 Las Vegas Blvd S ☎702 369 5000, ⓦwww.harrahslasvegas.com. Mon, Tues & Thurs–Sun 2–6pm. Free. MAP P.55, POCKET MAP G5

Las Vegas's biggest and best-loved Elvis impersonator, Pete Vallee, has shucked off the pounds in the last few years to become merely Large Elvis. His King-like voice still packs a powerful punch, though, and his mastery of Elvis's repertoire and easy audience rapport – requests welcome – make this the best free show in town.

IMPROV

Harrah's, 3475 Las Vegas Blvd S ☎ 702 777 7776, ⓦ www.harrahslasvegas.com. Daily except Mon 8.30pm & 10pm. $29 or $45. MAP P.55, POCKET MAP G5

This veteran spin-off of the legendary Chicago original continues to rank as Las Vegas's best comedy club. Despite the name, bills always consist of three individual stand-ups and often feature big names trying out new material.

JERSEY BOYS

Paris, 3655 Las Vegas Blvd S ☎702 777 7776, ⓦwww.jerseyboysvegas.com. Tues 6.30pm & 9.30pm, Wed–Fri & Sun 7pm, Sat 5pm & 8.15pm. $53–185. MAP P.55, POCKET MAP G6

Broadway shows tend to come and go in Las Vegas, but *Jersey Boys*, the musical story of Frankie Valli and the Four Seasons, has run and run, first at the Palazzo and now in Paris. More than just a vehicle for some magnificent music, it's a truly engaging two-hour theatre piece, playing at an exuberant fast-talking pace that sweeps audiences along.

JUBILEE!

Bally's, 3645 Las Vegas Blvd S ☎ 800 237 7469, ⓦ www.ballyslasvegas.com. Daily except Fri 7.30pm & 10.30pm (topless). $58–118. MAP P.55, POCKET MAP H7

Don't come to *Jubilee* expecting cutting-edge class. Come to enjoy the illusion that the last forty or so years never happened and that high-kicking showgirls in ostrich feathers – and, for the late shows, no bras – still represent the pinnacle of world entertainment. There's nothing quite like it left anywhere else in the city – don't miss it.

MAC KING

Harrah's, 3475 Las Vegas Blvd S ☎ 702 369 5222, ⓦ www.mackingshow.com. Tues–Sat 1 & 3pm. $33. MAP P.55, POCKET MAP G5

Just so there's no doubt, Mac King is billed as a comedy magician. With his clownish country-boy persona, clean-talking patter, easy way with his audience and family-friendly prices – plus of course his stunning sleight of hand – he's Las Vegas's best daytime entertainment bargain.

V – THE ULTIMATE VARIETY SHOW

Miracle Mile, Planet Hollywood, 3663 Las Vegas Blvd S ☎702 932 1818, ⓦwww.vtheshow.com. Daily 7pm & 8.30pm. $60 or $80 with dinner. MAP P.55, POCKET MAP H8

Rather than wide-eyed hopefuls, this enjoyable, long-running variety show features established acts happy to run through crowd-pleasing routines. Regular stars include Melinda, the "first lady of magic"; gloriously deadpan Mexican juggler Wally Eastwood; and the uproarious Russ Merlin, whose Halloween mask audience-volunteer stunt brings the house down.

JUBILEE!

The North Strip

Along the North Strip a vibrant cluster of high-end properties compete to grab visitors' attention with gimmicks like volcanoes (the Mirage); battling pirate ships (Treasure Island); Renaissance bridges (the Venetian); and all-round gilded opulence (Wynn Las Vegas). This part of the Strip is where things turn personal, with the giant casinos owned by fiercely competitive tycoons: specifically, Sheldon Adelson, owner of the Venetian and the Palazzo, is locked in fierce rivalry with Steve Wynn, of the similarly twinned Wynn Las Vegas and Encore. Until recently, the North Strip was regarded as stretching almost all the way to downtown. Since the recession kicked in, however, almost all the veteran casinos that lay further north have either closed down or been blown up, while projects scheduled to replace them have been abandoned.

THE MIRAGE

3400 Las Vegas Blvd S ☎ 702 791 7111,
🌐 www.mirage.com. MAP P.70, POCKET MAP F4

Unveiled as entrepreneur Steve Wynn's first Strip venture, in 1989 – when Las Vegas seemed to be in decline, and no new Strip hotels had been built for sixteen years – the **Mirage** can justly claim to have changed the city overnight. Proving that by investing in luxury, glamour and spectacle, casinos could bring back the crowds, it

spawned such a host of imitators that now, ironically, it no longer stands out from the pack. Following endless mergers and buy-outs, it now belongs to MGM Resorts, which tends to concentrate its attention on its string of properties further south, while the long-departed Wynn himself has built his latest opulent resort, Wynn Las Vegas (see p.72), a short way north.

There's still plenty to like about the Mirage, from its

glassed-in atrium, complete with towering tropical trees, via its well-judged array of restaurants and bars, to its huge complex of pools and gardens, part of which is home to the **Secret Garden and Dolphin Habitat** (see p.69). It's also still at the top of the entertainment tree, having replaced uber-camp Austrian magicians Siegfried and Roy with the Beatles showcase, *Love* (see p.84) and amazing impressionist Terry Fator (see p.85).

Steve Wynn's most radical innovation was to target the Mirage at pedestrians wandering the Strip in search of things to do. Hence the artificial **volcano** outside, which erupts at hourly intervals, on the hour, after dark.

SECRET GARDEN AND DOLPHIN HABITAT

Mirage, 3400 Las Vegas Blvd S ☎ 702 791 7188, ⓦ www.miragehabitat.com. Daily 10am–7pm. Adults $20, ages 4–12 $15. MAP P.70, POCKET MAP E4

Although a wayward tiger sadly curtailed the performing careers of Siegfried and Roy in 2003, the menagerie of big cats that featured in their magic is still here. Cages in the **Secret Garden and Dolphin Habitat** contain everything from black leopards and golden tigers to their signature white lions and tigers. There are also two pools of bottlenose dolphins, which interact with visitors.

TI (TREASURE ISLAND)

3300 Las Vegas Blvd S ☎ 702 894 7111, ⓦ www.treasureisland.com. MAP P.70, POCKET MAP G3

TI (Treasure Island) was built in 1993 as a sort of kid brother to the Mirage (see p.68) next door, with an all-pervasive pirate theme aimed at family visitors. While it's still

SIRENS OF TI

physically connected to the Mirage by a free **monorail**, it's now under separate ownership, and distances itself from its yo-ho-ho past by using the anodyne acronym TI.

The most obvious feature of Treasure Island remains the two **pirate ships** outside. Originally they were moored in front of a Caribbean village and crewed by battling buccaneers. Architectural theorists tied themselves in knots deciding whether Treasure Island was a building, a performance space or a theme park and now the village has been replaced by a crass Mexican "party restaurant", *Senor Frog's*, while the ships are now (wo)manned by the gyrating **Sirens of TI** (daily: spring & summer 7pm, 8.30pm, 10pm & 11.30pm; autumn & winter 5.30pm, 7pm, 8.30pm & 10pm; free).

Phil Ruffin, former owner of the now-vanished New Frontier, bought TI in 2008, when MGM Resorts ran short of cash to build CityCenter. He's steadily turning it into a blue-collar joint, home to nightspots like *Gilley's Saloon* (see p.81), though he's hung on to Cirque's first-ever Las Vegas show, *Mystère* (see p.84).

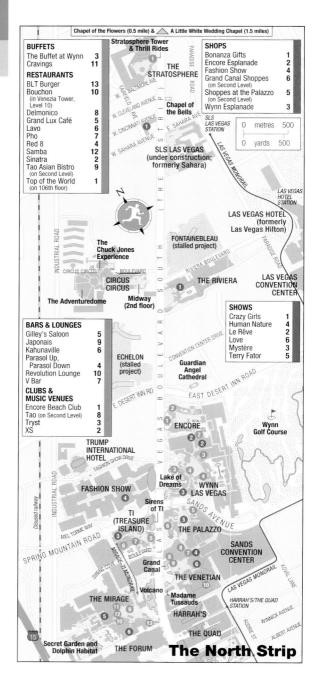

Chapel of the Flowers (0.5 mile) & ⬠ A Little White Wedding Chapel (1.5 miles)

BUFFETS

The Buffet at Wynn	3
Cravings	11

RESTAURANTS

BLT Burger	13
Bouchon (in Venezia Tower, Level 10)	10
Delmonico	8
Grand Lux Café	5
Lavo	6
Pho	7
Red 8	4
Samba	12
Sinatra	2
Tao Asian Bistro (on Second Level)	9
Top of the World (on 106th floor)	1

SHOPS

Bonanza Gifts	1
Encore Esplanade	2
Fashion Show	4
Grand Canal Shoppes (on Second Level)	6
Shoppes at the Palazzo (on Second Level)	5
Wynn Esplanade	3

BARS & LOUNGES

Gilley's Saloon	5
Japonais	9
Kahunaville	6
Parasol Up, Parasol Down	4
Revolution Lounge	10
V Bar	7

CLUBS & MUSIC VENUES

Encore Beach Club	1
Tao (on Second Level)	8
Tryst	3
XS	2

SHOWS

Crazy Girls	1
Human Nature	4
Le Rêve	2
Love	6
Mystère	3
Terry Fator	5

Stratosphere Tower & Thrill Rides

THE STRATOSPHERE

Chapel of the Bells

SLS LAS VEGAS STATION

SLS LAS VEGAS (under construction; formerly Sahara)

LAS VEGAS HOTEL STATION

LAS VEGAS HOTEL (formerly Las Vegas Hilton)

FONTAINEBLEAU (stalled project)

THE RIVIERA

LAS VEGAS CONVENTION CENTER

The Chuck Jones Experience

CIRCUS CIRCUS

Midway (2nd floor)

The Adventuredome

ECHELON (stalled project)

Guardian Angel Cathedral

ENCORE

Wynn Golf Course

TRUMP INTERNATIONAL HOTEL

FASHION SHOW

Lake of Dreams

WYNN LAS VEGAS

TI (TREASURE ISLAND)

Sirens of TI

THE PALAZZO

SANDS CONVENTION CENTER

Grand Canal

THE VENETIAN

Volcano

Madame Tussauds

HARRAH'S

HARRAH'S/THE QUAD STATION

THE MIRAGE

THE QUAD

Secret Garden and Dolphin Habitat

THE FORUM

The North Strip

metres 500

yards 500

THE VENETIAN

3355 Las Vegas Blvd S ☎702 414 1000,
🖲www.venetian.com. MAP P.70, POCKET MAP G4

The hugely successful **Venetian**
casino opened in 1999 on the
site of the much-mourned
Sands, the former Las Vegas
home of Frank Sinatra and the
Rat Pack. Even if its owner,
Sheldon Adelson, may lack the
design flair of Steve Wynn, he
has an unarguable genius for
making money. After buying
the Sands in 1988, he amassed
a billion-dollar fortune from
the annual tech-industry trade
show COMDEX and has more
recently expanded his casino
operations into Macau, as well
as ploughing huge sums into
conservative politics at home.

The Venetian itself is a
re-creation of the ultimate
honeymoon photo album;
Adelson returned from his 1991
honeymoon trip to Venice with
the idea of building a vast replica
of the city. Around a dozen
distinct Venetian landmarks
squeeze side by side into the
casino's Strip facade, while its
main entrance lies between two
columns, modelled on a pair
brought to Venice's Piazza San
Marco from Constantinople in
1172. One is topped by St
Theodore, the city's original
patron, the other by a winged
lion representing St Mark, who
became its patron in 1204.

The interior of the Venetian
holds fewer specific echoes of
the city. While it's the **Grand
Canal** upstairs that draws in
the sightseers, it's the sheer
opulence elsewhere, from the
huge staircases and resplen-
dent frescoes to the endless
hallways of marble tiles, which
makes this the most impressive
public space on the Strip.
It's also among the busiest,
thanks to an excellent crop of
restaurants, shops and theatres,
and the Sands Convention
Center at the back.

When it first opened, the
Venetian out-trumped Bellagio's
Gallery of Fine Art (see p.49) by
opening two separate
Guggenheim art museums. Both
have long since disappeared, but
the exhibition space near the
hotel lobby is still used for
occasional temporary art shows.

THE GRAND CANAL

Venetian, 3355 Las Vegas Blvd S ☎702 414
4300, 🖲www.venetian.com. Gondola rides
indoors Mon–Thurs & Sun 10am–11pm, Fri &
Sat 10am–midnight; outdoors daily 11am–10pm.
$16/person, under-13s $8, $64 for a 2-person
private ride. MAP P.70, POCKET MAP G4 & K5

You can't have Venice without
the **Grand Canal**. The Venetian
has it twice – outdoors beside
the Strip and as the centrepiece
of its shopping and dining mall
upstairs. While neither section
is particularly large, let alone
authentic, you have to admire
the sheer nerve. With its
artificial sky, the indoor
segment is obviously modelled
on the Forum and holds a large
plaza based on St Mark's
Square. Singing gondoliers take
paying customers on short
gondola rides along the canal.

THE GRAND CANAL

MADAME TUSSAUDS

Venetian, 3377 Las Vegas Blvd S ☎866
841 3739, ⓦwww.mtvegas.com. Mon–Thurs
& Sun 10am–9.30pm, Fri & Sat
10am–10.30pm. $26, ages 7–12 $16;
twenty percent discount online. MAP P.70,
POCKET MAP G4

Entered directly from the Strip,
just off the Venetian's attractive
covered Rialto Bridge,
Madame Tussauds taps into
Las Vegas's craving for close
celebrity contact by allowing
visitors to get personal with
waxworks ranging from Brad
Pitt and Daniel Craig to the
bizarre body-painted Blue Men
(even though they're not
actually recognizable as
individuals). With the single
exception of Barack Obama in
the White House, for whom
there's an extra fee, you're free
to take unlimited photos of,
and with, all of your friendly,
new-found waxy friends.

THE PALAZZO

3325 Las Vegas Blvd S ☎702 607 7777,
ⓦwww.palazzo.com. MAP P.70, POCKET MAP H3

Even if owner Sheldon Adelson
insists that his **Palazzo** resort
is entirely separate from the
Venetian next door, no one
takes the distinction seriously;
broad internal walkways enable

visitors to step from one
property to the other and
barely notice the transition.
Counted as a single unit, with
over seven thousand rooms,
this would be the largest hotel
in the world.

Considered on its own, on
the other hand, the Palazzo is
among the least interesting
casinos in Las Vegas. As well as
its own very high-end shopping
mall and a decent crop of
restaurants, it's home to the
Lavo nightclub, but nothing of
any interest for casual
sightseers. Even the giant
butterflies added to jazz up its
central waterfall feature look
more like one of rival Steve
Wynn's cast-off ideas than
anything truly original.

WYNN LAS VEGAS

3131 Las Vegas Blvd S ☎702 770 7000,
ⓦwww.wynnlasvegas.com. MAP P.70,
POCKET MAP J2

Steve Wynn, the man who's
credited with inventing the new
Las Vegas by opening first the
Mirage and then Bellagio,
bounced back from losing
control of the Mirage
organization by building his
own self-named resort, **Wynn
Las Vegas**, in 2005. Like his
great rival at the Venetian-
Palazzo next door, Sheldon
Adelson, Wynn swiftly
complemented Wynn Las Vegas
with Encore, and now runs two
nominally distinct resorts on
the same site.

When Wynn bought this
prime slice of real estate, it
held the fabled *Desert Inn*,
where Howard Hughes lived
out his final years in paranoid
seclusion. Steve Wynn doesn't
do secondhand, though; he
blew the whole place up and
set to work building bigger
and better than ever. The
result, a majestic bronze

crescent soaring skywards alongside the similar Encore, is breathtaking. Rendered almost blind by a degenerative eye disease, Wynn loves to fill his casinos with vibrant, dazzling swathes of colour – hence the plush red carpets that sweep through the interior, leading to a flower-packed **central garden** where the trees are bedecked with fairy lights and lanterns.

Because Steve Wynn wanted every Las Vegas visitor to come and admire Bellagio and the Mirage, he gave them all sorts of crowd-pleasing novelties. Wynn Las Vegas being targeted more exclusively at the luxury end of the market, with an array of consistently high-end restaurants and nightspots, holds fewer specific attractions and is therefore not quite so much of a must-see. Its most unusual feature is the **Lake of Dreams**, an expanse of water illuminated at night with changing projections, and peopled by mysterious mannequins. Unlike the Mirage's volcano, it was deliberately designed to only be visible to visitors from inside the property.

ENCORE

3121 Las Vegas Blvd S ☎ 702 770 8000, ⓦ www.encorelasvegas.com. MAP P.70, POCKET MAP J1

Encore stands in the same relation to Wynn Las Vegas as does the Palazzo to the Venetian. Erected three years after its elder brother, in 2008, and joined to it seamlessly via plush corridors, it's every bit as lavish – this is where Prince Harry was photographed naked in 2012 – but offers little sense of identity in its own right. In a deliberate

piece of provocative one-upmanship, Steve Wynn built it 11ft taller than rival Sheldon Adelson's Palazzo, unveiled earlier the same year. Adelson, it's widely believed, responded by opening a large, downmarket Walgreens pharmacy at the Palazzo's Strip-level corner, thumbing his nose at the pretentious shops preferred by Wynn.

Like all Wynn's properties, Encore is ablaze with colour, like an episode of *Sesame Street* that's brought to you by the colour Red and the insects Butterfly and Dragonfly. Other than the general air of luxury, its main strategy to bring in visitors is via entertainment.

The indoor-outdoor, day-night **Encore Beach Club** (see p.82) has been a huge hit, not least with visiting British royalty, while Steve Wynn pulled off a genuine coup by luring country superstar Garth Brooks out of retirement for a long-term deal. Brooks unexpectedly ended his run in 2012, but more big-name acts are expected to follow in his wake.

ENCORE

GUARDIAN ANGEL CATHEDRAL

GUARDIAN ANGEL CATHEDRAL

302 Cathedral Way ☎ 702 735 5241, ⓦ www
.lasvegas-diocese.org. Masses Sun 8am,
9.30am, 11am, 12.30pm & 5pm. MAP P.70,
POCKET MAP K1

Of all the Strip's eye-catching
architectural wonders, perhaps
the most unexpected stands
just north of Encore – the
Roman Catholic **Guardian
Angel Cathedral**. It was built
in 1963, on land donated by the
former owner of both the
Desert Inn and Stardust
casinos, Moe Dalitz, a Jewish
gangster from Detroit. Seeking
to improve his public image, he
paid modernist architect Paul
Revere Williams to design this
sloping tent-like structure. A
stained-glass window inside
shows the Strip's 1960s skyline.

THE RIVIERA

2901 Las Vegas Blvd S ☎ 702 734-5110,
ⓦ www.rivierahotel.com. MAP P.70,
POCKET MAP L9

One of the great names of Las
Vegas, now fallen on hard
times, the **Riviera** is stranded a
hot, bleak half-mile north of
Encore, with only Circus
Circus across the street for
company. Built in 1955 as the
Strip's first high-rise resort –
with nine storeys, it was also

home to the Strip's first elevator
– its original owners ranged
from mobsters to Marx
Brothers. Liberace was paid an
astonishing $50,000 per week
to open its showroom.

Despite repeated bankruptcies,
the Riviera is gamely soldiering
on. Behind its spectacular
reflective, neon starburst facade,
it still focuses primarily on
entertainment, putting on
tasteless shows like "insane
midget wrestlers" or shock
comedian Andrew Dice Clay.

CIRCUS CIRCUS

2880 Las Vegas Blvd S ☎ 702 734 0410,
ⓦ www.circuscircus.com. MAP P.70,
POCKET MAP K8

Guarded by the giant figure of
Lucky the Clown – if you suffer
from coulrophobia, or fear of
clowns, you won't like Lucky
one bit – the candy-striped big
top of **Circus Circus** has
loomed beside the Strip for half
a century. In recent years,
however, and despite being
owned by MGM Resorts,
Circus Circus has been battered
and isolated by the recession.
Former neighbours including
the New Frontier and the
Sahara have disappeared, while
the fancy new developments
that were supposed to replace
them have failed to materialize.
Pedestrian traffic hereabouts
has dwindled to nothing, to
leave Circus Circus cut off from
the Strip in general, and from
MGM Resorts' other properties
in particular.

Circus Circus has always been
a strange, unsettling hybrid of
circus and casino. It famously
attracted the scorn of Hunter S
Thomson, who wrote in *Fear
and Loathing in Las Vegas* that
"Circus Circus is what the
whole hep world would be
doing on Saturday night if the
Nazis had won the war". When

it opened, in 1968, as Jay Sarno's attempt to repeat his success with Caesars Palace, it didn't include any hotel rooms and charged customers an entry fee. At first it was very much an adult playground, reflecting the sleazier side of carnival attractions. It took a few years to hit on the formula it still follows, of catering largely to families by offering **live circus acts** and other child-oriented attractions. Coupled with its low room rates, the result has been that Circus Circus has become the tackiest of the major Strip casinos.

Circus Circus is so huge that it's the only Strip casino to have an internal **monorail system**, to take guests to their rooms. With its low ceilings and endless corridors, lined with fast-food outlets and novelty stores, it's quite a maze, and it can be hard to find the mezzanine area that's home to the **Midway**. The circular stage here plays host to a constant succession of free circus acts, from trapeze artists and jugglers to tightrope walkers and, yes, clowns. Old-fashioned sideshows offer kids the chance to kick-start a lifetime's gambling habit by winning stuffed toys.

THE ADVENTUREDOME

Circus Circus, 2880 Las Vegas Blvd S
📞 702 734 0410, 🌐 www.adventuredome
.com. Daily 10am–midnight during school
holidays, otherwise Mon–Thurs 11am–6pm,
Fri & Sat 10am–midnight, Sun 10am–9pm.
$5–8 individual attractions, $28 all-day
wristband, children under 4ft $17. MAP P.70,
POCKET MAP J8

Las Vegas's largest theme park, the **Adventuredome**, is housed in a giant pink enclosure at the back of Circus Circus, a long walk from the Strip. Entirely indoors and on a much smaller scale than say Disney World or Universal Studios, it's aimed very much at children. Adults may well enjoy the twisting, looping **Canyon Blaster** roller coaster or getting soaked in the **Rim Runner** water slide, but most of the space is given over to SpongeBob Squarepants simulator rides and the like.

THE CHUCK JONES EXPERIENCE

Circus Circus, 2880 Las Vegas Blvd S 📞 702
224 2580, 🌐 www.chuckjonesexperience.com.
Daily 10am–10pm. $20, ages 5–17 $15.
MAP P.70, POCKET MAP K8

A loving tribute to one of Hollywood's greatest animators, the **Chuck Jones Experience** occupies a substantial gallery space near the back of Circus Circus. Despite video clips and giant cut-outs of Jones's creations, such as Bugs Bunny and Daffy Duck, and the opportunity to draw your own cartoons, it's most likely to appeal to Chuck's adult fans. Fascinating displays detail the ground rules for the eternal rivalry between Wile E. Coyote and the Roadrunner, and illuminate Jones's creative influences, like Charlie Chaplin and Mark Twain.

THE ADVENTUREDOME

THE STRATOSPHERE

2000 Las Vegas Blvd S ☎702 380 7777,
🌐www.stratospherehotel.com. Tower
Mon–Thurs & Sun 10am–1am, Fri & Sat
10am–2am. $18, discounts for guests.
MAP P.70, POCKET MAP L2

The 1149ft **Stratosphere** makes
a conveniently colossal
landmark to denote the
northern limit of the Strip,
even if strictly speaking it's
located in the city proper, a full
mile north of Circus Circus, its
nearest active neighbour. It
took quite a feat of engineering
to build the tallest structure
west of the Mississippi in the
shifting sands of Nevada;
amazingly, its foundations are
only 12ft deep.

Served by Deuce buses, but
not the city's Monorail system,
the Stratosphere holds nothing
for sightseers apart from the
Stratosphere Tower itself. Two
observation decks, one
outdoors at the very summit
and the other indoors on the
floor below, offer fabulous
views over the city and hold
fascinating displays explaining
everything you can see. Most
visitors are up here strictly for
kicks, however, to dice with
death on the array of **Thrill
Rides** at the very top.

STRATOSPHERE THRILL RIDES

STRATOSPHERE THRILL RIDES

Stratosphere, 2000 Las Vegas Blvd S ☎702
380 7711, 🌐www.stratospherehotel.com.
Mon–Thurs & Sun 11am–1am, Fri & Sat
11am–2am. X-Scream, Big Shot & Insanity $15
each; combination tickets up to $34 for an
all-day unlimited package. SkyJump $110,
minimum age 14. MAP P.70, POCKET MAP L2

The top of the Stratosphere
serves as the launching point for
several terrifying **thrill rides**,
for daredevils only. **X-Scream** is
a sort of giant boat that tips
upside down a thousand feet
above the Strip, while **Insanity**
is a crane that spins riders out
over the abyss, and **Big Shot** is a
glorified sofa that free falls a
couple of hundred feet. Worst of
all is the **SkyJump**, in which
harnessed jumpers step off a
platform to fall 855ft.

The end of the Sahara

A Strip fixture since 1952 and home to Elvis Presley and the Beatles in
the 1960s, the veteran **Sahara** finally closed its doors in 2011. Back in
the day, Las Vegas casinos loved to play up their desert setting with
Arabian Nights touches like domed minarets and comedy camels, but the
Sahara had come to seem very dated and an attempt to reinvent itself as
"the Las Vegas home of NASCAR racing" came to naught.

The Sahara has not actually been demolished, though. When this book
went to press, it was scheduled to reopen in due course as a 1600-room
"boutique resort", **SLS Las Vegas**. As well as hotels in Beverley Hills and
South Beach, the SLS brand is also used for clubs and restaurants in other
American cities, so the new resort is likely to be an entertainment-based
property pitched a rung or two below the Strip's top tier. Architectural
mock-ups show the revamped building looking like a dull suburban mall.

Shops

BONANZA GIFTS

2440 Las Vegas Blvd S ☎ 702 385 7359,
Ⓦ www.worldslargestgiftshop.com. Daily
8am–midnight. MAP P.70, POCKET MAP L3

The self-proclaimed "World's
Largest Gift Shop", where
Sahara Avenue meets the
Strip, is *the* place to buy Las
Vegas souvenirs. Trinkets
celebrating the city, old and
new, include countless
variations on the iconic
"Welcome to Fabulous Las
Vegas" sign and memorabilia
from individual casinos, such
as packs of used playing cards.

FASHION SHOW

3200 Las Vegas Blvd S ☎ 702 369 8362,
Ⓦ www.thefashionshow.com. Mon–Sat
10am–9pm, Sun 11am–7pm. MAP P.70,
POCKET MAP G2

The only stand-alone shopping
mall on the Strip, and for most
Las Vegas visitors the only
serious rival to in-casino malls
such as the Forum, the Fashion
Show is spread across two
two-storey buildings across from
Wynn Las Vegas. Despite the
eye-catching circular sculpture
that dangles over the pavement,

it's in no sense an attraction,
simply a functional shopping
destination. Unlike its Strip
rivals, it's large enough to hold
department stores including
Macy's, Sak's Fifth Avenue,
Nordstrom and Dillard's, as well
as an Apple Store and the usual
clothing chains.

GRAND CANAL SHOPPES

Second Level, Venetian, 3355 Las Vegas
Blvd S ☎ 702 414 4500, Ⓦ ww
w.thegrandcanalshoppes.com. Mon–Thurs &
Sun 10am–11pm, Fri & Sat 10am–midnight.
MAP P.70, POCKET MAP K5

Arrayed along the waterfront
upstairs in the Venetian, the
Grand Canal Shoppes may
surpass Caesars' Forum for
sheer chutzpah, but as a
shopping destination the mall
is not a serious match. It does
hold a handful of clothing
chains, such as Kenneth Cole,
but consists largely of souvenir
and impulse-purchase stores,
with a big emphasis on showy
jewellery. After all, this was
where Michael Jackson went on
the celebrated million-dollar
shopping spree that's recorded
in Martin Bashir's 2003 TV
documentary about the star.

SHOPPES AT THE PALAZZO

Second Level, Palazzo, 3325 Las Vegas Blvd
S ☎ 702 414 4525, Ⓦ www.theshoppes
atthepalazzo.com. Mon–Thurs & Sun
10am–11pm, Fri & Sat 10am–midnight.
MAP P.70, POCKET MAP K5

More in keeping with the smart
stores of Wynn Las Vegas next
door than the gimmicky tone of
the nearby Grand Canal, the
Shoppes at the Palazzo are
scattered around the resort's
second floor. Few casual visitors
pass this way, so the atmosphere
tends to be hushed. Exclusive
fashion boutiques include Jimmy
Choo and Diane von Fursten-
berg, and there are also several
expensive jewellery outlets.

FASHION SHOW

WYNN ESPLANADE

WYNN AND ENCORE ESPLANADES

Wynn Las Vegas, 3131 Las Vegas Blvd S
☎ 702 770 7000, ⓦ www.wynnlasvegas.com.
Mon–Thurs 10am–11pm, Fri & Sat 10am–
midnight. MAP P.70, POCKET MAP H2 & J1

There's a separate Esplanade of shops in both Wynn Las Vegas and Encore, though they're all but identical in their opulent looks and high-end prices. For ordinary mortals, fashion boutiques like Alexander McQueen and Manolo Blahnik, and the Penske-Wynn Ferrari- and Maserati-only car dealership, make for great window shopping.

Buffets

THE BUFFET AT WYNN

Wynn Las Vegas, 3131 Las Vegas Blvd S
☎ 702 770 7000, ⓦ www.wynnlasvegas.com.
Breakfast Mon–Fri 8am–11pm $20; brunch
Sat & Sun 8am–3.30pm $32; lunch Mon–Fri
11am–3.30pm $23; dinner Mon–Thurs & Sun
3.30–10pm $37, Fri & Sat 3.30–10.30pm $40.
MAP P.70, POCKET MAP J2

Buffets are always a high priority for Steve Wynn and at Wynn Las Vegas he's got the best buffet in town. In a plush room that oozes belle époque excess, this is buffet food at its finest, with

dishes from lamb osso bucco and smoked duck salad to scallop ceviche and sushi rolls. While serious foodies will always prefer a real restaurant, if you've got a large appetite or are in a group with varying tastes, you won't be disappointed.

CRAVINGS

Mirage, 3400 Las Vegas Blvd S ☎ 702 792
7777, ⓦ www.mirage.com. Breakfast Mon–Fri
8–11am $16; brunch Mon–Fri 11am–3pm $19,
Sat & Sun 8am–3pm $25; dinner daily
3–10pm $27. MAP P.70, POCKET MAP F4

With its contemporary design aesthetic – rare indeed for a Las Vegas buffet, and resembling some futuristic space-age diner – *Cravings* is on a smaller scale than most of its rivals. Where possible, dishes such as stir-fries or omelettes are cooked to order; others are beautifully presented on gleaming platters. This is still mass catering – but it's a good option for a quick meal.

Restaurants

BLT BURGER

Mirage, 3400 Las Vegas Blvd S ☎ 702 792
7888, ⓦ www.mirage.com. Mon–Thurs & Sun
11am–2am, Fri & Sat 11am–4am. MAP P.70,
POCKET MAP F5

So-called "gourmet burger" joints are all the rage in Las Vegas. Lively long after midnight, this one, in a former tiger pen near the front of the Mirage, serves a delicious *wagyu* beef burger for $17 or a "classic" for $12, along with variations like a zesty $13 lamb tandoori burger.

BOUCHON

Level 10, Venezia Tower, Venetian, 3355
Las Vegas Blvd S ☎ 702 414 6200, ⓦ www
.bouchonbistro.com. Mon–Fri 7am–1pm &
5–10pm, Sat & Sun 8am–2pm & 5–10pm. MAP
P.70, POCKET MAP H4

Thomas Keller's scrupulous evocation of a French bistro,

hidden away on the tenth floor of the Venetian's Venezia tower, may not have novelty value, but it's a lovely, relaxed spot, with plentiful outdoor seating and food that's nothing short of *magnifique*. Brunch is the best value, with sandwiches or quiche for under $20; dinner mains like *steak frites* or *sole marinière* cost $37.

BOUCHON

DELMONICO

Casino Level, Venetian, 3355 Las Vegas Blvd S ☎702 414 3737, ⓦwww.venetian.com. Mon–Thurs 11.30am–1.45pm & 5–10pm, Fri & Sat 11.30am–1.45pm & 5–10.30pm, Sun 5–10pm. MAP P.70, POCKET MAP H3

Renowned for bringing New Orleans food to the nation, chef Emeril Lagasse has made the Venetian the setting for a sophisticated steakhouse with a strong contemporary flavour. While the lunch menu centres on salads ($10) and sandwiches ($17), the big guns come out in the evening, with giant juicy steaks ($50) and starters like barbecue shrimp ($18).

GRAND LUX CAFE

Casino Level, Palazzo, 3325 Las Vegas Blvd S ☎702 733 7411, ⓦwww.grandluxcafe.com. Mon–Thurs & Sun 6am–2am, Fri & Sat 6am–3am. MAP P.70, POCKET MAP H3

Although it's owned by the Cheesecake Factory chain, and has itself gone national, the *Grand Lux Cafe* was originally created as a casual, but nonetheless classy, 24-hour coffee shop for the Venetian, and swiftly added this slightly smarter branch in the Palazzo. Both offer wide-ranging menus of fresh, well-prepared favourites from around the world at good prices – pizza and salad costs $12, Jamaican pork tenderloin or Yankee pot roast $19 – and have their own on-site bakeries.

LAVO

Casino Level, Palazzo, 3325 Las Vegas Blvd S ☎702 791 1800, ⓦwww.lavolv.com. Mon–Thurs & Sun 5pm–midnight, Fri 5pm–1am, Sat 6.30pm–1am. MAP P.70, POCKET MAP H3

Considering it's attached to the exclusive *Lavo* nightclub, this is an oddly traditional Italian restaurant, dark and romantic rather than loud or brash. The food too is rich and authentic, and the prices relatively restrained, with pizzas for $20, pasta specials a little more and Mediterranean classics like veal *parmigiano* for $30.

PHO

TI, 3300 Las Vegas Blvd S ☎702 894 7111, ⓦwww.treasureisland.com. Mon–Thurs & Sun 11am–11.30pm, Fri & Sat 11am–2.30am. MAP P.70, POCKET MAP G3

You could easily fail to notice that half the time, half of TI's 24-hour *Coffee Shop* is given over to this inexpensive and excellent Vietnamese diner. The *phô* of the name is steaming noodle soup; prices start at $12 and increase depending on the of meat or fish you add. They also serve spring rolls and dry noodle dishes, and sneak in some sushi options and Chinese favourites too.

RED 8

Wynn Las Vegas, 3131 Las Vegas Blvd S ☎702 770 7000, ⓦwww.wynnlasvegas.com. Mon–Thurs & Sun 11.30am–midnight, Fri & Sat 11.30am–1am. MAP P.70, POCKET MAP J2

This decadent, deep-red, pan-Asian restaurant makes a stylish retreat from Wynn's adjoining casino floor and serves a full menu of Chinese classics, from dim sum dumplings at $10 to chow mein or *ho fun* noodles for around $20, as well as Thai fish cakes and Malysian satay and laksa.

SAMBA

Mirage, 3400 Las Vegas Blvd S ☎866 339 4566, ⓦwww.mirage.com. Daily 5–10.30pm. MAP P.70, POCKET MAP F4

With its bright playful decor and billowing couches, open to the main walkway through the Mirage, you can't but be drawn towards this enticing, high-quality Brazilian steakhouse. Hefty meat dishes typically cost around $30, with starters like ceviche or coconut prawns more like $10, while $40 buys an all-you-can-eat feast of barbecued meats, from sirloin to turkey, plus black beans and rice.

SAMBA

SINATRA

Encore, 3121 Las Vegas Blvd S ☎702 770 3463, ⓦwww.wynnlasvegas.com. Mon–Thurs & Sun 5.30–10pm, Fri & Sat 5.30–10.30pm. MAP P.70, POCKET MAP J1

The Sinatra name, licensed by Frank's family, is of course a gimmick, but it tells you what to expect – the kind of idealized Italian restaurant the Rat Pack might have frequented back in the 1960s, formal and romantic and not in the slightest bit calorie-conscious. Ol' Blue Eyes is everywhere from the speakers to the menu, with his favourite spaghetti and clams for $29 and Ossobuco "My Way" for $48.

TAO ASIAN BISTRO

Second Level, Venetian, 3355 Las Vegas Blvd S ☎702 388 8338, ⓦwww.taorestaurantlv.com. Mon–Thurs & Sun 5pm–midnight, Fri & Sat 5pm–1am. MAP P.70, POCKET MAP J5

By far the busiest and most profitable restaurant in the entire USA, *Tao* is a place to come for the experience – the over-the-top opium-den decor, the giant Buddha statue, the crowds of dressed-up clubbers getting ready to party in the *Tao* nightclub next door – as much as the showy Asian food. Calm down a moment, though, and you can enjoy a good meal – pork or duck with sizzling fried rice costs $15, and steak or sea bass is around $35.

TOP OF THE WORLD

Stratosphere, 2000 Las Vegas Blvd S ☎702 380 7711, ⓦwww.topoftheworldlv.com. Lunch and dinner Mon–Thurs & Sun 11am–10.30pm, Fri & Sat 11am–11pm. MAP P.70, POCKET MAP L2

While it's a lot classier than the hotel-casino far below, this restaurant only stands out from the pack for the compelling reason that it's over 800ft up in the air, and revolves every 80 minutes to give magnificent views over the Strip. Lunchtime is the cheapest time to come, for

a $15 or $30 steak, but dinner is much more romantic, even if the cheapest main is $40.

WAZUZU

Encore, 3121 Las Vegas Blvd S ☎702 770 3463, ⓦwww.wynnlasvegas.com. Mon–Thurs & Sun 11.30am–10.30pm, Fri & Sat 11.30am–1am. MAP P.70, POCKET MAP J1

Approached by an avenue of six colossal gilt pears, and featuring a colossal crystal dragon squirming along its back wall, *Wazuzu* is by far the best-looking restaurant in Encore, and it serves the best food too. As well as sushi, it draws on Asian cuisines from Korea (short ribs $25) and Mongolia (wok-tossed-beef $21) to Thailand (chicken basil stir-fry $17). Be sure to try the *sake* too.

Bars and lounges

GILLEY'S SALOON

TI, 3300 Las Vegas Blvd S ☎702 894 7111, ⓦwww.gilleyslasvegas.com. Mon–Thurs & Sun 11am–2am, Fri & Sat 11am–4am. $10 cover for live bands. MAP P.70, POCKET MAP G3

This raucous, no-nonsense country and rodeo saloon practically defines the new TI. Bikini-clad "Gilley Girls" ride the mechanical bulls, and you can join a free line-dancing lesson most nights at 7pm, drink two-for-one rum cocktails until 10pm, or dance to honky-tonk bands until long after midnight.

JAPONAIS

Mirage, 3400 Las Vegas Blvd S ☎702 792 7970, ⓦwww.japonaislasvegas.com. Mon–Thurs & Sun 2pm–midnight, Fri & Sat 2pm–2am. MAP P.70, POCKET MAP F4

While the dining room at *Japonais*, at the heart of the Mirage, serves everything from steak to sushi, the separate lounge and bar area is a stunning, glamorous spot for pre- or after-show drinks, swathed in flowing, spotlit fabrics and offering surprisingly intimate seating areas.

KAHUNAVILLE

TI, 3300 Las Vegas Blvd S ☎702 894 7390, ⓦwww.kahunaville.com. Mon–Thurs & Sun 11am–2am, Fri & Sat 11am–3am. $10 cover for live bands. MAP P.70, POCKET MAP G3

Tiki-tinged and loud in looks and decibels alike, *Kahunaville* is not exactly the place for a contemplative drink. If you're looking for Las Vegas at its liveliest, however, why not kick things off with one of its super-sized frozen margaritas or "Big Kahuna" flavoured rums?

PARASOL UP, PARASOL DOWN

Wynn Las Vegas, 3131 Las Vegas Blvd S ☎702 770 7000. Mon–Thurs & Sun 11am–4am, Fri & Sat 11am–5am. MAP P.70, POCKET MAP J2

A quintessential example of the Wynn way with design, these twin upstairs-downstairs bars, festooned with richly coloured umbrellas and filling Wynn's central stairway, are the perfect place to admire the Lake of Dreams. A cocktail or two, and you'll feel right at Las Vegas's absurd and exhilarating heart.

REVOLUTION LOUNGE

Mirage, 3400 Las Vegas Blvd S ☎702 693 8300, ⓦwww.mirage.com. Bar daily noon–4am, free; lounge Thurs–Sun 10pm–4am, cover varies. MAP P.70, POCKET MAP F4

Indulge your inner Austin Powers with a psychedelic Sixties moment in this upbeat, flamboyant bar-lounge combo. Supposedly a joint venture between the Cirque du Soleil and the Beatles, it's split between the free-access *Abbey Road Bar*, where the wall consists of huge letters that spell out LOVE, and the *Revolution Lounge* itself, which puts on live band showcases and DJ sets that usually kick off with the Fab Four themselves.

V BAR

Casino Level, Venetian, 3355 Las Vegas Blvd S ☎702 740 6433. Mon–Wed & Sun 5pm–2am, Thurs & Sat 5pm–3am. Cover from $10 after 10pm. MAP P.70, POCKET MAP H4

Sophisticated lighting and decor turns this simple rectangular room near the back of the Venetian into one of the city's most elegant and sophisticated bars, filled with beautiful people both early and late, and specializing in a selection of smoky martinis and delicious rum cocktails.

Clubs and music venues

ENCORE BEACH CLUB

Encore, 3121 Las Vegas Blvd S ☎702 521 4005, ⓦwww.encorebeachclub.com. Late April to Oct Fri noon–7pm, Sat & Sun 11am–7pm. Cover $20–60. MAP P.70, POCKET MAP J1

This luxurious multilevel complex of pools, patios, bars and private bungalows, in front of Encore but thoroughly screened from the Strip, is the definitive expression of Las Vegas's craze for DJ-fuelled daytime poolside parties. Thanks to the worldwide publicity it received as the scene of Prince Harry's 2012 antics, it's now even more packed than ever. You can escape the crowds either on pristine white "lily pads" out in the water or in your own cabana, but the pounding music will follow you everywhere. Expect ultra-high prices for drinks, let alone table service.

REVOLUTION LOUNGE

TAO

Second Level, Venetian, 3355 Las Vegas Blvd S ☎702 388 8588, ⓦwww.tao lasvegas.com. Nightclub Thurs–Sat 10pm–5am; Tao Beach Mon–Thurs 10am–sunset, Fri–Sun 10am–5am. Cover Thurs & Fri $20, Sat $40; weekend wristband $100. MAP P.70, POCKET MAP J5

An immediate hit in 2005 and still very much the place to be seen, this dynamic high-concept Asian-style nightclub inevitably attracts larger crowds than its small dance floor can handle. Even on the guest list you'll have to wait to get in and you'll pay heavily for any private space. The open-air *Tao Beach* pool club is a great place to gear up for the evening. Weekend wristbands also give admission to the same owners' *Lavo* club in the adjacent Palazzo.

TRYST

Wynn Las Vegas, 3131 Las Vegas Blvd S ☎702 770 3375, ⓦwww.trystlasvegas.com. Thurs–Sun 10pm–4am. Cover varies. MAP P.70, POCKET MAP H2

Very much in keeping with Wynn's overall decor, with its plush red sofas and drapery, the lounge areas of *Tryst* look more like an old-fashioned gentlemen's club than a twenty-first-century Las Vegas nightspot. Though it's on the small side compared with its mega-rivals and tends to attract an older, more well-heeled crowd, it also boasts a great indoor-outdoor dance floor, with an open-air terrace that faces a spectacular illuminated waterfall.

XS

Encore, 3121 Las Vegas Blvd S ☎702 521 4005, ⓦwww.xslasvegas.com. Fri–Sun 10pm–4am. Cover $20–30, men $50 Sat. MAP P.70, POCKET MAP J1

Where do Encore's beautiful people go after a hard day at the *Beach Club*? To the even more decadent *XS* nightclub, of course, to stay in the tropical mood, throw some moves on the massive dance floor, drink some very classy cocktails and cool off in yet more pools.

Shows

CRAZY GIRLS

Riviera, 2901 Las Vegas Blvd S ☎702 794 9433, ⓦwww.rivierahotel.com. Mon & Wed–Sun 9.30pm, $45 & $60. No under-21s. MAP P.70, POCKET MAP L9

The crowd at the Strip's best-known "adult revue" consists largely of excitable frat boys and middle-aged couples, crammed in at little tables and emitting the occasional squeal when the dancers come too close. Urged on by a lacklustre comedienne, eight world-weary and none-too-crazy showgirls, not only topless but also sexless for good measure, dance their way through a set of hackneyed chestnuts.

HUMAN NATURE

Venetian, 3355 Las Vegas Blvd S ☎ 702 414 1000, ⓦ www.humannaturelive.com. Mon & Thurs–Sun 7pm. $73–117. MAP P.70, POCKET MAP H4

Having enjoyed huge success with their own material back home, this wholesome Australian vocal quartet moved to Las Vegas, where their show has proved enough of a smash to transfer from the Imperial Palace to the Venetian in 2013. Their unlikely Stateside mission, to add a down-under twist to the Motown sound, enjoys the personal blessing of Smokey Robinson himself. And no wonder – with their fabulous voices and very likeable energy, they really are superb. A smokin' live band plays the music, and the boys simply soar.

LE RÊVE

Wynn Las Vegas, 3131 Las Vegas Blvd S ☎ 702 770 9966, ⓦ www.wynnlasvegas.com. Mon, Tues & Fri–Sun 7pm & 9.30pm. $105–195. MAP P.70, POCKET MAP J2

Le Rêve – "The Dream" – is also the title of Steve Wynn's favourite personal Picasso and was the working name of his casino too. For the show itself, Wynn dreamed of hiring former Cirque du Soleil talent

to out-Cirque Cirque with an even more unbelievable extravaganza of colour and spectacle, featuring more water than *O* and wilder costumes than *Mystère*. In terms of sheer looks it succeeds, with astonishing coups de théâtre that have the audience gasping; you'll need to overlook the vacuity of the plot, though, in which the endlessly bemused protagonist dreams of finding "the answer to life". Note that the cheapest seats are in the aptly named front-row "Splash Zone".

LOVE

Mirage, 3400 Las Vegas Blvd S ☎ 702 792 7777, ⓦ www.cirquedusoleil.com. Mon & Thurs–Sun 7pm & 9.30pm. $79–180. MAP P.70, POCKET MAP F5

A genuinely triumphant collaboration between Cirque du Soleil and the Beatles, in which Cirque perform superbly choreographed dancing and acrobatics to a crystal-sharp Beatles soundtrack, *Love* is much, much more than just another "jukebox musical". There's no story and no attempt to depict the Beatles as actual people – though eerily we hear their voices in retrieved studio chatter – just a dazzling celebration of their music and the times and places that made them who they were.

MYSTÈRE

TI, 3300 Las Vegas Blvd S ☎ 702 894 7722, ⓦ www.cirquedusoleil.com. Mon–Wed, Sat & Sun 7pm & 9.30pm. $69–119. MAP P.70, POCKET MAP G3

Twenty years since it first opened at Treasure Island, Las Vegas's original Cirque du Soleil show is still arguably the best – you can see why it changed the Strip's entertainment scene forever, overnight.

LOVE

TERRY FATOR

Mystère is pure spectacle, from its gorgeous costumes and billows of cascading silk to its jaw-dropping circus skills and phenomenal feats of strength.

TERRY FATOR

Mirage, 3400 Las Vegas Blvd S ☎ 702 792 7777. Ⓦ www.mirage.com. Tues–Sat 7.30pm. $66–143. MAP P.70, POCKET MAP F4

Yes, this middle-American ventriloquist swaps corny jokes with soft-toy puppets, but he also has an extraordinary talent: an astonishing five-octave singing voice that delivers perfect impressions of artists from Ozzy Osbourne to Etta James – all without moving his lips. Despite winning *America's Got Talent* in 2007 he is still likeable and down-to-earth.

Wedding chapels

CHAPEL OF THE BELLS

2233 Las Vegas Blvd S ☎ 702 735 6803, Ⓦ www.chapelofthebellslasvegas.com. Mon–Thurs & Sun 9am–10pm, Fri & Sat 9am–1am. MAP P.70, POCKET MAP L3

Crammed up against the singularly unprepossessing *Fun City Motel*, just north of Sahara Avenue, this little chapel conceals a romantic heart beneath its garish exterior. Draped in white silk, with the sun streaming in, it's really quite attractive – and if it was good enough for Pele, it's good enough for you. Non-denominational weddings start at $145; pay $255 or more and you get free transport to and from your hotel plus a DVD of the service.

CHAPEL OF THE FLOWERS

1717 Las Vegas Blvd S ☎ 702 735 4331, Ⓦ www.littlechapel.com. Mon–Thurs 9am–8pm, Fri & Sat 9am–10pm. MAP P.70, POCKET MAP M1

With three separate chapels opening onto the same garden and couples queuing to take snaps at the waterfall, things can get a bit hectic at peak times, but in principle it's all surprisingly tasteful. Most popular is the Victorian chapel, with its marble floors and mahogany pews. Packages, categorized as Intimate, Elegant or Legendary, range from $195 to $15,000.

A LITTLE WHITE WEDDING CHAPEL

1301 Las Vegas Blvd S ☎ 702 382 5943, Ⓦ www.alittlewhitechapel.com. Daily 8am–midnight. MAP P.70, POCKET MAP F14

The definitive only-in-Vegas wedding chapel, as used by Joan Collins and Michael Jordan, not to mention Britney, has grown and grown to include five separate chapels. Four resemble reasonably pleasant areas in, say, a chain hotel; the fifth, the notorious "Tunnel of Love", is basically the former driveway, roofed over with angels painted on the ceiling, and hosts drive-through weddings from as little as $40 (bring your own car).

Downtown Las Vegas

Amounting, as far as visitors are concerned, to little more than three or four blocks, downtown is where Las Vegas started out when the railroad arrived in 1905 and also held its first casinos back in the 1930s. Many visitors prefer downtown to the Strip, feeling that by offering serious gambling, plus cheap bars, restaurants and buffets, its no-nonsense casinos represent the "real" Las Vegas. With its old-style neon signs and garish arrays of multicoloured light bulbs, it also looks much more like the Las Vegas of popular imagination than the high-tech Strip, while in the artificial sky of the Fremont Street Experience canopy it boasts a genuine must-see attraction. What's more, thanks to revitalization efforts like the opening of the intriguing Mob Museum, the highbrow Smith Center arts centre and the world's largest gay nightclub, Krave Massive, downtown finally appears to be thriving again.

FREMONT STREET EXPERIENCE

Fremont St, between Main and Fourth sts
☎ 702 678 5777, ⓦ www.vegasexperience
.com. Nightly, on the hour from sunset until
1am. Free. MAP P.87, POCKET MAP G12

Wanting to give downtown a large-scale spectacle to match the Strip and make visitors feel safer outdoors at night, the downtown casinos came up with an amazing rebranding scheme – they put a roof over four city blocks and renamed downtown the **Fremont Street Experience**. After dark, the sky itself seems to become a giant movie screen – a dazzling light show of monsters and mayhem. Live bands pump out rock classics on stages set up at the main intersections – typically tribute acts to the likes of Bon Jovi or the Doors – and downtown parties until long after midnight.

FREMONT STREET EXPERIENCE

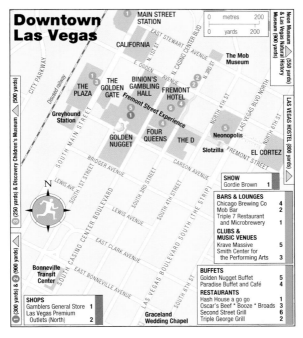

SLOTZILLA

Fremont St. Hours vary. Lower line $20, upper line $30, one ride on each $40. Maximum and minimum weight restrictions apply. MAP P.87, POCKET MAP G12

Unveiled in 2013, **Slotzilla** is an extraordinary two-tier zipline that centres on the world's biggest slot machine, which the 120ft-tall Slotzilla itself, which ejects four riders at a time on each level. Riders on the lower level have seats; those on the upper level hang prone, enabling them to fly like Superman and pass through the canopy of the Fremont Street Experience.

THE PLAZA

1 Main St ☎702 386 2110, ✆www.plazahotel casino.com. MAP P.87, POCKET MAP F11

Once Las Vegas's railroad station, the huge **Plaza** casino looked set to shut shop in 2010. Surprisingly, it reopened within

a year following a $35 million face-lift. Its owners cannily bought up the furnishings of and the abandoned Fontaine-bleu, the re-vamped Plaza now holds some of downtown's best bars and restaurants, including former mayor Oscar Goodman's glass-domed steakhouse (see p.92).

THE GOLDEN GATE

1 Fremont St ☎702 385 1906, ✆www .goldengatecasino.com. MAP P.87, POCKET MAP G11

Having opened in 1906, the **Golden Gate** is only a year younger than the city itself. A railroad hotel before becoming a casino, it still has only a hundred rooms and remains an appealing historic anomaly. Recent modernizations have stripped away some of its charms, however, including the 99¢ shrimp cocktail bar; they're now $2.99 from the 24-hour bakery.

GOLDEN NUGGET

129 E Fremont St ☎ 702 385 7111, ⓦ www
.goldennugget.com/lasvegas. MAP P.87,
POCKET MAP G12

Downtown's largest and
highest-profile casino, the
Golden Nugget has more in
common with the Strip than its
neighbours. Built in 1946, it's
among the city's oldest casinos,
but its current incarnation owes
more to the 1970s, when it was
acquired by a young man who
was to become the leading
entrepreneur of modern Las
Vegas: Steve Wynn. Downtown
has traditionally been
characterized by hard-bitten,
"sawdust joints"; Wynn gave the
Golden Nugget the bright,
glittery feel it retains to this day.

The most visible result of
remodelling by its latest owners
is the open-air swimming pool
at its heart; guests who plummet
down its towering waterslide
pass in a clear tube through a
shark-filled aquarium.
Most recently, the casino
opened up its Fremont Street
facade, adding *Bar 46* to create a
prime vantage point for the light
show on Fremont Street. The
casino holds little for sightseers
other than an actual golden
nugget; the 62-pound,
million-dollar Hand of Faith
was found in Australia in 1980.

BINION'S GAMBLING HALL

128 E Fremont St ☎ 702 382 1600, ⓦ www
.binions.com. MAP P.87, POCKET MAP G12

If you think owning a casino is a
sure-fire way to make money,
Binion's Gambling Hall offers a
salutary lesson. When its
original owner, Benny Binion,
died in 1989, this was, as
Binion's Horseshoe, Las Vegas's
most profitable casino. His heirs
ran the place so badly that it lost
its rooms and even its name.
Caesars Entertainment briefly
bought it to acquire the
Horseshoe name and the World
Series of Poker, but sold it on.

Binion's today is in a sorry
state, with big empty spaces
devoid even of slot machines. Its
one gimmick is that visitors can
pose for free photos with a
million dollars in cash; it takes
half an hour to get your print.

FOUR QUEENS

202 E Fremont St ☎ 702 385 4011, ⓦ www
.fourqueens.com. MAP P.87, POCKET MAP G12

Opened in 1966 and named for
its owner's four daughters, the
Four Queens fills a whole block
of Fremont Street. Its basic role
is to soak up any spillover from
the Golden Nugget; it holds
little apart from a decent pub,
the *Chicago Brewing Company*
and the *Canyon Club*
showroom/nightclub.

FREMONT HOTEL

200 E Fremont St ☎ 702 385 3232, ⓦ www .fremontcasino.com. MAP P.87, POCKET MAP G12

Ranking a distant second behind the Golden Nugget in terms of glitz and glamour, but still ahead of its other downtown neighbours, the **Fremont Hotel** is a smart but otherwise unremarkable casino. Back in 1956 this was Nevada's tallest building; now it's noteworthy as the home of above-par restaurants, and little else.

THE D

301 E Fremont St ☎ 702 388 2400, ⓦ www .thed.com. MAP P.87, POCKET MAP G12

A rare example of a casino completely changing both its image and its name, **The D** was until a couple of years ago a fake-Irish joint called Fitz-geralds, guarded by Mr O'Lucky the leprechaun. The "D" stands for downtown and Detroit, hometown of owner, Derek Stevens. He's taken advantage of the most unusual feature (that the casino boasts two storeys) to give each a different character – contemporary at street level, where go-go dancers gyrate in the "party pit", and vintage upstairs. Entertainment includes a Prince tribute show and murder-mystery dinner theatre.

EL CORTEZ

600 E Fremont St ☎ 702 385 5200, ⓦ www .ecvegas.com. MAP P.87, POCKET MAP H12

Long celebrated as downtown's most cheerfully downmarket casino, the seventy-year-old **El Cortez** is looking remarkably spruce thanks to a freshly remodelled facade. For a taste of days gone by and a possible glimpse of its nonagenarian former owner, Jackie Gaughan, who lives on site, it's worth braving the slightly intim-idating five-minute walk east of the Fremont Street Experience.

EL CORTEZ

MAIN STREET STATION

200 N Main St ☎ 702 387 1896, ⓦ www .mainstreetcasino.com. MAP P.87, POCKET MAP G11

At just twenty years old, **Main Street Station**, just north of the Plaza, is downtown's youngest casino. Despite its antique-filled Victoriana theme, it's also among the lightest and brightest casinos. While it doesn't belong to the Station chain ubiquitous elsewhere in the city, it offers a similar range of restaurants and bars.

THE NEON MUSEUM

770 Las Vegas Blvd N ☎ 702 387 6366, ⓦ www.neonmuseum.org. Tours Tues–Sat 10am onwards; call or check website for details as precise schedules vary. $18. MAP P.87, POCKET MAP H10

If your appetite is whetted by the vintage signs displayed along Fremont Street, east of Las Vegas Boulevard, take a tour of the **Neon Museum** half a mile north. Treasuring signs and sculptures salvaged from long-lost casinos like the Desert Inn and the Hacienda, this is basically a junkyard, without restrooms or other facilities. Its visitor centre was once the space-age lobby of *La Concha Motel*, which stood alongside the Riviera on the Strip.

THE MOB MUSEUM

300 Stewart Ave ☎ 702 229 2734, ⓦ www
.themobmuseum.org. Mon–Thurs & Sun
10am–7pm, Fri & Sat 10am–8pm. $18, ages
5–17 $12. MAP P.87, POCKET MAP G11

Opened on February 14, 2012,
the 83rd anniversary of the Saint
Valentine's Day Massacre, Las
Vegas's **Mob Museum** was
designed as the lynchpin of a
campaign by then-mayor Oscar
Goodman – a former lawyer
who defended many underworld
figures – to revitalize downtown
as a tourist destination. Its full
name, the National Museum of
Organized Crime and Law
Enforcement, reflects its dual
goal of chronicling the mobsters
who once controlled the city and
the lawmen who eventually
brought them down.

The museum takes up three
storeys of the imposing former
federal courthouse, two blocks
north of Fremont Street. One
upstairs courtroom has been
restored to how it looked in
1950 when it hosted hearings by
Senator Estes' Senate committee
investigating organized crime.

With its comprehensive
displays giving the inside
stories on all sorts of Las Vegas
characters and conspiracies, the
Mob Museum is a fascinating
place to spend a few hours.
While it likes to pitch itself as
being much more serious than
the rival Mob Attraction (see
p.35) at the Tropicana, it has a
similar propensity for
trivializing or glamorizing the
city's gangster past. Lurid
panels detail, for example, the
"Mob's Greatest Hits", while
waxworks depict gory corpses.

DISCOVERY CHILDREN'S MUSEUM

Symphony Park ☎ 702 382 5437, ⓦ www
.ldcm.org. See website for hours and prices.
MAP P.87, POCKET MAP F12

As this book went to press,
downtown's long-established

Discovery Children's
Museum was about to move
to spacious new premises,
next to the Smith Center (see
p.93), half a mile west of
Fremont Street. Always a
favourite with younger
children in particular, with
interactive play areas based,
for example, on supermarkets
or airports, it's expected to be
better than ever.

LAS VEGAS NATURAL HISTORY MUSEUM

900 Las Vegas Blvd N ☎ 702 384 3466,
ⓦ www.lvnhm.org. Daily 9am–4pm. $10, ages
3–11 $5. MAP P.87, POCKET MAP H10

Collections at the **Las Vegas
Natural History Museum**, a
mile north of downtown,
range from stuffed lions to
animatronic dinosaurs,
complemented by tanks of live
sharks and snakes. One
remarkable specimen, a
dinosaur that was naturally
mummified before it became a
fossil, prompts an intriguing
CSI-style investigation into its
life and death. There's also a
replica of Tutankhamun's
tomb, donated by the Luxor
when it stripped away its
former Egyptian theme.

LAS VEGAS NATURAL HISTORY MUSEUM

Shops

GAMBLERS GENERAL STORE

800 S Main St ☎ 702 382 9903, ⓦ www
.gamblersgeneralstore.com. Daily 9am–5pm.
MAP P.87, POCKET MAP F13

If you love gambling, but
sometimes wish you got
something back for your money,
this is the place to come. You
can buy anything from a $1.99
pack of playing cards used at
your favourite casino to a $3600
roulette wheel, strategy books
and non-gaming souvenirs.

LAS VEGAS PREMIUM OUTLETS (NORTH)

875 S Grand Central Parkway ☎ 702 474 7500,
ⓦ www.premiumoutlets.com. Mon–Sat
10am–9pm, Sun 10am–8pm. MAP P.87,
POCKET MAP E13

A mile west of downtown and
served by SDX buses (see p.125)
from the Strip, this huge mall
consists of over 150 stores
accessed via outdoor walkways.
Unlike the south-Strip branch
(see p.38), most are genuinely
"outlets" of well-known brands
– Disney, Tommy Hilfiger, Nike
– so you can find real bargains.

Buffets

GOLDEN NUGGET BUFFET

Golden Nugget, 129 E Fremont St ☎ 702 385
7111, ⓦ www.goldennugget.com/lasvegas.
Breakfast Mon–Fri 7–10.30am, $11;
champagne brunch Sat & Sun 8am–3.30pm,
$19; lunch Mon–Fri 10.30am–3.30pm, $13;
dinner daily 3.30–10pm, Mon–Thurs $19, Fri–
Sun $22. MAP P.87, POCKET MAP G12

As you might expect of a casino
once owned by Steve Wynn,
the Golden Nugget boasts
downtown's best buffet, offering
a wide array of cuisines in a
humdrum space that at least
enjoys a pool view. The
weekend "seafood and more"
dinners are the best bargain.

PARADISE BUFFET AND CAFÉ

Fremont Hotel, 200 Fremont St ☎ 702 385
3232, ⓦ www.fremontcasino.com. Breakfast
Mon–Fri 7–10.30am, $7; champagne brunch
Sat & Sun 7am–3pm, $12; lunch Mon–Fri
11am–3pm, $8; dinner Mon–Thurs & Sun
4–10pm, Fri & Sat 4–11pm, Wed, Thurs,
Sat & Sun $14, Tues & Fri $20. MAP P.87,
POCKET MAP G12

Downtown has always been
popular with Hawaiian visitors,
and with palm trees and bright
colours, the Fremont's buffet
gives a taste of the islands
themselves. The food concen-
trates on American classics;
prices go up for the "seafood
bonanza" (Tues and Fri). There
is also a separate café menu.

Restaurants

HASH HOUSE A GO GO

The Plaza, 1 Main St ☎ 702 386 7227,
ⓦ www.hashhouseagogo.com/vegas. Mon–
Thurs & Sun 7am–11pm, Fri & Sat 7am–1am.
MAP P.87, POCKET MAP F11

This gleaming, all-day diner is
hardly the place for a romantic
rendezvous, but its "twisted farm
food" – obscenely large portions
of wholesome American country
classics like pot pie – tastes good
and is great value. It's best for
breakfast, with a varied menu.

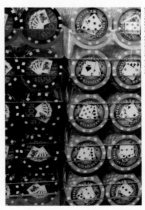

OSCAR'S BEEF * BOOZE * BROADS

The Plaza, 1 Main St ☎702 386 7227, ⓦwww
.plazahotelcasino.com. Mon–Thurs & Sun
5–10pm, Fri & Sat 4.30pm–midnight. MAP P.87,
POCKET MAP F11

Perched in a glass bubble
overlooking Fremont Street, this
shameless bid by former mayor
Oscar Goodman to cash in on
his larger-than-life image is a
favourite with all who remember
the old Las Vegas with affection.
Primarily a New York-style
steakhouse, serving top-quality
filet mignon or bone-in steaks
($40-plus), it also has a full
Italian-heavy menu. The
"broads" are the hostesses, also
available as dinner companions.

SECOND STREET GRILL

Fremont Hotel, 200 E Fremont St ☎702 385
3232, ⓦwww.fremontcasino.com. Mon, Thurs
& Sun 5–10pm, Fri & Sat 5–11pm. MAP P.87,
POCKET MAP G12

Despite its dreary, windowless
setting, this gourmet restaurant
offers downtown's most
inventive cuisine. Asian-influenced fish dishes like the tuna
sashimi starter or sesame-
crusted *mahi-mahi* reflect its
Hawaiian roots, while dishes like
chicken breast with risotto and
pesto are also on offer. Mains
cost $25-plus, but the nightly
special steak dinner is just $21.

TRIPLE GEORGE GRILL

201 N Third St ☎702 384 2761, ⓦwww
.triplegeorgegrill.com. Mon–Fri 11am–10pm,
Sat 4–10pm. MAP P.87, POCKET MAP G11

Its speakeasy decor, mixing
exposed brickwork with wood
panelling, might not be
genuine, but this downtown
steakhouse is a real-life
hangout for local politicos and
lawyers. Come early for lunch
and watch them wheeling and
dealing in the back room over
$12 Caesar salads, $13 chicken
fettuccini or $17 steaks.

Bars and lounges

CHICAGO BREWING CO

Four Queens, 202 E Fremont St ☎702 924
5222, ⓦwww.fourqueens.com. Mon–Fri
11.30am–1.30am, Sat & Sun 10am–1.30am.
MAP P.87, POCKET MAP G12

Fremont Street's best bar and
the pick of Las Vegas's few
microbreweries is a noisy and
upbeat spot to enjoy American,
German and English-style
beers, brewed on site and sold
individually or in 64-oz, $14
"Growlers". They also serve
pizzas, wings and sandwiches.

MOB BAR

201 N Third St ☎702 259 9700, ⓦwww
.mobbarlv.com. Mon–Thurs 11am–midnight,
Fri & Sat 11am–2am, Sun 1–8pm. MAP P.87,
POCKET MAP G11

Part of the complex that
includes the *Triple George Grill*
(see p.92), the former *Sidebar*
has been given a tasteful revamp
to lure in tourists heading for
the nearby Mob Museum. With
waiters in formal 1920s-style
attire and impeccably
concocted classic cocktails, it's
downtown's classiest bar.

TRIPLE GEORGE GRILL

SMITH CENTER FOR THE PERFORMING ARTS

361 Symphony Park Ave ☎ 702 749 2000, ⓦ www.thesmithcenter.com. See website for programme and prices. MAP P.87, POCKET MAP F12

Las Vegas acquired a performing arts centre in 2012 with the opening of this showpiece Art-Deco influenced theatre half a mile west of downtown. Its 2000-seat auditorium hosts classical concerts, ballet and touring Broadway shows, while smaller showrooms put on live music and theatre.

TRIPLE 7 RESTAURANT AND MICROBREWERY

Main Street Station, 200 N Main St ☎ 702 386 4442, ⓦ www.mainstreetcasino.com. Daily 11am–7am. MAP P.87, POCKET MAP G11

This cavernous pub and restaurant, at the heart of the antique-filled casino, is always full of lively, cheery drinkers savouring European brews along with substantial portions of good pub grub.

Clubs and music venues

KRAVE MASSIVE

Neonopolis, 450 Fremont St ☎ 702 836 0830, ⓦ www.kravelasvegas.com. Daily from 10.30pm. Cover varies. MAP P.87, POCKET MAP G12

As *Krave*, the world's largest gay nightclub was based in Planet Hollywood until 2012. It added *Massive* when it became downtown's first major club, taking over this colossal space in the Neonopolis mall. Its sheer scale is unbelievable; a former fourteen-screen cinema has been redivided to feature four dance floors, including one devoted to hip-hop and one to Latin music.

Show

GORDIE BROWN

Golden Nugget, 129 E Fremont St ☎ 866 946 5336, ⓦ www.gordiebrown.com. Tues–Sat 7.30pm. $33–71.50. MAP P.87, POCKET MAP G12

High-octane impressionist Gordie Brown has an unflagging urge to please everyone. Above all he's a singer, firing off on-the-note parodies of artists from Neil Diamond to Elvis. The 50-plus demographic means some material is a bit dated.

Wedding chapel

GRACELAND WEDDING CHAPEL

619 S Las Vegas Blvd ☎ 702 382 0091, ⓦ www.gracelandchapel.com. Daily 9am–11pm. MAP P.87, POCKET MAP G13

This pretty chapel, just south of downtown, is "the home of the original Elvis wedding". You can't marry Elvis, and he's not a minister, so he can't marry you, but he can renew your vows. In the basic $199 package, the King walks you down the aisle and sings two songs; pay $799 and you get two "duelling Elvises", young and old.

The rest of the city

A glance at any map will tell you that there's a lot more to Las Vegas than simply downtown and the Strip; well over a million people live in the valley as a whole. This is not a city where under-explored neighbourhoods hold fascinating and little-known attractions, however. It's a vast and overwhelmingly residential sprawl that you'll need a car and plenty of time to explore at all thoroughly. Even then, almost all you'll find will be casinos, malls, bars and restaurants; this chapter highlights the pick of the bunch. In addition to the few that genuinely compete with the best of the Strip – the Hard Rock Hotel, the Palms and the Rio – it focuses on the so-called "locals casinos" throughout the city. While these can't match the wow factor of the Strip giants, they find their own niche by offering good-value food, drink and entertainment.

DIG THIS!

3012 S Rancho Drive ☎ 702 222 4344, Ⓦ www.digthisvegas.com. Daily 8am–5pm; advance reservations essential. Big Dig $249, Mega Dig $449. MAP P.95, POCKET MAP A11

Las Vegas has always specialized in making adult fantasies come true, but it took a truly inspired entrepreneur to come up with the idea for **Dig This!**. On a patch of desert waste ground, a mile west of the Strip, customers get to operate their very own piece of heavy machinery. On payment of a substantial fee, anyone aged 14 and over can drive either a bulldozer or an excavator for ninety minutes; that's a Big Dig, while a Mega Dig lets you do both. Not only do you not need a driving licence, you don't even need to be old enough to have one.

After a few minutes' training you're allowed to sit alone in your vehicle, linked via headphones to an instructor who has an override switch. In a bulldozer, you pile up a huge mound of sand and then power

HARD ROCK HOTEL

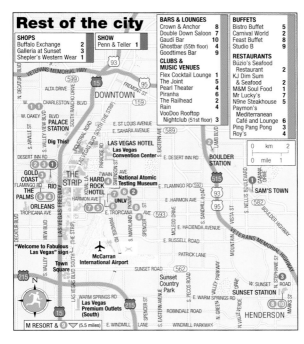

Rest of the city

SHOPS	
Buffalo Exchange	2
Galleria at Sunset	3
Shepler's Western Wear	1

SHOW	
Penn & Teller	1

BARS & LOUNGES	
Crown & Anchor	8
Double Down Saloon	7
Gaudi Bar	10
Ghostbar (55th floor)	4
Goodtimes Bar	9

CLUBS & MUSIC VENUES	
Flex Cocktail Lounge	1
The Joint	5
Pearl Theater	4
Piranha	6
The Railhead	2
Rain	4
VooDoo Rooftop Nightclub (51st floor)	3

BUFFETS	
Bistro Buffet	5
Carnival World	2
Feast Buffet	8
Studio B	9

RESTAURANTS	
Búzio's Seafood Restaurant	2
KJ Dim Sum & Seafood	2
M&M Soul Food	1
Mr Lucky's	7
N9ne Steakhouse	5
Paymon's Mediterranean Café and Lounge	6
Ping Pang Pong	2
Roy's	4

the dozer over the top; in an excavator, you dig trenches and play "basketball" using your scoop. The point, of course, is that it's all fantastic fun. Whether they do it as a retirement treat or a hen party escapade, everyone who has a go seems to come away exhilarated.

GOLD COAST

4000 W Flamingo Rd ☎702 367 7111, ⓦwww .goldcoastcasino.com. MAP P.95, POCKET MAP G15
One of Las Vegas's first "locals casinos", targeted at city residents themselves, the **Gold Coast** was erected half a mile west of the Strip in 1986. While it swiftly acquired much fancier neighbours, in the shape of the Rio and the Palms, it's hung on to its rather staid Western decor, and remains geared towards a local crowd, especially from the city's Chinatown immediately to the

north. As well as some good Asian restaurants, it also holds a seventy-lane bowling alley.

HARD ROCK HOTEL

4455 Paradise Rd ☎702 693 4000, ⓦwww .hardrockhotel.com. MAP P.95, POCKET MAP B16
Flagged by two enormous guitars, the **Hard Rock Hotel** clamours for attention a mile east of the Strip. Best seen as a self-sufficient party resort it fills every weekend with southern Californians who come to soak up the rock'n'roll atmosphere of its clubs, music venues and "daylife"-oriented pool. For sightseers there's little here apart from endless display cabinets of stage clothes and instruments, from Elvis to Bruce and beyond. Spend a night or two, though (ideally to coincide with a big gig), and enjoy its excellent bars and restaurants, and you might just have the time of your life.

M RESORT

LAS VEGAS HOTEL

3000 Paradise Rd ☎ 702 732 5111, Ⓦ www
.thelvh.com. MAP P.95, POCKET MAP L5

The **Las Vegas Hotel** used to be
the largest and most famous
hotel in the world. Built by
legendary entrepreneur Kirk
Kerkorian in 1969, half a mile
east of the Strip, it was originally
the International Hotel.
Renamed the Las Vegas Hilton
four years later, it hosted Elvis
Presley for 837 sell-out concerts.
Neither having its own Monorail
station nor standing next to the
city's Convention Center spared
it a battering by the current
recession, however, and in 2012
it went into foreclosure and lost
the Hilton name. Its restaurants
and music venues are still just
about ticking along, but it feels
very peripheral indeed.

M RESORT

12300 Las Vegas Blvd S, Henderson ☎ 702
797 1000, Ⓦ www.themresort.com. MAP P.95,
POCKET MAP B14

Surveying the city from its
hillside perch near the southern
end of the Las Vegas Valley, ten
miles south of Mandalay Bay,
the shiny **M Resort** opened in
2009. Sadly, the economic
climate was far from ideal for
the smartest new off-Strip casino
to be built in many years, so
despite its impressive contemporary architecture and well
considered amenities it was soon
struggling. Within two years, it
was snapped up by Penn
Gaming for barely a quarter of
its original billion-dollar cost.

Through it all, the M is
looking as good as ever – almost
in the Wynn class. With lavish
public spaces including a lovely
Palm Springs-style pool complex
and great restaurants like the
hugely popular *Studio B* buffet
and irresistible *Baby Cakes*
bakery, it's unusual in appealing
to locals and visitors alike.

ORLEANS

4500 W Tropicana Ave ☎702 365 7111, Ⓦwww
.orleanscasino.com. MAP P.95, POCKET MAP A12

Owned by the same manage-
ment as the Gold Coast (see
p.95), to which it's linked by
free shuttle buses, the **Orleans**
is roughly a mile due west of
New York–New York. Several
of its restaurants and bars play
on the New Orleans connection
suggested by its name, but
really the emphasis is on
catering to more local tastes,
via such means as an 18-screen
cinema and 24-hour bowling
alley. As a place to gamble at
above-average odds then relax
over cheap food and entertainment, it's hard to beat.

THE PALMS

4321 W Flamingo Rd ☎ 702 942 7777, ⓦ www.palms.com. MAP P.95, POCKET MAP F16

It's a cruel drawback of running a relatively small off-Strip casino that as soon as you come up with brilliant ideas to lure visitors the big boys simply copy your innovations and entice your customers back. When it opened across from the Rio in 2001, the **Palms** became the first Las Vegas casino to tap into the twenty-first-century's mix of street and celebrity culture, with an array of youth-oriented clubs and theatres that made it the hippest hangout in the city. Since then, the Strip giants have added their own state-of-the-art nightclubs and the Palms has had to keep upping its game.

Despite recent money worries, the basic elements of the Palms' winning formula remain pretty intact. Nightlife options including the penthouse *Moon* club and the *Ghostbar* still draw in the crowds, while the Pearl Theater ranks among the city's premier concert venues. The Palms even holds a recording studio, used by artists from Lady Gaga and Katy Perry to Tony Bennett. And with its own cinema and some decent budget restaurants, it's careful not to neglect locals either.

RIO

3700 W Flamingo Rd ☎ 866 746 7671, ⓦ www.riolasvegas.com. MAP P.95, POCKET MAP H15

A proud purple beacon, half a mile west of Caesars Palace across the interstate, when it opened in 1990, the **Rio** looked as though it might become the first casino in a generation to threaten the Strip's domination. It was independently owned and played on its Rio de Janeiro theme to build a reputation as the city's premier party scene for locals and visitors alike. Then, as now, all its guest rooms were sizeable suites, sold at highly competitive rates.

In 1999, however, the Rio was sold for almost a billion dollars to what later became Caesars Entertainment. Now run as an adjunct to its sister properties on the central Strip – to which it's linked by free shuttle buses (daily 10am–1am) from Harrah's (see p.61) and Bally's (see p.57) – it can therefore seem like something of an afterthought.

The Rio's Brazilian connection is most apparent in the Masquerade Village section of the casino, which stages its own free twelve-minute carnival on weekend evenings (Thurs–Sat, hourly 6–11pm). Models dressed in Victoria's Secret lingerie dance on a podium, while adults can pay $13 to ride colourful carnival "floats" that dangle from overhead rails.

Every June and July, the Rio hosts the high-profile **World Series of Poker**; Caesars acquired the rights to the tournament when it purchased its previous home, Binion's Horseshoe, in 2004. For the rest of the year, it's best known for its sky-high *Voodoo Rooftop Nightclub* (see p.103), the Penn and Teller magic show (see p.103) and its fine selection of restaurants and buffets.

SAM'S TOWN

5111 Boulder Hwy ☎ 702 456 7777, ⊕ www.samstownlv.com. MAP P.95, POCKET MAP D12

Best known these days as the name of an album by Las Vegas's favourite home-grown band, the Killers, **Sam's Town** is a locals casino that stands six miles east of the Strip, alongside the main road out to the Hoover Dam. In the last few years, it's updated its long-standing Wild-West image by adding a new affiliation with NASCAR racing, which includes hosting the Sam's Town 300 race every March. It has also roofed over its central courtyard, adding gardens and waterfalls to create Mystic Falls Park, the scene of regular sound-and-light shows (daily 2pm, 6pm, 8pm & 10pm).

SUNSET STATION

1301 W Sunset Rd, Henderson ☎ 702 547 7715, ⊕ www.sunsetstation.sclv.com. MAP P.95, POCKET MAP D13

The self-styled "Spanish Mediterranean" **Sunset Station** casino was the first major casino to be built in the fast-growing suburb of Henderson, eight miles southeast of the Strip. It opened in 1997 as the flagship property of the so-called "Stations chain" of locals casinos, and while the chain as a whole has struggled to stave off bankruptcy in recent years, Sunset Station itself is still looking good.

Its primary customers being drawn from its own neighbourhood, Sunset Station is crammed with community assets like the huge 72-lane, 24-hour StrikeZone bowling alley, a 13-screen cinema, and, rather more questionably, the Kids Quest daycare centre that'll look after children while their parents are gambling. Some of its features would be impressive even on the Strip, however, including the amazing undulating *Gaudí Bar* (see p.102) that's the centrepiece of the casino floor.

NATIONAL ATOMIC TESTING MUSEUM

755 E Flamingo Rd ☎ 702 794 5151, ⊕ www.nationalatomictestingmuseum.org. Mon–Sat 10am–5pm, Sun noon–5pm. $14, or $20 with Area 51; senior citizens, students and ages 7–17 $11/$17; under-6s free. MAP P.95, POCKET MAP B12

Between 1951 and 1958, a remote desert area sixty miles northwest of Las Vegas, designated as the Nevada Test Site, was used for above-ground tests of atomic bombs. Mushroom clouds were visible from the city and tourists would time their holidays so they could watch the blasts. That astonishing saga is explored in the **National Atomic Testing Museum**, which covers not only the political, scientific and military background, but also the kitschy ways in which popular culture celebrated the bomb. A separate **Area 51** exhibit examines the even more unbelievable story of supposed "alien autopsies" in the same general vicinity.

NATIONAL ATOMIC TESTING MUSEUM

Shops

BUFFALO EXCHANGE

4110 S Maryland Parkway ☎ 702 791 3960,
Ⓦ www.buffaloexchange.com. Mon–Sat
10am–8pm, Sun 11am–7pm. MAP P.95,
POCKET MAP B12

Many of downtown's antique-
clothing stores having closed
down in recent years, this
national chain, two miles east of
the Strip, is as good as Las
Vegas now gets for used men's
and women's clothes and shoes.

BUFFALO EXCHANGE

GALLERIA AT SUNSET

1300 W Sunset Rd, Henderson ☎ 702 434
0202, Ⓦ www.galleriaatsunset.com. Mon–Sat
10am–9pm, Sun 11am–6pm. MAP P.95,
POCKET MAP D13

Massive suburban shopping mall
across from Sunset Station, eight
miles southeast of the Strip, with
five department stores and a
host of middle-American chains.

SHEPLER'S WESTERN WEAR

Sam's Town, 5111 Boulder Hwy ☎ 702 454
8017, Ⓦ www.samstownlv.com. Mon–Fri
10am–9pm, Sat & Sun 10am–10pm. MAP P.95,
POCKET MAP D12

This in-casino store holds the
city's finest array of Western
wear. As you'd expect, there's a
vast assortment of jeans and
Stetsons, but the boots are the
real stunners, with python- and
ostrich-skin pairs from $220.

Buffets

BISTRO BUFFET

The Palms, 4321 W Flamingo Rd ☎ 702 953
7679, Ⓦ www.palms.com. Breakfast Mon–Sat
8–10am, $9; brunch Sun 8am–3pm, $20;
lunch Mon–Sat 11am–3pm, $13; dinner daily
4–9pm, $21. MAP P.95, POCKET MAP F16

A bright, modern space
adjoining the main casino
floor, the Palms' buffet is
popular with locals for its ease
of access and range of world
cuisines; be sure to sample the
succulent ham hocks.

CARNIVAL WORLD

Rio, 3700 W Flamingo Rd ☎ 702 777 7777,
Ⓦ www.riolasvegas.com. Breakfast Mon–Fri
8–11am, $19; champagne brunch Sat & Sun
8am–3.30pm, $30; lunch Mon–Fri
11am–3.30pm, $22; dinner daily 3.30–10pm,
$27. MAP P.95, POCKET MAP H15

Crowds flock to the Rio's
all-day buffet (as opposed to its
separate dinner-only *Village
Seafood* buffet) to pile their
plates high with almost any
food they can think of, from
sushi to corndogs; the choice is
endless, even if the quality is
predictably dependable rather
than particularly delicious.

FEAST BUFFET

Sunset Station, 1301 W Sunset Rd ☎ 702 547
7777, Ⓦ www.sunsetstation.sclv.com. Breakfast
Mon–Sat 8–11am, $9; brunch Sun 8am–4pm,
$15; lunch Mon–Sat 11am–4pm, $11; dinner
daily 4–9pm, $15. MAP P.95, POCKET MAP D13

Unlike their Strip rivals, all the
Stations casinos still offer
cut-price buffets to lure Las
Vegans out to eat and gamble.
Sunset Station has the nicest
dining room; pick carefully and
you can get a great-value meal
including dishes like Indian
curries, seldom seen elsewhere.

STUDIO B

M Resort, 12300 Las Vegas Blvd S ☎ 702 797 1000, ⓦ www.themresort.com. Breakfast Mon–Fri 8–10.30am, $11; brunch Sat & Sun 9am–2.30pm, $40; lunch Mon–Fri 10.30am–2.30pm, $16; dinner Mon–Thurs 4–9pm $24, Fri 4–9pm $40, Sat & Sun 2.30–10pm $40. MAP P.95, POCKET MAP B14

Primarily this is a buffet, with food (and prices) to match the very best on the Strip, but it's also a "studio" because chefs demonstrate their art here on stage and TV screens. Prices include free wine and beer; the higher evening and weekend rates cover seafood spreads that include raw oysters. Allow time to get here – it's ten miles south of the Strip – and expect to queue to get in.

Restaurants

BÚZIO'S SEAFOOD RESTAURANT

Rio, 3700 W Flamingo Rd ☎ 702 777 7923, ⓦ www.riolasvegas.com. Mon–Thurs & Sun 5–10.30pm, Fri & Sat 5–11pm. MAP P.95, POCKET MAP H15

The menu at this classy dinner-only fish restaurant, looking out over the Rio's pool, draws from the best of American and Mediterranean seafood traditions, with fish stews like bouillabaisse and cioppino alongside steamed New England lobster or crab. With mains around $30 it's likely to cost $50-plus per head, but it's well worth it.

KJ DIM SUM & SEAFOOD

Rio, 3700 W Flamingo Rd ☎ 702 777 7777, ⓦ www.riolasvegas.com. Daily 10am–2am. MAP P.95, POCKET MAP H15

This offshoot of a popular restaurant in Las Vegas's nearby Chinatown has been an instant hit, especially for lunching locals who come to select succulent $3–6 dumplings and seafood

specialities from the gleaming dim sum trolleys. Later on, full-sized mains like sizzling scallops or whole steamed fish cost from $20–30.

M&M SOUL FOOD

3923 W Charleston Blvd ☎ 702 453 7685, ⓦ www.mmsoulfoodcafe.com. Daily 7am–8pm. MAP P.95, POCKET MAP A11

Genuine soul food being hard to come by in Las Vegas, this neighbourhood diner is a godsend. Four miles west of downtown, it's best reached by car; you won't be in a fit state to walk anywhere once you've filled up on their succulent chicken, ribs, gumbo or cornbread.

MR LUCKY'S

Hard Rock Hotel, 4455 Paradise Rd ☎ 702 693 5000, ⓦ www.hardrockhotel.com. Daily 24hr. MAP P.95, POCKET MAP A16

A refreshing modern take on the traditional Las Vegas all-night casino coffeeshop, with an open kitchen and stylish patio seating. Whether you grab a pastrami and rye New York sandwich for lunch ($18) or stumble in for 4am spaghetti and meatballs ($14), *Mr Lucky's* offers a round-the-clock break from the Hard Rock frenzy.

N9NE STEAKHOUSE

Palms, 4321 W Flamingo Rd ☎ *702 942 6832*, ⓦ www.n9negroup.com. Mon–Thurs & Sun 5–10pm, Fri & Sat 5–11pm. MAP P.95, POCKET MAP F16

With its waterfalls, constant play of lights and glass-walled celebrity areas, this glitzy, high-concept restaurant is very much a place to see and be seen, but its beautifully presented resort cuisine, which includes sushi and sashimi as well as steak, cannot be faulted. You can pay well over $50 for a steak, but the $65 early-evening prix fixe menu (served 5–7pm) includes unlimited wine.

PAYMON'S MEDITERRANEAN CAFÉ AND LOUNGE

4147 S Maryland Parkway at Flamingo Rd ☎ *702 731 6030*, ⓦ www.paymons.com. Daily 11am–1am. MAP P.95, POCKET MAP B12

A truly local restaurant, busy until late with students from the nearby university. While not exclusively vegetarian – meat-eaters can enjoy dishes like the $13 Persian chicken-and-walnut *fesenjan* – it's especially recommended for its extensive array of Middle Eastern classics such as falafel, hummus and baba ghanoush, available singly or in a $13 combination platter.

PING PANG PONG

Gold Coast, 4000 W Flamingo Rd ☎ *702 367 7111*, ⓦ www.goldcoastcasino.com. Daily 10am–3pm & 5pm–3am. MAP P.95, POCKET MAP F15

You can tell straight away this is the best Chinese restaurant in any Las Vegas casino; most of the diners are Chinese and the menu is written in Chinese characters as well as English. Dim sum makes a lunchtime treat, while later on you can get chicken noodles for just $8 or half a roast duck for $13.

ROY'S

620 E Flamingo Rd ☎ *702 691 2053*, ⓦ www.roysrestaurant.com. Mon–Thurs 5.30–9.30pm, Fri 5.30–10pm, Sat 5–10pm, Sun 5–9.30pm. MAP P.95, POCKET MAP B12

Generally considered the best non-casino restaurant in Las Vegas, Hawaiian chef Roy Yamaguchi's dazzling, dinner-only Pacific Rim showcase serves exquisite Asian-influenced cuisine. Mains like beef short ribs or *misoyaki* butterfish cost around $30 on average, but there's also a three-course $37 set menu.

ROY'S

Bars and lounges

CROWN & ANCHOR

1350 E Tropicana Ave ☎ *702 739 8676*, ⓦ www.crownandanchorlv.com. Daily 24hr. MAP P.95, POCKET MAP B12

The closest Las Vegas comes to having a genuine British pub, complete with Cornish pasties and Sunday roasts, although most of its customers, even when it's showing European soccer games, are students from the nearby university.

DOUBLE DOWN SALOON

4640 Paradise Rd ☎ 702 791 5775, ⓦ www
.doubledownsaloon.com. Daily 24hr. MAP P.95,
POCKET MAP C17

Archetypal hole-in-the-wall
dive bar, one block south of the
Hard Rock, with funky murals,
a hard-edged punk jukebox,
no-cover live bands most
nights, plus slots, blackjack and
pool, and signature drinks like
"ass juice" and bacon martinis.

GAUDÍ BAR

Sunset Station, 1301 W Sunset Rd,
Henderson ☎ 702 547 7777, ⓦ www
.sunsetstation.sclv.com. Daily 24hr. MAP P.95,
POCKET MAP D13

The coolest bar in any Las Vegas
casino, created in honour of
Catalan architect Antoni Gaudí,
this bizarre fungoid excrescence
undulates through the heart of
Sunset Station, with cracked-up
mosaics across its cave-like
walls and light courtesy of the
colourful stained-glass panels in
the ceiling.

GHOSTBAR

Palms, 4321 W Flamingo Rd ☎ 702 942
6832, ⓦ www.ghostbar.com. Daily 8pm–dawn.
Cover Mon–Thurs & Sun $10, Fri & Sat $20.
MAP P.95, POCKET MAP F16

What do you call a club with
DJs and a cover charge but no

dancing? It must be an
ultra-lounge – and there's no
better place to appreciate Las
Vegas at night than from the
deck of this 55th-floor bar,
where the glass floor is replaced
every two weeks.

GOODTIMES BAR

1775 E Tropicana Ave ☎ 702 736 9494,
ⓦ www.goodtimeslv.com. 24hr. MAP P.95,
POCKET MAP B12

This long-established and
very friendly neighbourhood
gay bar has increasingly
established a late-night alter
ago as a fully fledged club; the
big night of the week is
Thursday for the "Carpe
Noctem" Goth extravaganza.

Clubs and music venues

FLEX COCKTAIL LOUNGE

4371 W Charleston Blvd ☎ 702 385 3539,
ⓦ www.flexlasvegas.com. Daily 24hr. No cover.
MAP P.95, POCKET MAP A11

Lively gay bar and club, with
pool tables, slots and an
emphasis on upbeat action.
Free entertainment nightly,
including late-night drag
shows Thurs–Sat, plus
half-price Happy Hours
4–7pm and 4–7am.

THE JOINT

Hard Rock Hotel, 4455 Paradise Rd ☎ 702
693 5066, ⓦ www.thejointlasvegas.com. See
website for schedule and prices. MAP P.95,
POCKET MAP B16

Totally revamped in 2009, the
Hard Rock's theatre attracts
four-thousand-strong crowds
to see big-name touring acts.
In addition, groups like
Guns'n'Roses take up
residence for a month or more
at a time, with typical ticket
prices of around $100.

DOUBLE DOWN SALOON

GAUDI BAR

THE RAILHEAD

Boulder Station, 4111 Boulder Hwy ☎ 702 547 5300, Ⓦ www.boulderstation.sclv.com. Daily 24hr. Concert tickets typically $15–40. MAP P.95, POCKET MAP C11

A run-of-the-mill member of the Stations chain of locals casinos, Boulder Station's one bright spot is this large lounge/theatre, which hosts Latin nights on Fridays and Sundays, but also puts on solid mid-range country, soul and blues acts.

VOODOO ROOFTOP NIGHTCLUB

Rio, 3700 W Flamingo Rd ☎ 702 777 7776, Ⓦ www.riolasvegas.com. Mon–Thurs & Sun 5pm–3am, Fri & Sat 5pm–4am. Cover $20 and up. MAP P.95, POCKET MAP J15

Long famed for its stunning 51st-floor views, this New Orleans-tinged rendezvous made its reputation as an ultra-hip drinking spot. Now a fully fledged nightclub, it's smaller than its newer rivals on the Strip, but the location is as good as ever and offers a great night out at more affordable prices.

Show

PENN & TELLER

Rio, 3700 W Flamingo Rd ☎ 702 777 7776, Ⓦ www.pennandteller.com. Mon–Wed, Sat & Sun 9pm. $75–95. MAP P.95, POCKET MAP H15

Magicians Penn (the talkative one) and Teller (the other one) have been performing at the Rio since 2000 – while still keeping up their TV careers – but the show remains fresh, whether you simply want to swoon at the magic or you love the behind-the-scenes tricks-of-the-trade patter. They're also great with their audiences, posing and signing happily for groups of fans after the show.

PEARL THEATER

Palms, 4321 W Flamingo Rd ☎ 702 944 3200, Ⓦ www.palmspearl.com. See website for current schedule and prices. MAP P.95, POCKET MAP F16

The Palms' start-of-the-art theatre may be smaller than the Hard Rock's Joint, but with its great sound and atmosphere it attracts its fair share of major-league acts across the spectrum, from hip-hop and R&B to reggae and rock.

PIRANHA

4633 Paradise Rd ☎ 702 791 0100, Ⓦ www.piranhavegas.com. Daily 10pm–5am. Cover varies, typically $20. MAP P.95, POCKET MAP B17

The jewel of the so-called "Fruit Loop" and the pulsating heart of Las Vegas's gay nightlife, the spectacular *Piranha* club is approached via either a fiery waterfall or a piranha-filled aquarium. The similarly lavish *8½ Ultra Lounge* alongside makes a perfect spot to kick off the night.

The deserts

Las Vegas stands close to some of the most extraordinary landscapes on the planet – the stark, sublime deserts of the American Southwest. It's possible to get a taste of this red-rock wonderland on brief forays from the city, either to Red Rock Canyon, Hoover Dam and Lake Mead, or to the Valley of Fire. To appreciate its full splendour, however, you need to venture further afield. The primary goal for many visitors is the Grand Canyon, though you'd do better visit the canyon's South Rim, almost three hundred miles east, than Grand Canyon West, which is closer to hand. Utah's Zion Canyon arguably makes an even better destination for an overnight trip from Las Vegas.

RED ROCK CANYON

17 miles west of the Strip ☎ 702 515 5350, ⓦ www.redrockcanyonlv.org. Visitor centre daily 8am–4.30pm. Scenic Drive daily: March 7am–7pm, April–Sept 6am–8pm, Oct 6am–7pm, Nov–Feb 6am–5pm. $7/vehicle, $3 for bikes, motorbikes and pedestrians. MAP P.104–105

For a quick blast of dramatic Southwestern scenery and searing desert sun, simply drive

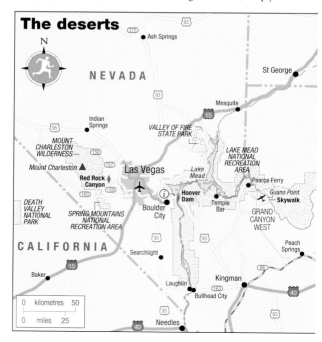

RED ROCK CANYON

west on any road from the Strip. Tucked behind the first low scrubby hills, the **Red Rock Canyon National Conservation Area** centres on a desert basin at the foot of towering 3000ft cliffs. Ideally, come in the morning, when the glowing red rocks are spotlit by the rising sun, and the day's heat has yet to set in. Staff at the visitor centre will introduce you to this unforgiving but beautiful wilderness and point out hiking trails and climbing routes that set off from the one-way, thirteen-mile **Scenic Drive** just beyond, which is the only way to see the canyon itself.

HOOVER DAM

30 miles southeast of the Strip ☎ 702 494 2517, ✆ www.usbr.gov/lc/hooverdam. Parking daily 8am–6.15pm; $7. Visitor Center daily: April–Sept 9am–6pm; Oct–March 9am–5pm; $8. Powerplant Tour April–Sept 9.25am–4.55pm; Oct–March 9.25am–3.55pm; $11 including Visitor Center, senior citizens & ages 4–16 $9. Dam Tour April–Sept Mon–Thurs 9.30am–4pm, Fri & Sat 9.30am–4.30pm; Oct–March daily 9.30am–3.45pm; all-inclusive fee $30, no reductions, minimum age 8. MAP P.104–105

The mighty **Hoover Dam** straddles the Colorado River and thus the Nevada–Arizona state line as well. While this graceful 726ft-tall concrete marvel does not, as many visitors imagine, supply a significant proportion of the electricity that keeps Las Vegas running, its construction during the 1930s triggered the growth spurt, and the gambling boom, that created the modern city.

The main highway to Arizona, US-83, crosses the Colorado on a new bridge, slightly downstream from the dam. To see the dam itself, leave the highway via the spur roads at either end. For a quick look you can park briefly on the Arizona side and walk out atop the dam. Otherwise, park in the multistorey garage on the Nevada side, and walk down to the Visitor Center. Displays there explain the story and inner workings of the dam, but paying just a little extra entitles you to join a Power-plant Tour, and ride an elevator down to its base. The hour-long Dam Tour takes you right into its bowels, exploring its dank and mysterious tunnels.

LAKE MEAD

30 miles southeast of the Strip ☎ 702 293 8990, ✆ www.nps.gov/lake. Visitor Center daily 8.30am–4.30pm. MAP P.104–105

Created by the construction of the Hoover Dam, **Lake Mead**, east of Las Vegas, is the largest artificial lake in the USA when full. Its deep blue waters make an extraordinary contrast against the arid sands and red-rock cliffs of the desert, and attract huge numbers of visitors. Only its Nevada shoreline is accessible by road, most easily via Boulder City, a thirty-mile drive from the Strip.

Call in at the **Visitor Center** just off US-93 (closed for renovation as this book went to press, it should have reopened by the time you read this), then follow the **Lakeshore Scenic Drive** down to the lake itself. How close it approaches the shore depends on current water levels, which have remained

HOOVER DAM

low since 2002. Both **Lake Mead Marina** (☎ 702 293 3484, ⓦ www.riverlakes.com) and the neighbouring **Las Vegas Boat Harbor** (☎ 702 293 1191, ⓦ www.boatinglakemead .com) rent out boats and jet-skis, while the **Desert Princess** paddle steamer offers lake cruises from the latter ($25–57.50; ☎ 702 293 6180, ⓦ www.lakemeadcruises.com).

MOUNT CHARLESTON

A real anomaly in the Nevada deserts, and one that tends to be appreciated more by locals than by visitors, the Spring Mountain range soars into the sky forty miles northwest of the Strip. Its highest peak, **Mount Charleston**, stands just under 12,000ft tall, so its forested slopes offer a welcome escape from the summer heat of the city. Several appealing hiking trails set off across the surrounding hillsides.

To reach the mountains, head northwest out of Las Vegas on US-95 then turn west onto Hwy-157, which snakes its way into **Kyle Canyon**. Up at the head of the canyon, the **Mary Jane Falls Trail** is a 2.5-mile round-trip trek that climbs via gruelling switchbacks to a pair of waterfalls. Half a mile further on, the three-mile **Cathedral Rock Trail** involves a demanding thousand-foot ascent to a promontory with onward views to Charleston Peak itself.

That's as far as most people go, but with a little more time you can drive north from Kyle Canyon to **Lee Canyon** along Hwy-158 to enjoy far-reaching views over the desert wasteland where Nevada's notorious A-bomb tests took place in the 1950s, and then return to US-95 via Hwy-56.

VALLEY OF FIRE STATE PARK

VALLEY OF FIRE STATE PARK

Just over 50 miles northeast of the Strip ☎ 702 397 2088, ⓦ www.parks.nv.gov/vf.htm. Visitor centre daily 8.30am–4.30pm. $10/ vehicle. MAP P.104–105

The most mind-blowing red-rock scenery you can see on a driving day-trip lies in the Valley of Fire State Park. To get there, follow I-15 for thirty miles towards Utah, then turn right onto Hwy-169. The park begins just after you cross the ridge of **Muddy Mountain** to look out over a magnificent sandscape of incandescent, multicoloured peaks and cliffs stretching all the way to Lake Mead.

A roadside visitor centre explains local history and geology, and displays live rattlesnakes. It marks the start of a five-mile, dead-end road that winds through amazing rock outcrops that can be explored on short hiking trails. The single most extraordinary formation, however, lies a further three miles along Hwy-169, where a natural arch – **Elephant Rock** – looks like a giant elephant poking its trunk into the sands.

Keep driving east, and you can loop back to Las Vegas along the north shore of **Lake Mead** – a total round trip of 130 miles.

Grand Canyon tours

The Grand Canyon is not as near Las Vegas as you might imagine. **Grand Canyon National Park** is 200 miles east of Las Vegas and the **South Rim** (see p.109), which holds the park's main tourist facilities and viewpoints, is a drive of almost 300 miles each way from the city. To see the canyon on a day-trip, there are two options: a long bus ride or an expensive flight. The majority of tours from Las Vegas therefore go to **Grand Canyon West** (see p.108), more like 100 miles from the city, which while less spectacular is also home to the **Skywalk**, and offers the chance to land by, and even take a rafting trip on, the **Colorado River**.

With most of the operators listed below, you can choose between taking a **tour** to Grand Canyon West or the South Rim, by bus, helicopter or plane. Bus tours to Grand Canyon West typically cost around $100, or $135 including the Skywalk. The entire round-trip takes at least 12 hours, including four hours at Grand Canyon West itself. A **bus tour** to the South Rim takes over sixteen hours, with less time at the canyon itself. Prices can be as low as $80, but expect to pay more like $150 for a de luxe coach.

Flight-seeing tours to Grand Canyon West start at around $135 by plane (without landing) or $250 by helicopter. Expect to pay at least $250 by plane or $300 by helicopter for a tour that includes walking on the Skywalk, and up to $500 for a helicopter tour that lands down by the river as well.

All **flights** to the South Rim are in fixed-wing planes. A flight with a ground tour of canyon viewpoints by bus will cost around $250. Tours that include a separate helicopter flight once you arrive cost around $400.

Note that many flights depart not from Las Vegas itself, but from **Boulder City**, thirty miles southeast. If you're hoping for an aerial view of the city into the bargain, check which airport your operator uses.

TOUR OPERATORS

Grand Canyon Airlines T 928 638 2359, W www.grandcanyonairlines.com.
Maverick T 702 261 0007, W www.maverickhelicopter.com.
Papillon T 702 736 7243, W www.papillon.com.
Scenic Airlines T 702 638 3300, W www.scenic.com.
Sundance T 702 736 0606, W www.sundancehelicopters.com.

GRAND CANYON WEST

125 miles west of Las Vegas W www.grandcanyonwest.com. If you drive here yourself you'll still have to join a ground tour, costing a minimum of $44/person, or $88 including the Skywalk. MAP P.104–105

The spot known as **Grand Canyon West** (or the West Rim) is not actually in Grand Canyon National Park, but on the Hualapai Indian Reservation to the west. Although it can be reached via a 125-mile one-way drive from Las Vegas, road conditions are so poor that almost all visitors fly (see box above).

At this point, close to the western end of the Grand Canyon shortly before the Colorado River spills into Lake Mead, the chasm has dwindled to around two miles wide and lacks the extraordinary sculpted rock formations you may be

expecting. Instead Grand Canyon West consists of a cluster of viewpoints above drops of up to 4000ft, and looking across to similar cliffs on the far side of the river.

The major attraction is the **Skywalk**, a glass-floored, horseshoe-shaped walkway that juts out over the rim of a side canyon at Eagle Point, close to the airstrip where tours begin. The best view of the canyon itself comes from **Guano Point**, a mile or so north. The Hualapai tribe, who have lived here for over a thousand years, offer various other activities, including dance performances and barbecue cookouts.

GRAND CANYON SOUTH RIM

270 miles west of Las Vegas ☎ 928 638 7888, Ⓦ www.nps.gov/grca. Entrance fee $25/ vehicle, valid for seven days. MAP P.104–105

To see the Grand Canyon in all its glory, you have to visit **Grand Canyon National Park**. This is the area familiar from a million movies and photographs, where the canyon is studded with mighty red-rock buttes and pyramids, and measures a mile deep and eleven miles wide.

Tourist facilities, concentrated around several magnificent viewpoints along the canyon's South Rim, can be reached either by road – a total drive from Las Vegas of 270 miles, via the I-40 interstate that crosses northern Arizona fifty miles south of the canyon – or by air, to Tusayan airport, six miles south of the canyon.

While it's possible to visit the **South Rim** on a day-trip (see box opposite), it makes much more sense to drive yourself and stay at least one night. That will give you the chance to spend some time beside the canyon at sunset and dawn, and to sample the evening atmosphere of the splendid old rim-edge *El Tovar* hotel (see p.121).

ZION NATIONAL PARK

160 miles northeast of Las Vegas ☎ 435 772 3256, ⊕ www.nps.gov/zion. Entrance fee $25/ vehicle, valid for seven days. MAP P.104–105

Any Las Vegas visitor hoping to see the stupendous desert scenery of the Southwest at its absolute best would do well to consider making a side trip to **Zion National Park**. Located in southwest Utah, a fast, direct drive of 160 miles northeast up I-15 from Las Vegas, it's every bit as impressive as the Grand Canyon, and offers much greater potential for an active weekend excursion from the city.

Named by nineteenth-century Mormon settlers, and carved by the Virgin River, Zion Canyon stands at the heart of the park. Unlike at the Grand Canyon, which is almost always seen from above, visitors enter by following the river upstream from the south and therefore see it from the verdant valley below. Astonishing sheer red-rock walls soar to either side, many of them topped by crests of paler sandstone that have been given fanciful names like the Court of the Patriarchs and the Great White Throne.

At the northern end of the canyon, visitors can follow the easy, mile-long **Riverside Walk** to the point where the Virgin River enters the valley. In the Zion Narrows beyond, accessible only to hardy hikers happy to wade waist-deep in ice-cold water, the towering canyon walls stand just a few feet apart. Other demanding trails switchback out of the valley to reach the desert uplands high above, and make wonderful day-hikes; the **West Rim Trail**, for example, climbs to a slender rock spur known as Angel's Landing, with a sheer quarter-of-a-mile drop to either side. Not surprisingly, Zion is also a favourite destination with rock climbers; several local operators offer guides.

Although it's possible to drive through the southern portion of the park, and continue east (towards Bryce Canyon) via an amazing 1930s tunnel, the only vehicles allowed into the narrowest part of the canyon are free shuttle buses, which depart from the visitor centre beside the park entrance.

In the canyon itself, the veteran *Zion Lodge* (see p.121) offers accommodation and dining, and the park runs large but very pleasant campgrounds. Otherwise, almost all facilities are in the gateway town of **Springdale**, in a magnificent setting just south of the park.

ZION NARROWS, ZION NATIONAL PARK

Restaurants

Mount Charleston

A CUT ABOVE

Resort on Mount Charleston, 2 Kyle Canyon Rd ☎702 872 5500, Ⓦwww.mtcharleston resort.com. Mon–Thurs & Sun 7am–8pm, Fri & Sat 7am–10pm. MAP P.104–105

Open for all meals daily – though note the early closing time on weekdays – the light, spacious restaurant at this grand old lodge serves hearty mountain specialities such as warming buffalo and boar stew ($10), plus tasty pizzas, pasta and $25 steaks.

MOUNT CHARLESTON LODGE

5375 Kyle Canyon Rd ☎702 872 5408, Ⓦwww.mtcharlestonlodge.com. Daily 8am–9pm. MAP P.104–105

The obvious place to stop for lunch on a Mount Charleston day-trip, where the road up the mountain reaches its dead end, featuring an outdoor patio that enjoys drop-dead views. The food itself is less enthralling, with pizzas and sandwiches for around $13, burgers a little more and a three-course dinner menu for $19.

Grand Canyon

ARIZONA ROOM

Bright Angel Lodge, Grand Canyon South Rim ☎928 638 2631, Ⓦwww.grandcanyon lodges.com. Daily: March–Oct 11.30am–3pm & 4.30–10pm; Nov & Dec 4.30–10pm. No reservations. MAP P.104–105

This good-value restaurant, near the rim but with no views, is the most convenient place to pick up a decent meal on the South Rim. Lunchtime burgers, sandwiches and salads cost $8–12, full dinners more like $16 for chicken and $24 for steak.

EL TOVAR DINING ROOM

El Tovar, Grand Canyon South Rim ☎928 638 2631, ext 6432, Ⓦwww.grandcanyonlodges .com. Daily 6.30am–10.45am, 11.15am–2pm & 4.30–10pm. MAP P.104–105

The stately splendours of the timber-built *El Tovar* make an impressive setting for great food. Only the front row of tables enjoy partial views of the canyon, but this grand century-old hotel oozes old-fashioned charm and the waiters are happy to let you linger. Reserve ahead for dinner, when rich mains like half a duck or veal *jaegerschnitzel* cost $30; lunch and breakfast are first-come first-served and significantly cheaper.

Springdale

BIT & SPUR RESTAURANT

1212 Zion Park Blvd, Springdale UT ☎435 772 3498, Ⓦwww.bitandspur.com. Daily 5–10pm. MAP P.104–105

With a cosy saloon-like interior, and a terrace facing Zion's red-rock cliffs, this relaxed but high-quality Mexican/ Southwestern restaurant makes a wonderful dinner spot. Chilli-rubbed steak costs $26, barbecued ribs $22 and a *chile relleno* (stuffed chilli) just $13.50, while the outdoor seating makes an ideal venue for a beer after a long day's hiking.

SPOTTED DOG CAFÉ

Flanigan's Inn, 428 Zion Park Blvd, Springdale UT ☎435 772 3244. Daily 7–11am & 5–10pm. MAP P.104–105

This very reasonably priced restaurant is attached to a motel near the Zion park entrance. In the morning it lays out a decent breakfast buffet, while the dinner menu ranges from a highly recommended $22 lamb shank to meatloaf or pasta at more like $15.

ACCOMMODATION

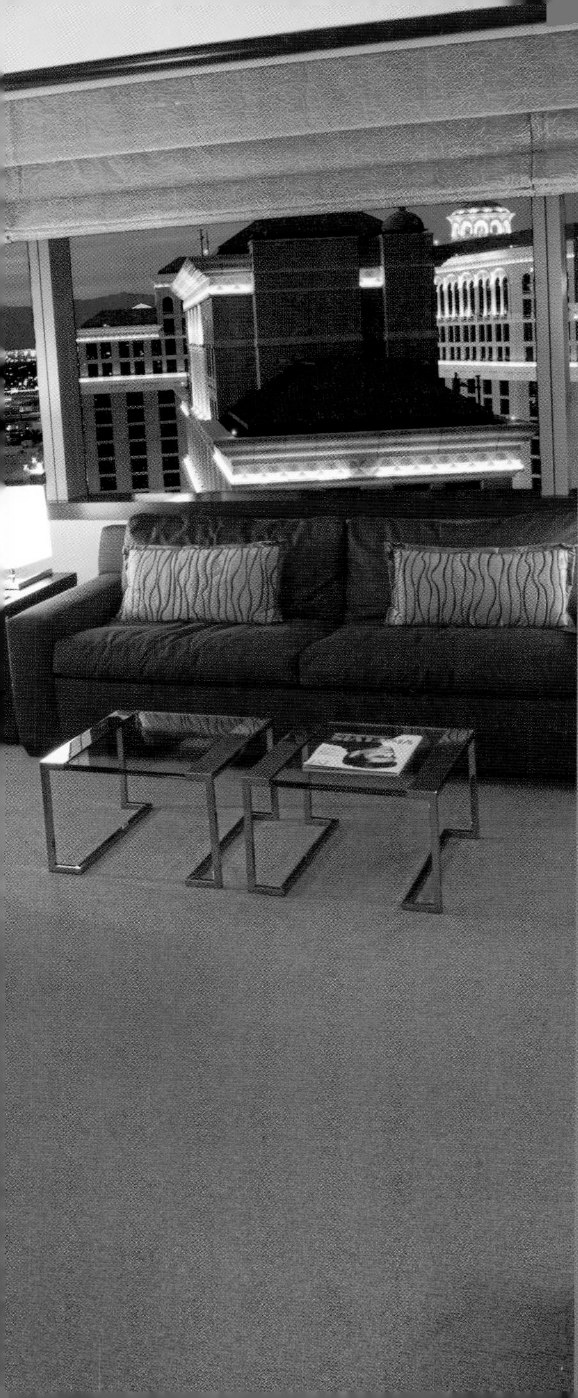

Accommodation

Choosing where to stay is the single biggest decision of any Las Vegas trip. Las Vegas is not like other destinations, where it's the city that you've come to see, and your choice of hotel makes little difference. In Las Vegas, it's the hotels that you've come to see – or rather the stupendously large casino resorts that hold not only the hotels, but also the restaurants, clubs, theatres and attractions, as well as the slot machines and gaming tables.

The fundamental choice is whether or not to stay on the **Strip**, which basically means staying in one of the colossal mega-casinos. Las Vegas is currently home to twenty of the world's 27 largest hotels, most along or very close to the Strip. Between them, they hold over 75,000 rooms, an average of almost four thousand each. All of those rooms are at least the standard of a good chain motel, invariably with en-suite bathrooms and with two queen-sized beds as the norm. Many are much more opulent; the standard rooms at places like Wynn, the Venetian and Bellagio are very plush, while every property offers **suites**.

However luxurious the rooms, the experience of staying in a hotel that has several thousand rooms has its drawbacks, including long **check-in queues** (half an hour is considered normal), a lack of personal service and endless walking to and fro. In, say, Caesars Palace or the MGM Grand, it can easily take twenty minutes to walk from your room out onto the Strip. The result is that most visitors spend their time in either their own hotel or its immediate neighbours.

The obvious alternative is to stay **downtown**, which is smaller and on a more manageable scale, with every hotel within easy walking distance from all the rest. While downtown has more affordable gambling and dining,

however, it has very few shops, shows or clubs, and lacks the jaw-dropping architecture of the Strip. It's also possible to find a room **elsewhere in the city**, either in a so-called locals casino, or in one of the many chain motels scattered around the periphery, but it's not recommended for visitors who want to experience all that makes Las Vegas unique.

As for **room rates**, it's essential to be aware that rooms change in price every night according to the level of demand. Just because a room costs $49 on Wednesday, it won't still be $49 on Saturday; it might well be $199. As a rule, Friday and Saturday are the most expensive nights, though exact rates also depend on factors such as whether there's a big convention in town; a concert at a specific casino; or even a sports event elsewhere, which gamblers want to bet on in Las Vegas.

The one sure way to find a cheap rate is to visit during the week. Beyond that, it's best to book via the hotel's own website a couple of months or more in advance, or, for weekday stays only, at the very last minute. Making a reservation at short notice is usually asking for trouble.

The **prices** given here are broad guidelines to suggest what you might pay during an ordinary, quiet week, and give some idea of how hotels compare.

Resort fees and taxes

Note that in addition to the room rates shown in this chapter, guests in almost every Las Vegas hotel are also required to pay so-called resort fees, listed here separately. These additional daily fees were introduced on the pretext of covering internet access – even if you don't use it – and generally also include such things as local or even long-distance (at Wynn and Encore) phone calls, use of a fitness centre and a daily newspaper. For many years, Caesars Entertainment made a big show of not having resort fees in its properties, but finally starting charging them in 2013.

All hotel bills are also subject to an additional room tax of twelve percent on the Strip and thirteen percent downtown; the room rates given here do not include these taxes.

The Strip

ARIA > 3730 Las Vegas Blvd S ☎866 359 7757 or ☎702 590 7111, ⓦwww .arialasvegas.com. MAP P.45, POCKET MAP B1 If you're more of a modernist than a traditionalist – and not only appreciate Aria's sleek contemporary aesthetic, but enjoy having on-screen digital controls for everything from the curtains to the air-conditioning – CityCenter's focal resort is the place for you. The rooms are classy rather than opulent, with great big beds and walk-in showers as well as tubs, but check-in tends to be slow and somewhat anarchic. **Resort fee $25/day. Mon–Thurs & Sun $169, Fri & Sat $259.**

BALLY'S > 3645 Las Vegas Blvd S ☎877 603 4390, ⓦwww.ballys lasvegas.com. MAP P.57, POCKET MAP G7 Staying at Bally's is not an experience anyone gets very excited about – the rooms are spacious but otherwise run of the mill – but it is in a great location to make the most of the Strip. Above all, it's intertwined with its younger sister Paris next door, so guests effectively get the benefits of staying there at significantly lower rates. **Resort fee $15/day. Mon–Thurs & Sun $94, Fri & Sat $174.**

BELLAGIO > 3600 Las Vegas Blvd S ☎888 987 6667 or ☎702 693 7111, ⓦwww.bellagio.com. MAP P.45, POCKET MAP F7 As Las Vegas is forever outdoing itself, Bellagio is no longer the cream of the crop, but by any normal standards, its opulent rooms epitomize luxury, while its location and amenities can't be beaten. The premium rooms naturally overlook the lake and its fountains, but actually the views from the back, over the pool, are great too. **Resort fee $25/day. Mon–Thurs & Sun $199, Fri & Sat $269.**

CAESARS PALACE > 3570 Las Vegas Blvd S ☎866 227 5938, ⓦwww .caesarspalace.com. MAP P.57, POCKET MAP F6 Fond memories of 1960s excess will always form part of the appeal of Caesars Palace, even if these days contemporary comfort tends to win out over kitsch. The sheer scale of the place can be overwhelming, but with its top-class dining and shopping, plus a fabulous pool and spa, it still has a real cachet. For serious luxury, pay $50–100 extra to stay in the newer Augustus and Octavius towers, which with their separate entrances also offer greater privacy and convenience. **Resort fee $25/day. Mon–Thurs & Sun $209, Fri & Sat $299.**

CIRCUS CIRCUS > 2880 Las Vegas Blvd S ☎800 634 3450 or ☎702 734 0410, ⓦwww.circuscircus.com. MAP P.70, POCKET MAP K8 Long a favourite with families and budget travellers, Circus Circus is showing its age; with its neighbours dropping like flies it feels like the casino time forgot. If you don't plan to linger and you have a car, its rock-bottom rates may prove irresistible. Pay a little extra to stay in its renovated towers, as opposed to the dingy Manor section. **Resort fee $9. Mon–Thurs & Sun $29, Fri & Sat $94.**

THE COSMOPOLITAN > 3708 Las Vegas Blvd S ☏702 698 7000, Ⓦwww .cosmopolitanlasvegas.com. MAP P.45, POCKET MAP F9 The stylish, contemporary Cosmopolitan makes a great option at the heart of the Strip. The guest rooms are classy and comfortable with colossal beds; even those that aren't suites have large living areas, while all except the cheapest have Strip-view balconies (a rarity in Las Vegas), and many overlook the Bellagio fountains. There's a good spa plus top-quality restaurants and clubs, and the hotel rooms aren't far from the lobby or the parking garage. **No resort fee. Mon–Thurs & Sun $180, Fri & Sat $270.**

ENCORE > 3121 Las Vegas Blvd S ☏888 320 7125 or ☏702 770 8000, Ⓦwww .encorelasvegas.com. MAP P.70, POCKET MAP J1 Las Vegas doesn't come any more luxurious than this; Encore truly is fit for a prince (just ask Harry Windsor). The huge, high-tech rooms are more subdued and earth-toned than the lurid reds the casino might lead you to expect, and all are considered suites, although the beds are screened off from the living areas rather than being separate rooms. **Resort fee $25. Mon–Thurs & Sun $209, Fri & Sat $399.**

EXCALIBUR > 3850 Las Vegas Blvd S ☏877 750 5464 or ☏702 597 7777, Ⓦwww.excalibur.com. MAP P.32, POCKET MAP B4 Cross the drawbridge to enter the Disney-esque castle, wheel your bag through the casino full of kids, ride the elevator to the top of the tower and...amazingly enough, so long as you pay a little extra for one of the renovated "wide-screen" rooms, you've found yourself a nice place to stay. The older rooms are looking very worn, though, and with its endless queues Excalibur itself can feel too big for comfort. **Resort fee $15. Mon–Thurs & Sun $36, Fri & Sat $120.**

THE FLAMINGO > 3555 Las Vegas Blvd S ☏888 902 9929 or ☏702 733 3111, Ⓦwww.flamingolasvegas.com. MAP P.55, POCKET MAP G6 So long as you stay at ground level, the Flamingo seems like a great place to stay – light, airy and very central, it's on a manageable scale, and has an attractive garden and pool area, and even live flamingos. The guest rooms upstairs are very hit and miss, however, and can be very grubby indeed; only consider staying here if you find a truly exceptional rate. **Resort fee $18/day. Mon–Thurs & Sun $85, Fri & Sat $175.**

HARRAH'S > 3475 Las Vegas Blvd S ☏800 214 9110 or ☏702 369 5000, Ⓦwww.harrahsvegas.com. MAP P.55, POCKET MAP G5 There's nothing to quicken the heart about Harrah's, the middle-of-the-Strip, middle-of-the-road casino that spent a couple of decades catering so assiduously to its long-standing repeat customers that it was able to buy all its fancier neighbours. With that kind of success, they haven't felt constrained to change much. The standard rooms remain rather gloomy and ordinary, though there are some fancier suites. **Resort fee $18/day. Mon–Thurs & Sun $60, Fri & Sat $150.**

LUXOR > 3900 Las Vegas Blvd S ☏877 386 4658 or ☏702 262 4444, Ⓦwww .luxor.com. MAP P.32, POCKET MAP B6 More than twenty years since this futuristic black-glass pyramid opened it's sadly feeling its age. It can still be a thrill to stay in one of the original rooms, with their sloping windows, but there's a reason rooms in the newer tower next door cost a little more – they're in much better condition, and also have baths and/or jacuzzis instead of showers. **Resort fee $20. Mon–Thurs & Sun $65, Fri & Sat $125.**

MANDALAY BAY > 3950 Las Vegas Blvd S ☏877 632 7800 or ☏702 632 7777, Ⓦwww.mandalaybay.com. MAP P.32, POCKET MAP B7 This far south of the central Strip, it makes sense to see Mandalay Bay as a self-contained resort. If you're happy to spend long days by its extravagant pool, and while away your evenings in its fine restaurants, bars, clubs and theatres, then it's well worth considering. Certainly the actual rooms are exceptionally comfortable, with both baths and walk-in showers. **Resort fee $25. Mon–Thurs & Sun $90, Fri & Sat $160.**

MGM GRAND > 3799 Las Vegas Blvd S ☏877 880 0880 or ☏891 7777, Ⓦwww.mgmgrand.com. MAP P.32, POCKET MAP C3 While it may not be the world's largest hotel any more, the MGM Grand feels too big for its own good; once you've queued to check in, and walked half a mile to your room, you may not feel up to venturing out to explore. Accommodation has been largely upgraded at the expense of its former character; the dark brown palette could be any convention hotel, anywhere. **Resort fee $25. Mon–Thurs & Sun $89, Fri & Sat $179.**

THE MIRAGE > 3400 Las Vegas Blvd S ☎800 374 9000 or ☎702 791 7111, ⓦwww.mirage.com. MAP P.70, POCKET MAP F4 Strangely enough, the casino that gave Las Vegas a new definition of luxury, twenty years ago, now seems like a relatively modest choice, in that its rooms are smaller than the norm, and bathrooms even smaller. They're still more than comfortable, though, with Strip and volcano views, and in a good location with excellent on-site amenities. **Resort fee $25. Mon–Thurs & Sun $125, Fri & Sat $240.**

MONTE CARLO > 3770 Las Vegas Blvd S ☎888 529 4828 or ☎702 730 7777, ⓦwww.montecarlo.com. MAP P.45, POCKET MAP C2 Anywhere else, the 3000-room Monte Carlo might seem like a big deal. In Las Vegas, it's barely visible, serving simply as an access route to CityCenter. Don't expect remarkable rooms, but in their anonymous way they're spruce and smart, and with the top-notch pool it's well worth considering if you can find a decent rate. **Resort fee $20. Mon–Thurs & Sun $84, Fri & Sat $160.**

NEW YORK–NEW YORK > 3790 Las Vegas Blvd S ☎866 815 4365 or ☎702 740 6969, ⓦwww .newyorknewyork.com. MAP P.32, POCKET MAP C3 Spending a night or two in Las Vegas's own Big Apple makes a more appealing prospect than a stay at most of its larger, less compact neighbours. Whether you opt for a "Park Avenue" or a slightly larger "Madison Avenue" room, the guest rooms are attractive and readily accessible, with some nice Art Deco touches, and the casino itself holds some excellent bars and restaurants. **Resort fee $18. Mon–Thurs & Sun $85, Fri & Sat $170.**

Las Vegas's most luxurious spas

Las Vegas's top casinos compete to offer state-of-the-art spas, with an array of pools, steam rooms, fitness facilities and massage services designed to pamper visitors to the nth degree. Spa entry normally costs around $30 per day, while massages and other treatments typically cost from around $100 for half an hour. While most accept non-guests, during busy periods you may find you can only use a particular spa if you're staying in the relevant casino or if you book a treatment there. The following are the very best the city has to offer:

Aria	The Spa	Daily 5.30am–8pm	☎702 590 9600
Bellagio	Spa Bellagio	Daily 6am–8pm	☎702 693 7472
Caesars Palace	Qua	Daily 6am–8pm	☎866 782 0655
Cosmopolitan	Sahra	Daily 7.30am–8pm	☎702 698 7171
Encore	Spa	Daily 7am–9pm	☎702 770 4772
Golden Nugget	Spa	Daily 6am–8pm	☎702 386 8186
Hard Rock	Reliquary	Daily 8am–8pm	☎702 693 5520
Mandalay Bay	Bathhouse	Daily 6am–8.30pm	☎877 632 9636
The Mirage	Spa	Daily 6am–7pm	☎702 791 7472
Planet Hollywood	Mandara	Daily 7am–7pm	☎702 785 5772
Venetian	Canyon Ranch	Daily 6am–8pm	☎702 414 3600
Wynn	Spa	Daily 9am–7pm	☎702 770 3900

THE PALAZZO > 3325 Las Vegas Blvd S ☎866 263 3001 or ☎702 607 7777, Ⓦwww.palazzo.com. MAP P.70, POCKET MAP H3 Staying at the Palazzo is fundamentally the same as staying at the Venetian (once you go downstairs, you're in the same building), but you'll find yourself slightly further from the heart of the action. The actual rooms are very similar, with plush sleeping and living areas at slightly different levels, and huge marble bathrooms, while the rates tend to be a little lower. **Resort fee $20. Mon–Thurs & Sun $209, Fri & Sat $249.**

PARIS > 3655 Las Vegas Blvd S ☎877 796 2096 or ☎702 946 7000, Ⓦwww .parislasvegas.com. MAP P.55, POCKET MAP G8 For many visitors, Paris represents an ideal compromise – you get to stay in an interesting big-name property, with excellent amenities plus "only in Vegas" features like the Eiffel Tower outside your window – without paying premium prices for opulent fittings you don't really need. The standard rooms are a little faded now; for a little more pampering, opt for a newer "Red Room". **Resort fee $20/day. Mon–Thurs & Sun $93, Fri & Sat $201.**

PLANET HOLLYWOOD > 3667 Las Vegas Blvd S ☎866 919 7472 or ☎702 785 5555, Ⓦwww.planethollywood resort.com. MAP P.55, POCKET MAP G9 While Planet Hollywood's confusing layout can make it a long trek from your car to your room, once you're here it's a great-value central location. The rooms are in a style they call "Hollywood Hip", which tends to mean black and gold carpets and wallpaper; movie stills on the wall; and walk-in showers as well as baths. **Resort fee $20/day. Mon–Thurs & Sun $79, Fri & Sat $159.**

THE RIVIERA > 2901 Las Vegas Blvd S ☎800 634 6753 or ☎702 734 5110, Ⓦwww.rivierahotel.com. MAP P.70, POCKET MAP L9 Assuming the Riviera even exists by the time you read this, it's a safe bet to assume it will still be rundown, with tired rooms and drab furnishings. The only reason to stay in this rather desolate part of the Strip is if you find a much better rate than anywhere else. **Resort fee $11. Mon–Thurs & Sun $35, Fri & Sat $95.**

THE STRATOSPHERE > 2000 Las Vegas Blvd S ☎800 998 6937 or ☎702 380 7777, Ⓦwww.stratosphere hotel.com. MAP P.70, POCKET MAP L2 Much too far to walk to from either the Strip or downtown, the Stratosphere is at least something of a destination in its own right – the rooms aren't in the 1000ft tower, but guests do get free admission. Find the right cut-price offer online, and its simple but sizeable rooms may suit your budget. **Resort fee $7.50. Mon–Thurs & Sun $39, Fri & Sat $99.**

TI (TREASURE ISLAND) > 3300 Las Vegas Blvd S ☎800 288 7206 or ☎702 894 7111, Ⓦwww .treasureisland.com. MAP P.70, POCKET MAP G3 Like the building itself, the rooms at TI remain in good condition – they're nothing fancy, but they look reasonably fresh and have good beds – and the location is great too. These days, the whole place, and the pool in particular, attracts a young party crowd. Look out for online discounts. **Resort fee $25. Mon–Thurs & Sun $79, Fri & Sat $149.**

THE TROPICANA > 3801 Las Vegas Blvd S ☎888 381 8767 or ☎702 739 2222, Ⓦwww.troplv.com. MAP P.32, POCKET MAP C4 Completely overhauled in 2010, this long-standing landmark can't quite match its Mirage-owned neighbours for dining and nightlife, but seen simply as a place to stay, it offers large, cream-and-orange-rooms with new furnishings, an excellent pool complex and a location handy for the airport. **Resort fee $15. Mon–Thurs & Sun $85, Fri & Sat $149.**

VDARA > 2600 W Harmon Ave ☎866 745 7767 or ☎702 590 2767, Ⓦwww .vdara.com. MAP P.45, POCKET MAP E9 Hedonist holidaymakers might feel ill at ease with the austere steel-and-chrome aesthetic of this CityCenter all-suite hotel and its lack of a casino, but if you're here to work or fancy an escape from the round-the-clock scene, it makes a peaceful and comfortable retreat. **Resort fee $25. Mon–Thurs & Sun $129, Fri & Sat $205.**

THE VENETIAN > 3355 Las Vegas Blvd S ☎866 659 9643 or ☎702 414 1000, ⓦwww.venetian.com. MAP P.70, POCKET MAP G4 In terms of amenities in the property as a whole, and sheer comfort in its guest rooms, the Venetian ranks in the very top tier of Strip hotels; slightly more old-fashioned than Wynn, but still a true pampering experience. All the rooms are suites; you step down from the sleeping area, with its huge bed, to reach a sunken living space near the panoramic windows. Unusually, the price for advance bookings often remains the same for weekends as for weekdays. **Resort fee $20. Daily $209.**

WYNN LAS VEGAS > 3131 Las Vegas Blvd S ☎877 321 9966 or ☎702 770 7000, ⓦwww.wynnlasvegas.com. MAP P.70, POCKET MAP J2 With the arguable exception of the all-but-identical Encore alongside, this is as opulent as it gets in Vegas. The super-large rooms are tastefully decorated and equipped with luxurious linens, and bathrooms feature marble tubs, walk-in showers and even TVs. **Resort fee $25. Mon–Thurs & Sun $259, Fri & Sat $399.**

Downtown

THE D > 301 E Fremont St ☎702 388 2400, ⓦwww.thed.com. MAP P.87, POCKET MAP G12 Since turning from Fitzgerald's into The D, this central downtown hotel has become a real bargain. All its rooms have had a top-to-bottom makeover (each has two queen beds) and the amenities downstairs are much improved. The one problem can be noise from the Experience outside. **No resort fee. Mon–Thurs & Sun $39, Fri & Sat $99.**

EL CORTEZ > 600 E Fremont St ☎800 634 6703 or ☎702 385 5200, ⓦwww .ecvegas.com. MAP P.87, POCKET MAP H12 Long renowned as Las Vegas's cheapest casino, El Cortez stands a short but, at night, potentially intimidating walk from the heart of Fremont Street. Once there, everything's in good shape, though the "Vintage" rooms, reached via the stairs, are no better than faded motel rooms. The "Cabana" suites,

across the street, are much more appealing. Online packages for first-time guests offset room rates with free meals and gaming. **No resort fee. Mon–Thurs & Sun $28, Fri & Sat.**

FOUR QUEENS > 202 E Fremont St ☎800 634 6045 or ☎702 385 4011, ⓦwww.fourqueens.com. MAP P.87, POCKET MAP G12 There's no real reason to pick this resolutely old-school downtown stalwart over any of its neighbours, though it has at least kept its rooms up to the adequate but unexciting level, say, of a $60-per-night national chain. **No resort fee. Mon–Thurs & Sun $35, Fri & Sat $79.**

FREMONT HOTEL > 200 E Fremont St ☎800 634 6460 or ☎702 385 3232, ⓦwww.fremontcasino.com. MAP P.87, POCKET MAP G12 As one of the few downtown casinos owned by a major corporation – Boyd Gaming – the Fremont keeps its standards pretty high. The rooms are small but up to date, with pleasant decor and linens, and it's really not a bad alternative if you fancy being in the thick of the Fremont Street action. **No resort fee. Mon–Thurs & Sun $50, Fri & Sat $89.**

THE GOLDEN GATE > 1 E Fremont St ☎800 426 1906 or ☎702 385 1906, ⓦwww.goldengatecasino. com. MAP P.87, POCKET MAP G11 Las Vegas's first ever hotel, 107 years old in 2013, has been restyled as a 106-room "boutique hotel", with the promise that more suites will soon be added in a new extension. Yes, the rooms are small and the floors strangely lumpy, but you do get a true taste of Vegas history – plus, unfortunately, a blast of noise from the Experience. **No resort fee. Mon–Thurs & Sun $39, Fri & Sat $69.**

GOLDEN NUGGET > 129 E Fremont St ☎800 846 5336 or ☎702 385 7111, ⓦwww.goldennugget.com. MAP P.87, POCKET MAP G12 Downtown's classiest option is the only hotel hereabouts with amenities – like its amazing pool – to match the Strip giants. The actual rooms, at their freshest but loudest in the Rush Tower overlooking Fremont Street, are smart and comfortable, if not all that exciting. **No resort fee. Mon–Thurs & Sun $69, Fri & Sat $129.**

LAS VEGAS HOSTEL > 1322 E Fremont St ☎800 550 8958 or ☎702 385 1150, Ⓦwww.lasvegashostel.net. MAP P.87, POCKET MAP J13 Popular with young travellers, this converted motel is almost a mile east of downtown in an area where walking is unadvisable. Adequate bare-bones accommodation includes four-, six- and eight-bed single-sex and mixed dorms, and en-suite private rooms. There's also a pool, hot tub and organized activities. Wi-fi, parking and breakfast included. **Dorms $13–17/person; doubles $36.**

MAIN STREET STATION > 200 N Main St ☎800 713 8933 or ☎702 387 1896, Ⓦwww.mainstreetcasino.com. MAP P.87, POCKET MAP G11 A short but safe walk north of Fremont Street, this large and reasonably modern casino is always good value, for accommodation, food and drink; it's particularly recommended as an affordable base for a busy weekend. Ask for a room away from the interstate. **No resort fee. Mon–Thurs & Sun $50, Fri & Sat $70.**

THE PLAZA > 1 Main St ☎800 634 6575 or ☎702 386 2110, Ⓦwww.plazahotel casino.com. MAP P.87, POCKET MAP F11 The veteran Plaza, at the end of Fremont Street on the site of Las Vegas's original railroad station, pulled off a real coup in 2011. It bought up the brand-new fixtures and fittings from the prestigious Fontaineblue on the Strip, so badly hit by the recession it never even opened, and used them to turn its rundown rooms into some of the smartest and best value lodgings around. **Resort fee $10. Mon–Thurs & Sun $40, Fri & Sat $79.**

The rest of the city

GOLD COAST >4000 W Flamingo Rd, ☎800 331 5334 or ☎702 367 7111, Ⓦwww.goldcoastcasino.com. MAP P.95, POCKET MAP G15 Sedate, old-fashioned locals casino, complete with bingo and a bowling alley, a hot half-mile west of the Strip (to which it's connected by free shuttle buses), but right by the fancier Rio and Palms. The rooms are not all bad, but there's no earthly reason to stay unless the price is right. **Resort fee $3. Mon–Thurs & Sun $34, Fri & Sat $99.**

HARD ROCK HOTEL > 4455 Paradise Rd ☎800 473 7625, Ⓦwww .hardrockhotel.com. MAP P.95, POCKET MAP B16 If you know what you're coming for – to mix with partying 20-somethings – the *Hard Rock* will suit you perfectly. The rooms are cool and comfortable, and you can even open the floor-to-ceiling windows. It's too far from the Strip, though, to make a good base for seeing the city as a whole. Weekends book up early; reserve in advance. **Resort fee $18. Mon–Thurs & Sun $62, Fri & Sat $249.**

LAS VEGAS HOTEL > 3000 Paradise Rd ☎702 732 5111, Ⓦwww.thelvh .com. MAP P.95, POCKET MAP L5 How the mighty are fallen. The only reason to stay in the former Hilton – once, as home to Elvis Presley, Las Vegas's premier hotel – is if you're attending a convention next door. Otherwise, the rooms just aren't good enough to compensate for the cut-off location and general air of decay. **No resort fee. Mon–Thurs & Sun $39, Fri & Sat $79.**

ORLEANS > 4500 W Tropicana Ave ☎800 675 3267 or ☎702 365 7111, Ⓦwww.orleanscasino.com. MAP P.95, POCKET MAP A12 Provided you get one of its freshly renovated rooms and you have a car to get around, the Orleans, a mile west of the Strip, can serve as an affordable base to explore Las Vegas. The on-site cinema is a real boon. **Resort fee $6. Mon–Thurs & Sun $40, Fri & Sat $75.**

THE PALMS > 4321 W Flamingo Rd ☎866 942 7777 or ☎702 942 7777, Ⓦwww.palms.com. MAP P.95, POCKET MAP F16 One of the very few off-Strip casinos that you might genuinely want to stay in, rather than simply find a good-value rate for, the Palms is renowned for its clubs, gigs and weekend buzz. Things are much quieter on weekdays, but with such comfortable rooms and great pools, it can be a real bargain. **Resort fee $20. Mon–Thurs & Sun $99, Fri & Sat $199.**

RIO > 3700 W Flamingo Rd ☎866 746 7671, Ⓦwww.riolasvegas.com. MAP P.95, POCKET MAP H15 Part of the Caesars Entertainment empire, but separated by half a mile from its Strip siblings, the Rio really isn't a bad accommodation option. As well as high-class amenities and entertainment, it offers comfortable rooms (large but not suites, as they claim). The Palms is over the road, but you may feel you're missing out on all the action. **Resort fee $18/day. Mon–Thurs & Sun $59, Fri & Sat $159.**

SAM'S TOWN > 5111 Boulder Hwy ☎800 897 8696 or ☎702 456 7777, Ⓦwww.samstownlv.com. MAP P.95, POCKET MAP D12 Quietly prospering from meeting its middle-American customers' needs with Wild-West shops, restaurants and NASCAR races, this old-fashioned local casino stands resolutely apart from modern Las Vegas. If you want to dip into town but stay somewhere more peaceful, its comfortable rooms may suit you fine. It's a six-mile shuttle ride to the Strip so you're better off with a car. **Resort fee $4.50. Mon–Thurs & Sun $30, Fri & Sat $95.**

SUNSET STATION > 1301 W Sunset Rd, Henderson ☎800 782 8466 or ☎702 547 7777, Ⓦwww.sunsetstation.com. MAP P.95, POCKET MAP D13 This huge, attractive and well-equipped casino, ten miles southeast of the Strip en route towards Arizona, would seem impressive anywhere else. Here, despite its pool and fine restaurants, it counts as low-key, and only worth considering if the price is right or you're passing through. **Resort fee $15. Mon–Thurs & Sun $48, Fri & Sat $114.**

Mount Charleston

MOUNT CHARLESTON LODGE > 5375 Kyle Canyon Rd ☎702 872 5408, Ⓦwww.mtcharlestonlodge.com. MAP P.104–105 Nineteen comfortably appointed log cabins, alongside the restaurant (see p.111) at the far end of Hwy-157. Lacking phones, wi-fi and TV reception, they're especially popular with honeymooners escaping Las Vegas. **$142.**

RESORT ON MOUNT CHARLESTON > 2 Kyle Canyon Rd ☎888 559 1888, ☎702 872 5500, Ⓦwww.mtcharleston resort.com. MAP P.104–105 Set below Hwy-157, facing a towering rocky outcrop 17 miles up from US-95, the best accommodation option in the mountains holds 61 very cosy, smart rooms, arranged around an artificial lake. **$99.**

Grand Canyon South Rim

BRIGHT ANGEL LODGE > Grand Canyon South Rim, AZ. Advance reservations ☎888 297 2757 or ☎303 297 2757, same-day reservations ☎928 638 2631, Ⓦwww.grandcanyonlodges.com. MAP P.104–105 Stretching along the South Rim and consisting of a grand lodge flanked by individual cabins, this fantastic-value option is usually booked up months in advance. Some units share bathrooms, while others enjoy canyon views. **Double with shared bathroom $83.**

EL TOVAR > Grand Canyon South Rim, AZ. Advance reservations ☎888 297 2757 or ☎303 297 2757, same-day reservations ☎928 638 2631, Ⓦwww.grandcanyonlodges.com. MAP P.104–105 At heart an overgrown log cabin, this magnificent, century-old hotel, a symphony in dark wood, is the definitive national park lodge. Although it's very close to the rim, only three of its 78 rooms offer substantial canyon views. **$178**

Zion National Park

DESERT PEARL INN > 707 Zion Park Blvd, Springdale UT ☎888 828 0898 or ☎435 772 8888, Ⓦwww.desertpearl.com. MAP P.104–105 An absolutely gorgeous hotel, ranged alongside the Virgin River just outside the park, with superb views. From the parking areas it may look like a regular motel, but the actual rooms are huge, modern and very attractive, and there's a good pool with hot tubs. **$158.**

ZION LODGE > Zion National Park, UT. Advance reservations ☎888 297 2757 or ☎303 297 2757, same-day reservations ☎435 772 7700, Ⓦwww.zionlodge.com. MAP P.104–105 The only accommodation option inside the national park, occupying pride of place on lush lawns in the heart of the Canyon. The forty en-suite cabins have gas fireplaces and private porches, while the 72 motel rooms are plainer, but still have porches or balconies. **Motel rooms $176, cabins $184.**

El Cort
HOTE
COFFEE SHOP &
FREE PARKING
SEPTEMBER GIVEAWAY
FREE PLAY
ALL THE
TIME!
$10 TO $1,000 IN FRE
SUBWAY

ESSENTIALS

Arrival

A very high proportion of visitors to Las Vegas **fly** into the city's only significant airport, not far east of the Strip, while all the rest **drive** across the empty desert from elsewhere in the USA. No passenger trains currently serve the city, though there's talk of constructing a high-speed link with Los Angeles.

By air

Las Vegas's ever-expanding **McCarran International Airport** (☎702 261 5211, ⊕www.mccarran .com) lies immediately southeast of the Strip; aircraft pass within a mile of Mandalay Bay and the Tropicana as they taxi. However, both its terminals – confusingly numbered 1 and 3, since the new Terminal 3, used by all international flights, replaced the former Terminal 2 in 2012 – are accessed from the east, via Paradise Road. That means the closest Strip casinos are around three miles by road from the airport; the Venetian and Wynn more like five miles; and downtown hotels around seven miles.

Assuming you're not renting a car – in which case, note that all the rental companies are based at a separate, off-site facility (see p.126) – much the best way to transfer from the airport to your hotel is by **taxi**. In principle, a cab ride to the southern Strip (10–20min) will cost $16 and upwards, and to the northern Strip (20–30min) more like $30. If the traffic's bad you may have to pay up to $10 more.

Lone travellers may prefer to pay for a seat in a shared **Bell Trans shuttle bus** (☎702 739 7990, ⊕www .bell-trans.com), which costs $7.50 to the Strip and $10 to downtown, but as these services drop off other passengers en route the journey time can be long, at an hour or more for properties on the North Strip.

It is also possible, but even slower, to use the **RTC bus network** (see p.125), by taking route #109 from the airport to the South Strip Transfer Terminal, and changing there onto the Strip And Downtown Express, for a total fare of $3. The total journey is likely to take at least half an hour for the South Strip, and over an hour for the North Strip and downtown.

Note that the **Las Vegas Monorail** (see p.126) does not serve the airport.

By car

The main driving route into Las Vegas is the **I-15** interstate, which connects the city with Los Angeles, 270 miles southwest, and Salt Lake City, 420 miles northeast. On Fridays especially, it tends to be clogged with cars arriving from southern California. Only if traffic is at a standstill is it worth leaving the interstate before you reach the exit closest to your final destina-tion. If you're coming from California, therefore, you wouldn't normally expect to drive the full length of Las Vegas Boulevard, which runs parallel to I-15 from the southern end of the valley, and becomes the Strip roughly ten miles along.

Driving to Las Vegas from the Grand Canyon or anywhere else in Arizona, you'll approach the city along **US-93**, via the Hoover Dam. Either follow the same road, as Boulder Highway, all the way to downtown, or turn west, most likely on Tropicana Road or Flamingo Avenue, to reach the Strip.

By bus

Long-distance **Greyhound buses** (☎800 231 2222, ⊕www.greyhound .com), which connect Las Vegas with other Southwestern cities including Los Angeles, Phoenix and Salt Lake City, stop downtown rather than on the Strip. The station is alongside the Plaza hotel, at 200 S Main St.

Getting around

If you're visiting Las Vegas specifically to spend time on the Strip and/or downtown – as is the case for most visitors – there's no point renting a car. Downtown is small enough to walk around, while a good **bus service** runs the full length of the Strip and continues to downtown, and there are also several separate **monorail systems** on the Strip. Only if you expect to explore any further afield, whether to outlying areas (see p.94), or to the surrounding desert (see p.104), does a car become essential.

On foot

It comes as a big surprise to most visitors quite how much **walking** you have to do in Las Vegas. The Strip might look like a simple straight line on the map, but it has a peculiar geography all its own; the colossal scale of the buildings tricks the eye, making them look smaller and nearer than they really are. Each individual casino can measure a mile end to end, while walking from, say, a restaurant in one property to a club in the next can take half an hour. Especially in summer, when the searing heat makes it all but impossible to walk more than a block or two outdoors, plotting a route from A to B becomes a real art, involving cutting through air-conditioned casinos, catching the occasional monorail and other such dodges.

By bus

While **RTC buses** (⊚www.catride .com) cover the whole city, two main routes meet the needs of almost all visitors. You must buy a ticket before you board; vending machines at stops along both routes sell a 2-hour pass for $5, a 24-hour pass for $7 or a 3-day pass for $20. All buses are wheelchair accessible.

The **Deuce on the Strip** (daily 24hr) runs the full length of the Strip, from Mandalay Bay to the Stratosphere, stopping outside all the casinos, and also loops around downtown, running north on Casino Center Boulevard and south on Las Vegas Boulevard. While its principal downtown stop is where the Fremont Street Experience meets Las Vegas Boulevard, it also stops in both directions at the Bonneville Transit Center (BTC), six blocks south at Bonneville and Casino Center, the main interchange for crosstown routes.

As the name suggests, the faster **Strip & Downtown Express**, or SDX, (daily 9am–12.30am) also connects the Strip with downtown, but with fewer stops. In addition, rather than follow the Strip between Wynn Las Vegas and the Stratosphere, it detours west to run past the Convention Center. Downtown is the most useful stop, where the Fremont Street Experience meets Casino Center Boulevard, though the route loops back west beyond Fremont Street to terminate at the Las Vegas Premium Outlets (North) mall, and it also stops at the Bonneville Transit Center. Southbound SDX buses stop on the Strip outside the Fashion Show mall, Bellagio, Excalibur and Mandalay Bay; northbound buses stop across from Mandalay Bay, and outside the MGM Grand, Paris and Wynn. The southern end of the route is the South Strip Transfer Terminal (SSTT), three miles southeast of Mandalay Bay at 6675 Gilespie Street, which connects with other bus routes and is also served by free airport shuttle buses.

In addition, various free **shuttle buses** connect the Strip with further-flung casinos. From Harrah's, buses run west to the Rio (half-hourly departures, daily 10am–1am; ☏800 214 9110) and east to Sam's Town (every 1hr 30min, daily 9.30am–9.30pm; ☏800 897 8696). From the intersection of Flamingo Road with the Strip, buses run via the Gold Coast to the Orleans (half-hourly departures, daily 9.30am–12.30am).

By monorail

Four separate monorail systems currently operate along different stretches of the Strip. The longest, but in some respects least useful, is the one officially called the **Las Vegas Monorail** (Mon–Thurs 7am–2am, Fri–Sun 7am–3am; single trip $5, 1-day pass $12, 3-day pass $28; www.lvmonorail.com). It runs behind the casinos on the eastern side of the Strip, from the MGM Grand to the former Sahara, detouring east en route to call at the Convention Center. Had the route been extended south to the airport, and downtown in the north, it could have relieved Las Vegas's traffic problems. As it is, it's only conceivably helpful for hops along the southern Strip. Even then, all the stations are located right at the back of the relevant casinos, ten minutes' walk from their Strip entrances, so it can be slower to catch the Monorail than to walk.

All the other three monorail systems are **free**, and link small groups of neighbouring casinos. The southernmost connects Mandalay Bay with Excalibur, via Luxor. The second runs from the Monte Carlo, via Aria and Crystals in CityCenter, to Bellagio; it's a futuristic ride, but be warned the Bellagio station is in that property's far southwestern corner, far from the casino floor and the Strip. Finally, the short link between the Mirage and TI now serves little practical function other than keeping pedestrians cool.

By car

Locals might find it hard to believe, but for visitors, **driving** in Las Vegas can be a real pleasure. The thrill of cruising along the Strip, with its sights and sounds and blazing signs, only wears

thin if you're actually trying to get somewhere by a certain time. Tourists tend naturally to avoid the worst times for traffic, like the morning rush hour.

Along the Strip, every casino offers **free parking**, albeit in an enormous multistorey garage around the back – somewhere that may well be a long walk from your destination. You can save a lot of time by using valet parking at the main entrance; in theory it's free, but you're expected to tip around $2. Most downtown casinos charge non-guests a parking fee, but it's often waived if you spend money in their restaurants or bars.

Car rental is available from almost every Strip or downtown hotel; as a rule each holds one or two outlets of the major rental chains. However, you can find a much wider choice, and usually better rates, if you pick up at the airport. That said, the major rental agencies are no longer based at the airport itself, but at the **McCarran Rent-A-Car Center**, three miles southwest at 7135 Gilespie Street, which is connected with the terminals by free shuttle buses. If you're already in the city and decide to rent a car, be sure to take a cab direct to the Rent-A-Car Center. Whether you book via the agencies' own websites, or online brokers like Travelocity or Expedia, you can expect to pay around $40 per day, or $200 per week, for a compact car.

By taxi

You can't hail a passing **taxi** on the street in Las Vegas, but long lines of cabs wait to pick up passengers at the casino entrances, as well as at the airport. Meters calculate fares on the basis of $3.30 for the first mile and $2.60 for each additional mile, but also run if you're delayed in traffic, charging $1 every two minutes. There's an additional $1.80 surcharge for trips to or from the airport (see p.124). Fifteen percent is the usual tip for the driver.

Gambling

Gambling, or as they like to call it these days "**gaming**", lies at the root of everything in Las Vegas. Only one visitor in ten doesn't gamble at all; the rest lose an average of $500 each in the casinos. Whether you're pumping coins into a slot machine or trying to beat the dealer at blackjack, the rules always mean the casino enjoys the "house edge". So long as you're 21 or over, and carrying ID to prove it, you can gamble anywhere you like. The glamour of the large **Strip casinos** can be seductive, but the minimum stake for each game tends to be higher, and the odds a little worse. Many visitors prefer to gamble **downtown**, where the atmosphere is a bit more down-and-dirty and their money holds out longer. Either way, decide in advance how much you're prepared to lose, and stop if you reach that point.

In all casinos waitresses will ply you with free drinks as long as you are gambling; tips are expected. If you gamble for any length of time, join the casino's free players club; it can earn you meals, freebies and future stays.

Baccarat

Formerly the preserve of high-rolling "whales", **baccarat** (pronounced bah-kah-rah) accounts for over forty percent of the casinos' revenue from table games. Played with an ordinary pack in which each numbered card counts its face value (aces are 1 not 11), except tens, jacks, queens and kings, all valued at zero, it's a simple game of luck. Only two hands are dealt, the "player" and the "bank". Each aims to reach a total value of nine; you can bet on either, but the bank has a slightly better chance of winning. The house advantage comes because the casino rakes off a small commission.

Blackjack

Also known as "21" or "pontoon", **blackjack** remains Las Vegas's favourite card game. Players compete against the bank, attempting to build a hand that adds nearly, or exactly, to 21. Tens, jacks, queens and kings count as ten points, aces as either one or eleven. Players make their bets before receiving two cards, then each in turn plays their hand through to completion, saying "hit" to receive additional cards, and either "stand" to stop, or "bust" if the total exceeds 21. The dealer plays last, according to fixed rules that preclude individual judgement. The house advantage comes because players who go bust lose their stakes whether or not the dealer does too. Players can minimize that advantage by learning the "correct" response to every situation – it's so hard that some casinos provide gamblers with the relevant charts.

Craps

If you don't know how to play the dice game **craps**, played on a high-walled baize table, take a lesson (freely available in most casinos) – you'll never be able to learn it from watching. The basic idea is that a different "shooter" throws a pair of dice each time around. Players bet on either "pass" or "don't pass" before the first throw, known as the "come-out roll". If that throw is 7 or 11, "pass" has won; if it's 2, 3 or 12, "don't pass" wins. Anything else, and the shooter throws again, and keeps doing so until either matching the original throw – a win for "pass" – or throwing 7 – a win for "don't pass". All sorts of side bets capture the imaginations of serious gamblers.

Poker

In **poker**, players compete against each other, not the house, to build the best five-card hand (see box, p.128). The two most popular variations are

Seven Card Stud, in which each player receives two cards face down, four face up, and then the last face down, and Texas Hold 'Em, in which your two face-down cards are supplemented by five face-up communal cards. The casino rakes off a percentage of each pot. You're therefore playing against whoever else happens to be around; it's possible to win, but it's a big risk to assume you're the best player at the table.

Casinos also offer what's effectively poker played in a **blackjack format**, in which each player attempts to beat the dealer. Formats include Let It Ride, Pai Gow Poker and Caribbean Stud.

Roulette

Roulette is the game in which a ball lands in a numbered slot in a rotating wheel. You can bet on the specific number, or group of numbers, and if the slot is "red" or "black". Winners are paid as though the wheel holds 36 slots, but it usually holds 38, thanks to two green slots, 0 and 00. Always look for wheels that hold only one extra slot, and thus offer better odds. You can't get your money back by repeatedly redoubling your stake; tables allow bets up to a quickly reached maximum.

Slot machines

Casinos make more money from **slot machines** than from anything else. All machines are programmed to pay out a percentage of their intake as winnings. On average, visitors feed $1600 per day into every single machine in the city, and win $1500 back again, leaving the casino $100 profit. The slots downtown offer better odds than on the Strip.

A "non-progressive" machine always pays the same for a specific winning combination and pays smaller but more frequent jackpots. "Progressive" slots, such as Wheel of Fortune, are linked into networks where the overall jackpot can climb into millions of dollars, before someone scoops the lot.

Video poker is an addictive cross between traditional slot machines and the table game. The odds can be so good that on certain machines, players who play a perfect strategy have a slight advantage over the house.

Sports betting

Las Vegas is all but unique in the USA in offering visitors the chance to bet on sports events legally, in the highly charged atmosphere of a major casino. Almost every casino holds either a **Sports Book**, or if it covers horse-racing as well, a Race and Sports Book, which vary from comfortable high-tech lounges to something more like a raucous neighbourhood sports bar. All offer much the same odds on any specific event and many offer "in-running" wagering, meaning moment-by-moment bets on games currently in progress.

Ranking of poker hands

Straight flush Five consecutive cards in the same suit.
Four of a kind Four aces, four sevens etc.
Full house Three of a kind and a separate pair.
Flush Any five cards in the same suit.
Straight Five consecutive cards not in the same suit.
Three of a kind Three Kings, three sixes etc.
Two pair Two fours and two Jacks etc.
One pair Two tens etc.

Directory A–Z

Cinemas

Typical ticket prices for cinemas in Las Vegas are around $8 for matinée performances, starting before 6pm, and $10 for evening shows.

Brenden Theatres & IMAX The Palms, 4321 W Flamingo Rd ☎702 507 4849, ⊚www.brendentheatres.com.

Century 18 Orleans, 4500 W Tropicana Ave ☎702 889 1220, ⊚www.cinemark.com.

Century 18 Sam's Town, 5111 Boulder Hwy ☎702 547 1732, ⊚www.cinemark.com.

Rave Motion Pictures Town Square, 6587 Las Vegas Blvd S ☎702 362 7283, ⊚www.mytownsquarelasvegas.com. Regal 13 Sunset Station, 1301 W Sunset Rd, Henderson ☎702 221 2283, ⊚www.regmovies.com.

United Artists Showcase 8 Next door to the MGM Grand at 3769 Las Vegas Blvd S ☎702 221 2283, ⊚www.regmovies.com. The only cinema on the Strip.

Crime

While you're safe in the major public spaces of Las Vegas, such as inside the security-conscious casinos, crime can be a problem elsewhere. Away from the crowded Strip, which has its own problems with **pickpockets** and bag-snatchers, you can feel exposed and vulnerable if you walk any distance outdoors. It's essential to keep your cash hidden at all times, not to flaunt valuables like cameras and iPads, and not to tell strangers your hotel room number. Be cautious in multistorey parking garages, especially at night, and try to park close to the exits.

Travellers with disabilities

The **Las Vegas Convention and Visitors Authority** offers detailed advice for disabled visitors; download the Access Las Vegas brochure from ⊚www.visitlasvegas.co.uk, or call their advice line on ☎702 892 7525.

All the casinos in Las Vegas are **wheelchair accessible** and offer hotel rooms designed to suit visitors with disabilities. Don't underestimate the sheer scale of each casino, let alone the Strip as a whole; an individual destination like a restaurant or a theatre may be a long way from the nearest parking space. If you need to rent specific mobility equipment, contact Ability Center, 6001 S Decatur Blvd (☎702 434 3030, ⊚www.abilitycenter.cAs). For public transport, both Bell Trans shuttle buses from the airport (☎702 739 7990, ⊚www.bell-trans.com) and RTC buses in the city itself (⊚www.rtcsnv.com) are wheelchair accessible. If you plan to drive yourself, the national rental chains offer adapted vehicles, and visitors can arrange temporary free **disabled parking permits** via the Nevada Department of Motor Vehicles (☎775 684 4750, ⊚ www.dmvnv.com).

Electricity

The **electricity** supply in Las Vegas, as in all of the USA, is 110 volts AC, and uses two-pin plugs. Bring or buy an adapter, and if necessary a voltage converter as well, if you're travelling from a country that uses a different system and need to use your own electrical appliances.

Gay and lesbian travellers

Although Las Vegas, or at least the parts of the city that visitors are at all likely to see, is a **gay-friendly** city, the casinos make little show of catering to gay travellers in any specific sense. Thus no casino holds a gay bar or club; instead, by far the largest gay club, **Krave Massive**, is in the Neonopolis mall on Fremont Street downtown (see p.93). Otherwise, the city's gay-oriented nightlife is focused around what's fondly known as the "**Fruit Loop**", a mile east of the Strip, where Paradise Road, running south from the Hard Rock, meets Naples Drive. Well-known clubs in the neighbourhood include Piranha (see p.103), but there are none exclusively geared towards women.

The best source of information on current issues and events in Las Vegas's gay community is the monthly magazine *QVegas*, distributed in a free printed version and also available online (⊙www.qvegas.com).

Nevada law does not recognize gay marriage, but gay couples can arrange **commitment ceremonies** at most major casinos, and also at the Gay Chapel of Las Vegas, 1205 Las Vegas Blvd S (☎702 384-0771 or ☎800 574 4450, ⊙www.gaychapelof lasvegas.com).

The annual **Las Vegas Pride** event, celebrated in early September (☎702 615 9249, ⊙www.lasvegaspride.org), kicks off with a Friday-night parade through downtown, while the Saturday sees an open-air festival in the grounds of the Clark County Government Center, a few blocks southwest.

In May, the **Nevada Gay Rodeo Association** (⊙www.ngra.com) holds the three-day BigHorn Rodeo at Horseman's Park, 5800 E Flamingo Rd.

Health

In any medical emergency, call ☎911. The front desk or phone operator at your hotel will be able to advise on sources of appropriate help. **Hospitals** that have 24hr emergency rooms include Sunrise Hospital, 3186 S Maryland Parkway (☎702 731 8000, ⊙www.sunrisehospital.com), and the University Medical Center, 1800 W Charleston Blvd (☎702 383 2000, ⊙www.umcsn.com). For more minor issues, head to the Harmon Medical Center, 150 E Harmon Ave (Mon–Fri

8am–8pm; ☎702 796 1116, ⊙www .harmonmedicalcenter.com).

Twenty-four-hour **pharmacies** on the Strip include the 24hr CVS Pharmacy, alongside the Monte Carlo at 3758 Las Vegas Blvd S (☎702 262 9284) and Walgreens, beside the main Palazzo entrance at 3339 Las Vegas Blvd S (☎702 369 8166).

To find a local **dentist**, contact the Nevada Dental Association (☎702 255 4211, ⊙www.nvda.org).

Internet

Every Las Vegas casino provides **wi-fi access** for its guests, but only very rarely is it free. In almost all, it's the main pretext for charging the compulsory "resort fee" (see p.115), which typically costs between $15 and $25 per day; elsewhere, guests can choose to pay a stand-alone fee of around $15 per day. That said, all the MGM Resorts properties now provide free wi-fi throughout their public areas (as opposed to simply within the guest rooms).

A few casinos do however offer **free wi-fi** access to everyone on site: the Tropicana, the Venetian and the Palazzo on the Strip; Main Street Station downtown; and the Hard Rock Hotel east of the Strip. In addition, a handful of shops and cafés along the Strip provide free wi-fi to customers (and anyone in the immediate vicinity): *Coffee Bean & Tea Leaf* in Planet Hollywood's Miracle Mile (see p.62); *Kahunaville* in TI (see p.81); *Sugar and Ice* in Wynn Las Vegas (see p.72); and the Apple Store and *Starbucks* in the Fashion Show Mall (see p.77).

There's also free wi-fi throughout McCarran International Airport.

Money

Las Vegas is not a budget destination in any meaningful sense. The days are gone when casinos used cut-price food and entertainment to lure in gamblers.

Now everything from restaurants to showrooms have to make a profit, and prices are high. A typical all-you-can-eat buffet costs $20 or more for dinner; a run-of-the-mill restaurant more like $40 per head, without drinks; and a gourmet place double that or more. Tickets for a show can easily cost $100 or more, while a night out in a big club is liable to cost hundreds, and potentially thousands, of dollars. Hotel room rates are generally good value, and on weekdays compare favourably with what you'd get for the same money elsewhere in the USA, but can run into hundreds per night on weekends. On top of that, of course, the average visitor also loses several hundred dollars gambling.

As for how you bring your money, it's totally assumed you'll use a **credit card** for all significant expenses. It's extremely easy to get cash anywhere on the Strip; ATMs are everywhere, though all tend to charge around $3 for withdrawals.

Travellers from overseas are advised not to bring foreign cash; there are no banks on the Strip, and while the casinos will gladly change your cash you won't get a good rate. Dollar **travellers' cheques** are accepted as cash everywhere, though few visitors bring them these days.

Phones

Foreign visitors can assume that their **mobile phones** (cellphones) will work in Las Vegas, though it's worth checking with your phone provider that your existing payment scheme will cover you there, and what the call charges are. Many providers offer short-term pricing packages designed to make holiday phone usage more affordable. If you plan to access the internet using your phone, make sure you know your provider's roaming charges, which may well be extremely expensive.

For all calls, you can make tremendous savings by using **Skype**, or similar programmes, to make free wi-fi calls from your phone or laptop. Alternatively, prepaid **phone cards** are widely available from casino convenience stores, petrol (gas) stations, supermarkets and other outlets. Many casinos, especially those that charge resort fees (see p.115), offer guests free local phone calls; making an international call from your hotel room phone is always liable to be very expensive.

Smoking

Smoking remains legal in the public areas of all casinos, and in bars that do not serve food. It is forbidden in restaurants, including those inside casinos, though smoke does waft into those restaurants that are open to the casino floor. All hotels offer non-smoking rooms.

Tax

Sales tax of 8.1 percent is charged on all purchases in Las Vegas. Hotel rates are subject to an additional **room tax** of twelve percent on the Strip, and thirteen percent downtown (see box, p.115).

Time

Las Vegas is in the **Pacific Time Zone**, three hours behind the Eastern Time Zone. It's almost always seven hours behind the UK, though clocks in the US move forward by one hour on the second Sunday in March and back one hour on the first Sunday in November, placing them briefly out of synch with clocks in the UK.

Emergency numbers

In any medical or security emergency, call ☎911.

131

Tipping

Tipping etiquette is not as complicated as many visitors imagine; if you find yourself wondering whether to tip, do. Servers in restaurants depend on tips for their income, and expect at least fifteen percent. So do cab drivers. If someone carries your bags, tip $1–2 per bag; valet parking attendants expect $2; and it's usual to leave a tip of $1 or $2 per day when you leave your hotel room. When gambling, it's considered appropriate to tip the dealer a chip or two if you win. Bar staff, or casino waitresses bringing free drinks, expect $1–2 per drink.

Tourist information

The best single source of information on the city is ⓦwww.visitlasvegas.com, the website of the **Las Vegas Convention and Visitor Authority** (LVCVA). They also run a visitor centre at 3150 Paradise Rd, half a mile east of the Strip (Mon–Fri 8am–5pm; ☏877 847 4858), but it holds nothing you can't find much more easily elsewhere.

Other useful websites include:
ⓦ**www.eatinglv.com** This long-running blog holds a huge archive of restaurant reviews.
ⓦ**www.lasvegascitylife.com** The website of the free weekly City Life magazine; useful for news as well as current listings.
ⓦ**www.lasvegassun.com** Las Vegas's best daily newspaper website.
ⓦ**www.lasvegasweekly.com** A good source of current listings.
ⓦ**www.lvol.com** Schedules, reservations and reviews for concerts and shows; a good place to find out what's happening while you're in town.
ⓦ**www.vegaschatter.com** Lively gossip about Las Vegas comings and goings.

ⓦ**www.vegastodayandtomorrow.com** Fascinating maps, statistics and diagrams, plus news of upcoming projects.

Tours

Las Vegas does not offer the kind of **sightseeing tours** familiar in other cities. Almost everything of interest in the city itself is in and around the casinos; you can't really appreciate them from a passing bus, and they're too big to explore more than one or two at a time on foot. **Bus tours** do however head further afield. Thus Gray Line (☏702 384 1234, ⓦwww.grayline.com) offers tours to the Hoover Dam (4hr 30min; $60); the Grand Canyon West Rim (11hr; $200); and the Grand Canyon South Rim (14hr; $170). Helicopter operators, including Maverick (☏702 261 0007, ⓦwww.maverickhelicopter.com) and Sundance (☏702 736 0606, ⓦwww.sundancehelicopters.com), offer brief day or night **"flight-seeing" tours** over the Strip, at typical prices of around $100 for a flight lasting less than fifteen minutes. They and other companies also fly day trippers east to the Grand Canyon (see p.108).

Travelling with children

In the early 1990s, Las Vegas flirted briefly with the idea that it might become a child-friendly destination to match Orlando, Florida. That dream was swiftly abandoned; gambling and kids don't make a good mix. Even so, many visitors bring their **kids** to the city; the Strip sidewalk is thronged until after midnight with parents pushing cumbersome buggies and struggling with exhausted children.

There's still a lot about Las Vegas that will appeal to kids, from the castles and pyramids, volcanoes and pirate battles on the Strip, to more specific paying attractions. Among the most popular with children are the Secret Garden and Dolphin Habitat at the Mirage; Shark Reef at Mandalay Bay; the Bodies and Titanic exhibitions at Luxor; the Mob Attraction at the Tropicana; CSI: The Experience at the MGM Grand; and the roller coasters and thrill rides at New York–New York, Circus Circus and the Stratosphere.

All the casinos welcome children as guests. Strictly speaking, **under-21s** are not allowed in gambling areas, which means that family groups have to keep walking rather than linger on the casino floor. Casinos do not offer babysitting services, but can provide details of babysitting agencies.

Note that in many casinos, some or all the swimming pools now operate as adults-only "day clubs", with drinking, dancing and partying; it's worth checking in advance before you go ahead and book your accommodation.

Weddings

Thanks to Nevada's notoriously minimal legal requirements, and especially the lack of an obligatory waiting period, around a quarter of a million people get married in Las Vegas each year.

At its simplest, arranging a Vegas wedding is very straightforward. First of all, you need a **Nevada marriage licence**. To get that, both parties must appear in person at the Clark County Marriage Bureau, 201 E Clark Ave, downtown (daily 8am–midnight; ☎702 671 0600, ⊛clarkcountynv.gov). So long as both are aged 18 or over, not married already and can show picture ID, they'll sell you a licence for $60 (credit cards $65, debit cards not accepted). Note that there isn't an office on the Strip.

If you've made an advance reservation, you can then walk with your licence to the office of the **Commissioner of Civil Marriages**, on the sixth floor at 330 S Third St (Mon–Thurs & Sun 2–6pm, Fri 10am–9pm, Sat 12.30–9pm; ☎702 671 0577, ⊛clarkcountynv.gov) and pay another $50 cash to have the actual ceremony performed. One witness is required; ideally you should bring your own, though what the Commissioner charmingly calls "unsavoury individuals" lurk outside the offices, hoping to sell their services as witnesses.

Just because it's possible to have a quick, cheap wedding in Las Vegas, however, doesn't mean that's what most couples actually do. Instead, most marriages are celebrated in wedding chapels, which can be stand-alone structures of the kind reviewed throughout this book or yet one more component in the huge casino-hotels. You can find full listings of chapels and wedding planners on the official Las Vegas CVB website, ⊛lasvegas.com, and also on the casinos' own websites.

Prices at **wedding chapels** range upwards from around $200 all-in for a bare-bones ceremony. For the full works, which in Las Vegas can include helicopter flights to the Grand Canyon or pretty much anything else you care to mention, the bill can of course run into thousands of dollars. The biggest hidden expense is likely to be photography; be sure to check whether you or your guests will be allowed to bring cameras, and if not, how much the official photos or footage will cost.

Finally, note that while gay marriage is not legal in Nevada, many chapels offer gay or lesbian **commitment ceremonies**, which have no legal force (see p.130).

Festivals

Compared to other American cities, Las Vegas does not have an extensive calendar of annual events. In terms of attracting crowds, the biggest events tend to be the opening of new casinos and, even more exciting, the implosions of old ones.

NASCAR WEEKEND

Early March ⓦ www.lvms.com
Three days of racing at the Las Vegas Motor Speedway, 7000 Las Vegas Blvd N at Speedway Blvd.

ST PATRICK'S DAY

March 17
Pubs, clubs, casinos and restaurants all celebrate St Patrick's Day.

WORLD SERIES OF POKER

Late May to mid-July ⓦ www.wsop.com
The world's premier poker tournament has been held at the Rio since 1995.

LAS VEGAS HELLDORADO DAYS

Mid-May ⓦ www.elkshelldorado.com
Four nights of pro rodeo action at

Public holidays

Jan 1 New Year's Day
Jan 15 Martin Luther King Jr's Birthday
3rd Mon in Feb Presidents' Day
Last Mon in May Memorial Day
July 4 Independence Day
1st Mon in Sept Labor Day
2nd Mon in Oct Columbus Day
Nov 11 Veterans' Day
Last Thurs in Nov Thanksgiving Day
Dec 25 Christmas Day

the Cashman Field stadium, a mile northeast of downtown at 7000 Las Vegas Blvd N, plus a Saturday night parade downtown.

NATIONAL FINALS RODEO

Early Dec ⓦ www.nfrexperience.com
Ten-day pro rodeo event at the Thomas & Mack Center, 4505 S Maryland Parkway.

NEW YEAR'S EVE

December 31
The biggest night in the city's calendar, marked by concerts and festivities.

Conventions and trade shows

When planning a visit, it's useful to know when the city's biggest **conventions** are happening as room rates can soar.

Mid-Jan Consumer Electronics Show

Mid-Feb Men's Apparel Guild (MAGIC) convention

Early April National Association of Broadcasters convention

Mid-August Men's Apparel Guild (MAGIC) convention (again)

Early Nov Specialty Equipment Manufacturers Association (SEMA) convention

Chronology

1598 > Spain claims what's now southern Nevada as part of the colony of New Mexico.

1829 > Mexican explorers name an unexpected oasis of grasslands "Las Vegas" – "The Meadows".

1847 > USA acquires New Mexico.

1855 > Mormons establish the colony of Bringhurst in the Las Vegas Valley; it lasts three years.

1864 > Nevada becomes a state.

1905 > The railroad arrives. Las Vegas is established on May 15, when forty newly drawn blocks are auctioned.

1909 > Nevada became the first US state to outlaw gambling.

1931 > Nevada marks the end of Prohibition by legalizing gambling – the only state to do so.

1935 > Hoover Dam completed. Las Vegas hosts first convention.

1938 > Guy McAfee, former chief of LA's vice squad, takes over the Pair-O-Dice Club, on what he dubs "The Strip".

1940 > Las Vegas's population reaches eight thousand.

1941 > El Rancho opens as the Strip's first fully fledged resort.

1946 > Mobster "Bugsy" Siegel opens the Flamingo; he's murdered six months later after heavy losses.

1950s > An unstoppable flow of new Strip resorts includes the Desert Inn, the Sands, the Riviera, the Dunes and the Hacienda. Desert A-bomb tests can be seen and heard from the city.

1966 > Caesars Palace, the first themed casino, opens. Howard Hughes asked to leave the Desert Inn because he isn't gambling; instead, he buys it, along with the Sands, the Silver Slipper, and the New Frontier, marking the end of Mob domination.

1969 > Kirk Kerkorian opens the world's largest hotel– the Las Vegas Hilton – which hosts Elvis's rebirth as a karate-kicking lounge lizard.

1973 > Kirk Kerkorian again opens the world's largest hotel – the original MGM Grand, now Bally's. Steve Wynn takes over downtown's Golden Nugget.

1983 > Following disastrous fires at the MGM Grand and the Hilton, Las Vegas seems about to be eclipsed by Atlantic City; direct flights between New York and Las Vegas are discontinued.

1989 > Steve Wynn opens the opulent Mirage, complete with volcano. Benny Binion dies, with his Horseshoe downtown still Las Vegas's most profitable casino.

1993 > In a short-lived bid to reinvent Las Vegas as a child-friendly destination, Luxor, Treasure Island and the MGM Grand all open.

1995 > Downtown roofed over to create Fremont Street Experience.

1997 > New York–New York opens; in a craze for building replica cities, it's followed by Bellagio in 1998 and the Venetian and Paris in 1999.

2000 > Steve Wynn sells the Mirage organization to MGM, which buys the Mandalay Bay Group in 2004.

2005 > Harrah's buys Caesars Entertainment, leaving the Strip largely owned by two huge corporations. Steve Wynn opens Wynn Las Vegas.

2009 > Recession hits hard. MGM Mirage completes CityCenter, but many projects are abandoned.

2011 > Former mob lawyer Oscar Goodman completes a twelve-year stint as mayor, succeeded by wife Carolyn.

2012 > The Mob Museum and the Smith Performing Arts Center open downtown.

PUBLISHING INFORMATION

This first edition published October 2013 by **Rough Guides Ltd**

80 Strand, London WC2R 0RL

11, Community Centre, Panchsheel Park, New Delhi 110017, India

Distributed by the Penguin Group

Penguin Books Ltd, 80 Strand, London WC2R 0RL

Penguin Group (USA) 375 Hudson Street, NY 10014, USA

Penguin Group (Australia) 250 Camberwell Road, Camberwell, Victoria 3124, Australia

Penguin Group (NZ) 67 Apollo Drive, Mairangi Bay, Auckland 1310, New Zealand

Penguin Group (South Africa) Block D, Rosebank Office Park, 181 Jan Smuts Avenue,

Parktown North, Gauteng, South Africa 2193

Rough Guides is represented in Canada by

Tourmaline Editions Inc., 662 King Street West, Suite 304, Toronto, Ontario, M5V 1M7

Typeset in Minion and Din to an original design by Henry Iles and Dan May.

Printed and bound in China

© Rough Guides, 2013

Maps © Rough Guides

144pp includes index

A catalogue record for this book is available from the British Library

ISBN 978-1-40936 414-6

MIX
Paper from
responsible sources
FSC™ C018179
www.fsc.org

ROUGH GUIDES CREDITS

Text editor: Alison Roberts

Managing editor: Mani Ramaswamy

Layout: Umesh Aggarwal

Cartography: Edward Wright

Picture editor: Mark Thomas

Photographer: Tim Draper

Production: Charlotte Cade

Proofreader: Susanna Wight

Cover design: Wilf Matos and Umesh Aggarwal

THE AUTHOR

Greg Ward has been writing about Las Vegas for more than twenty years. As well as four previous Rough Guides to the city, he's the author of separate Rough Guides to the Southwest USA and the Grand Canyon. He has also written many other Rough Guides, including those to the USA, the *Titanic*, Hawaii, Brittany & Normandy, Provence, Spain, Blues CDs and US History; edited many more; and written books for several other publishers. For more information, visit ⓦ www.gregward.info.

ACKNOWLEDGEMENTS

Greg Ward: Thanks as ever to my dear wife Sam, for her support, encouragement and wise words. At Rough Guides, thanks to Alison Roberts for her thoughtful and scrupulous editing, and Ed Wright for his exceptional dedication to producing great maps. And thanks to everyone in Las Vegas who helped me to find and enjoy the very best of the city, especially Kimberley Diller and David Gonzalez, as well as Hannah Allen, Jennifer Byles, Stephanie Capellas, Stephanie Chavez, Katie Conway, Maggie Feldman, Sara Gorgon, Andrew Ho, Alison Monaghan, Holly Olp, Jennifer Polito, Kellyann Roberts, Rochelle Samilin-Jurani, Josie Self, Melanie Shafer, Wendy Sloan, Eleni Stylianou, Melissa Warren and Cathy Wiedemer.

HELP US UPDATE

We've gone to a lot of effort to ensure that the first edition of the **Pocket Rough Guide Las Vegas** is accurate and up-to-date. However, things change – places get "discovered", opening hours are notoriously fickle, restaurants and rooms raise prices or lower standards. If you feel we've got it wrong or left something out, we'd like to know, and if you can remember the address, the price, the hours, the phone number, so much the better.

Please send your comments with the subject line "Pocket Rough Guide Las Vegas Update" to ✉ mail@roughguides.com. We'll credit all contributions and send a copy of the next edition (or any other Rough Guide if you prefer) for the very best emails.

Find more travel information, connect with fellow travellers and book your trip on Ⓦ www .roughguides.com

PHOTO CREDITS

Index

Maps are marked in **bold**.

AFFECT, ANIMATE,
AROUSE, CARRY,
CAUSE, COMMOVE,
ELATE, EMBOLDEN,
ENDUE, ENKINDLE,
ENLIVEN, EXALT, EXCITE,
EXHILARATE, FIRE UP,
GALVANIZE, GIVE IMPETUS,
GIVE RISE TO, HEARTEN,
IMBUE, IMPRESS, INFECT,
INFLAME, INFLUENCE,
INFORM, INFUSE, INSPIRE,
INSPIRIT, INSTILL,
INVIGORATE, MOTIVATE,
OCCASION, PRODUCE,
PROVOKE, QUICKEN,
REASSURE, SPARK, SPUR,
START OFF, STIR, STRIKE,
SWAY, TOUCH, TRIGGER,
URGE, WORK UP

Whatever you call it,
Rough Guides does it